IN THE LION'S
MOUTH

The Stackpole Military History Series

THE AMERICAN CIVIL WAR

Cavalry Raids of the Civil War
Ghost, Thunderbolt, and Wizard
In the Lion's Mouth
Pickett's Charge
Witness to Gettysburg

WORLD WAR I

Doughboy War

WORLD WAR II

After D-Day
Airborne Combat
Armor Battles of the Waffen-SS, 1943–45
Armoured Guardsmen
Army of the West
Arnhem 1944
Australian Commandos
The B-24 in China
Backwater War
The Battle of France
The Battle of Sicily
Battle of the Bulge, Vol. 1
Battle of the Bulge, Vol. 2
Beyond the Beachhead
Beyond Stalingrad
The Black Bull
Blitzkrieg Unleashed
Blossoming Silk against the Rising Sun
Bodenplatte
The Brandenburger Commandos
The Brigade
Bringing the Thunder
The Canadian Army and the Normandy Campaign
Coast Watching in World War II
Colossal Cracks
Condor
A Dangerous Assignment
D-Day Bombers
D-Day Deception
D-Day to Berlin
Destination Normandy
Dive Bomber!
A Drop Too Many
Eagles of the Third Reich
The Early Battles of Eighth Army
Eastern Front Combat
Europe in Flames
Exit Rommel
The Face of Courage
Fist from the Sky
Flying American Combat Aircraft of World War II
For Europe

Forging the Thunderbolt
For the Homeland
Fortress France
The German Defeat in the East, 1944–45
German Order of Battle, Vol. 1
German Order of Battle, Vol. 2
German Order of Battle, Vol. 3
The Germans in Normandy
Germany's Panzer Arm in World War II
GI Ingenuity
Goodwood
The Great Ships
Grenadiers
Guns against the Reich
Hitler's Nemesis
Hold the Westwall
Infantry Aces
In the Fire of the Eastern Front
Iron Arm
Iron Knights
Kampfgruppe Peiper at the Battle of the Bulge
The Key to the Bulge
Knight's Cross Panzers
Kursk
Luftwaffe Aces
Luftwaffe Fighter Ace
Luftwaffe Fighter-Bombers over Britain
Luftwaffe Fighters and Bombers
Massacre at Tobruk
Mechanized Juggernaut or Military Anachronism?
Messerschmitts over Sicily
Michael Wittmann, Vol. 1
Michael Wittmann, Vol. 2
Mountain Warriors
The Nazi Rocketeers
Night Flyer / Mosquito Pathfinder
No Holding Back
On the Canal
Operation Mercury
Packs On!
Panzer Aces
Panzer Aces II
Panzer Aces III
Panzer Commanders of the Western Front
Panzergrenadier Aces
Panzer Gunner
The Panzer Legions
Panzers in Normandy
Panzers in Winter
The Path to Blitzkrieg
Penalty Strike

Poland Betrayed
Red Road from Stalingrad
Red Star under the Baltic
Retreat to the Reich
Rommel's Desert Commanders
Rommel's Desert War
Rommel's Lieutenants
The Savage Sky
Ship-Busters
The Siege of Küstrin
The Siegfried Line
A Soldier in the Cockpit
Soviet Blitzkrieg
Stalin's Keys to Victory
Surviving Bataan and Beyond
T-34 in Action
Tank Tactics
Tigers in the Mud
Triumphant Fox
The 12th SS, Vol. 1
The 12th SS, Vol. 2
Twilight of the Gods
Typhoon Attack
The War against Rommel's Supply Lines
War in the Aegean
Wolfpack Warriors
Zhukov at the Oder

THE COLD WAR / VIETNAM

Cyclops in the Jungle
Expendable Warriors
Fighting in Vietnam
Flying American Combat Aircraft: The Cold War
Here There Are Tigers
Land with No Sun
MiGs over North Vietnam
Phantom Reflections
Street without Joy
Through the Valley

WARS OF AFRICA AND THE MIDDLE EAST

Never-Ending Conflict
The Rhodesian War

GENERAL MILITARY HISTORY

Carriers in Combat
Cavalry from Hoof to Track
Desert Battles
Guerrilla Warfare
Ranger Dawn
Sieges

IN THE LION'S MOUTH

Hood's Tragic Retreat from Nashville, 1864

Derek Smith

STACKPOLE
BOOKS

Published by
STACKPOLE BOOKS
5067 Ritter Road
Mechanicsburg, PA 17055
www.stackpolebooks.com

Cover design by Tracy Patterson

Printed in the United States of America

10 9 8 7 6 5 4 3 2 1

Library of Congress Cataloging-in-Publication Data

Smith, Derek, 1956 Nov. 3–
  In the lion's mouth : Hood's tragic retreat from Nashville, 1864 / Derek Smith.
      p. cm. — (Stackpole military history series)
  Includes bibliographical references and index.
  ISBN 978-0-8117-1059-6
  1. Nashville, Battle of, Nashville, Tenn., 1864. 2. Tennessee—History—Civil War, 1861–1865—Campaigns. 3. Hood, John Bell, 1831–1879. 4. Confederate States of America. Army of Tennessee. I. Title.
  E477.52.S65 2011
  976.8'04—dc22
                                    2011005360

Table of Contents

Introduction

"You may talk about your Beauregard and sing of
General Lee, but the gallant Hood of Texas played
hell in Tennessee."

From its headwaters where the French Broad and Holston
Rivers blend at Knoxville, the Tennessee River twists like a
water moccasin for more than 600 miles. Geologic time and
erosion carved its bed, endless water grinding through mountains and orange clay in a relentless rush to the Ohio River.
Even before it was named, the Tennessee was a byway for
Choctaw, Cherokee, Creek, and the prehistoric nomadic peo-
ples who preceded them, fishing and gathering berries along
its banks. It also was a likely passage for the Spanish explorer
Hernando de Soto and his conquistadores as they plunged into
the wilds of sixteenth-century North America on a quest for
gold and empire.

In the fall and winter of 1864—one of the harshest on
record in the region—the Tennessee was a river of war. Generals and navy officers pored over maps of its bends, shoals, and
crossings, much as their counterparts in the east studied the
Potomac, Rapidan, Rappahannock, and James, all glamorized
in headlines heralding the exploits of Grant, Sheridan, and
Meade.

The Tennessee had been a critical waterway throughout
the war in the west, from Fort Henry and the bloodbath at
Shiloh to the battles around Chattanooga. Now it would witness whether one of the Confederacy's two main armies could

muster a final offensive to regain momentum for the South's reeling fortunes.

The hourglass was draining for the Confederacy. Gen. Robert E. Lee's Army of Northern Virginia was mired in the miles of trenches around Richmond and Petersburg, starving and dying in a hopeless numbers game with besieging Federal armies. Atlanta had fallen, and 60,000 Union veterans under Maj. Gen. William T. Sherman were poised to lash out from there to any coastal point from Alabama to South Carolina. In Missouri, an October offensive by Confederates under Gen. Sterling Price had been stymied. The Union naval blockade continued its anaconda-like constriction of the few seaports still open. And all Confederates in uniform were tormented by the fact that loved ones at home were suffering since the Union had started to inflict major devastation in every state of the Confederacy.

Yet there was a dim sparkle of hope that the vast wave of bad tidings could be reversed, this seemingly inevitable free fall averted. But Sherman had to be cast out of Atlanta before he could do even more harm.

With Lee and his army pinned in Virginia, the Confederacy's fate rested with its other main military force, the Army of Tennessee, commanded by the thirty-three-year-old John Bell Hood. This army had been roundly battered in the fighting withdrawal across northern Georgia the previous summer and in the siege and battles for Atlanta, which were lost. The Army of Tennessee was a hard-luck bunch that fought tough but was usually in disarray because of a dysfunctional command system—and always operated in the shadows of its brothers in arms in Lee's army. There had been disharmony in the ranks since the one-legged Hood replaced the popular Joseph E. Johnston in July, and various feuds among its other generals seethed.

Still, Hood and his troops moved north in late September, intent on destroying Sherman's vital railroad supply line between Chattanooga and Atlanta and possibly drawing Sherman after them. Indeed, Sherman did follow for a few weeks,

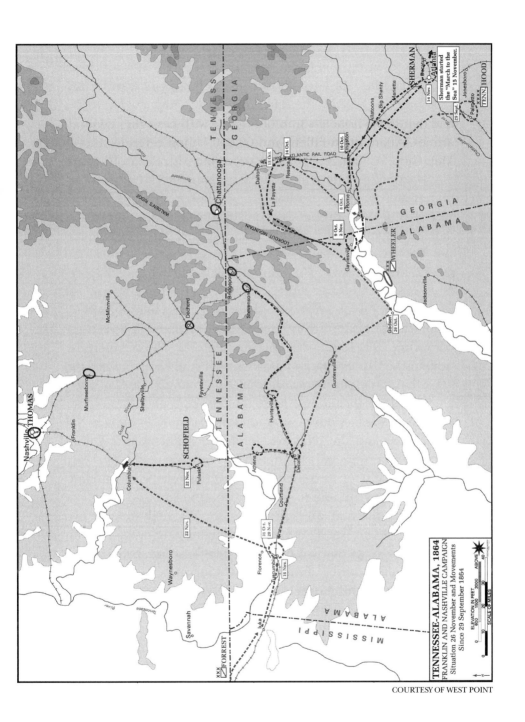

TENNESSEE-ALABAMA, 1864
FRANKLIN AND NASHVILLE CAMPAIGN
Situation 26 November and Movements
Since 29 September 1864

COURTESY OF WEST POINT

but unable to catch Hood, he returned to Atlanta to finalize plans for his fiery march to the sea. Hood wrecked some railroads and, with ever-changing plans, continued into northern Alabama, where by late October he was poised for a strike into Tennessee to reclaim the state for the Confederacy. There was wild optimism that such an offensive could pave the way for a thrust farther north into Kentucky or perhaps—even wilder— for Hood to turn his army east and unite with Lee in Virginia.

Delayed by rainy weather for about three weeks, the Confederates did not begin moving into Tennessee until late November, giving their prime antagonist critical time to prepare a lethal welcome. In the fall, Sherman had sent Maj. Gen. George H. Thomas to Nashville to assemble an army in case Hood aimed for Tennessee. The hero of Chickamauga, Thomas gathered troops and further fortified the already strong defenses of the capital. Amid controversy that still swirls, Hood missed an opportunity to capture or destroy a portion of the Federal army at Spring Hill, Tennessee, on November 29. The next day, he fought the battle of Franklin—essentially the Gettysburg of the west. This five-hour holocaust resulted in about 7,000 Confederate casualties, including a large number of generals and other officers. It was a crippling wound to the Army of Tennessee, but Hood resumed the offensive, following the retreating Union forces to Nashville, where Thomas awaited him.

Facing the formidable Federal fortifications, the Confederates dug in as the winter worsened; ice and snow proved to be worse enemies than any soldier in blue. Through the first two weeks of December, Thomas faced heightening pressure from his superiors, primarily Lt. Gen. Ulysses S. Grant, commander of all Union armies, and Abraham Lincoln, to attack Hood immediately. Thomas held firm in his decision to wait for a break in the frigid, stormy weather as he gathered troops to make the assault. During this lull, Union brigadier general James Wilson assembled a cavalry corps of 15,000, which would play a key role in the campaign.

Finally, the weather eased, and Thomas launched his offensive on December 15, driving the Confederates from their positions. After a brief withdrawal, Hood managed to dig in again during the night, awaiting the next blow. It came the following day when Thomas attacked again. The southerners held firm until the afternoon, when their left flank was suddenly broken. With shocking speed, the rest of the line folded like a house of cards, and much of the army disintegrated in rout as Hood watched in horror.

What followed over the next twelve days would be one of the most spellbinding and tragic episodes in American military history as hunters and hunted left bloody footprints on the bayonet-sharp ice for more than 100 miles. Grizzled Confederates who survived claimed it was worse than the patriots' sufferings at Valley Forge. One general wrote that it was "a most painful march, characterized by more suffering than it had ever before been my misfortune to witness."

Thomas sent Wilson's cavalry after the disorganized Confederates while the Federal infantry slogged south in knee-deep mud. In desperation, Hood organized a temporary rear guard led by Nathan Bedford Forrest to stave off the enemy while his tattered columns tried to reach the Tennessee River. Meanwhile, Union gunboats were chugging upriver, trying to seal off Hood's crossing point and bag or destroy the Confederates at the Tennessee. As his miserable troops tramped south amid rain, sleet, snow, and stinging cold, Hood and his engineers worried if they had enough pontoon boats to span the river.[1] Slowed by Forrest's ambushes and other delaying actions, Thomas also was held up by flooded creeks and streams. But an order he gave after just being awakened resulted in a logistical error that may have cost him his best chance to bring Hood to bay, trapped with his back to the Tennessee.

Missed opportunities haunted both sides in November and December 1864. This is the story of that terrible retreat from Nashville when men in blue and gray alike suffered privations and tribulations few American soldiers have ever endured—and hopefully never will again.

CHAPTER 1

Preamble to Catastrophe

Confederate president Jefferson Davis knew he was climbing into a den of rattlesnakes when he stepped from his train at Palmetto, Georgia, on a rainy Sunday, September 25, 1864, making his way through the orange mud to the nearby encampment of the Army of Tennessee. Realizing the fragility not only of military affairs in Georgia, but of the army—and his nation—as well, Davis had traveled more than 600 miles from Richmond to confer with John Bell Hood; his three corps commanders, lieutenant generals William J. Hardee, Alexander P. Stewart, and Stephen Dill Lee; and other officers.

Less than a month had passed since the Confederates had evacuated Atlanta, and nerves were worn raw among all ranks. The army's upper-level infighting—never far from boiling over—was especially bitter now between Hood and Hardee. Hood placed much of the blame for the loss of Atlanta on his senior corps commander and wanted Hardee relieved. These quarrels aside, Hood realized the army could not remain stationery for long and told Davis about a plan to retake the offensive and deal decisively with Union general William Tecumseh Sherman. Hood wanted to march north of Atlanta, aiming to sever Sherman's supply lines from Chattanooga to Atlanta, the most vital of which was the Western & Atlantic Railroad. If Sherman pursued, perhaps there would be a chance to defeat him in the north Georgia wilds. If Sherman ignored Hood and moved south out of Atlanta, Hood could pounce on the enemy—or at least remain within striking distance—and await his next move.

With scant options, Davis agreed to let Hood attack Sherman's iron umbilical cord, a strategy that had been on his mind

1

as well. En route to Palmetto on September 24, Davis had made a speech in Macon, Georgia, urging renewed determination to stop the Federal invaders and win the war. He told the crowd that Sherman's long communications and supply chain could not be maintained and that Union forces would have to retreat sooner or later. "And when that day comes, the fate that befell the army of the French Empire in its retreat from Moscow will be re-enacted," he said. "Our cavalry and our people will harass and destroy his army as did the Cossacks of Napoleon, and the Yankee general, like him, will escape with only a bodyguard."[1]

Thus, as autumn began to kiss the Deep South with its colorful majesty, Hood's legions started north on September 29, but this was not an army that had full faith in its general or vice versa. During a review of the troops at Palmetto, some soldiers had shouted to the president, "Give us Joe Johnston"—which had embarrassed Hood, who later wrote, "I regretted I should have been the cause of this uncourteous reception to his Excellency. At the same time, I could recall no offence [sic] save that of having insisted that they fight for and hold Atlanta forty-six days, whereas they had previously retreated one hundred miles within sixty-six days." The latter remark was not only a swipe at his troops, but also at Johnston, who had repeatedly withdrawn from mountain strongholds in the face of Sherman's relentless onslaught toward Atlanta. Davis also promptly acted on Hood's request to relieve Hardee, sending the Georgian to command the Department of South Carolina, Georgia, and Florida. Thus, as Hood headed north, he had a new corps commander, Maj. Gen. Benjamin F. Cheatham of Tennessee.[2]

By the first week of October, Hood's army of about 43,000—excluding Maj. Gen. Joseph Wheeler's cavalry corps, off on an extended raid—was well north of Atlanta, had destroyed miles of railroad, and had captured several hundred Union prisoners. On October 5, one of his divisions attacked the strong Union outpost and major supply depot at Allatoona Pass, but it was repelled after a sharp fight. Hood then continued farther into northern Georgia, gobbling up Federal garrisons at Tilton, Dalton, and Mill Creek Gap. Even at this early

Jefferson Davis.

point in the campaign, the Confederates were in poor shape in terms of rations, uniforms, and other equipment. Spirits, however, were high for the most part. Three Union officers captured at Dalton observed the army as it passed, one of them writing a description that appeared in newspapers on both sides:

> Everything in their language and bearing indicated that they were determined to fight a while longer. . . . They were ragged and thinly clad, having as a general thing, only pantaloons, shirt and hat in their inventory . . . the first too greasy and tattered, the last shocking affairs in multitudinous variety. As a general thing they were tolerably shod; though in one of Stewart's divisions one of our officers counted over three hundred barefooted privates. Not more than one in ten have blankets, and much suffering must have ensued through the keen, frosty nights now prevailing. . . . Regimental discipline seemed a little loose, and privates appeared to comment upon the commands of their immediate officers with an unction and broadness of diction. . . . The guns were nearly all Napoleons, of the average calibre [*sic*]. The public animals were in pretty good condition— quite equal to pulling along light field batteries, empty wagons, and careering under the wiry, not over fat, grizzled, and besmeared cavaliers.[3]

With Hood on the march, Sherman was far from idle. As the Confederates hoped, he had indeed marched north from Atlanta with about 60,000 troops, basically backtracking over old battlegrounds where he had dueled with Johnston the previous summer as he tried to overtake Hood. Yet a decision Sherman made in late September, about the time the Confederates left Palmetto, would prove to have the most far-reaching consequences on the upcoming campaign. Southern cavalry led by Maj. Gen. Nathan Bedford Forrest had boiled up from Mississippi on a raid into northern Alabama and eventually

into middle Tennessee. Sherman received a September 26
order from Lt. Gen. Ulysses S. Grant, commander of all Union
armies, that Forrest had to be driven out of Tennessee. Three
days later, Sherman's choice for this assignment, Maj. Gen.
George H. Thomas, the hero of Chickamauga, was headed
north, with two infantry divisions to follow. Thomas epito-
mized the Union bulldog in appearance and action, even
though he was a Virginian by birth. He had led the Army of
the Cumberland in the Atlanta campaign, where his troops
constituted more than half of Sherman's entire force. Thomas
and Sherman were old friends, having been roommates at
West Point. Now, far from the parade grounds above the Hudson, they were poised to be twin knights in one of the war's last
and most decisive stages.[4]

By early October, Thomas had reached Nashville, the state
capital, where he would direct operations against Forrest and
reorganize Union forces in Tennessee. He settled into rooms
at the St. Cloud Hotel and conducted his military affairs from
the Cunningham House on High Street. If he believed he had
been placed on the back burner of Sherman's camp stove,
Thomas did not voice it, concentrating instead on his assignment and the myriad duties it involved.

The Federals had little luck corralling Forrest, who ripped
up some railroad, captured about 1,200 prisoners, and, by
October 6, had escaped south after a two-week foray. For
Thomas, however, there was a more menacing threat as Hood's
army recoiled from Allatoona Pass and churned northward, its
course as unpredictable as a killer hurricane. Piecing together
a patchwork of units in the event he had to face Hood, Thomas
was confident at this stage that he and Sherman would confront the enemy together. "Am making such disposition of my
force as will, I hope, prevent him [Hood] crossing the Tennessee," he wrote to U.S. Secretary of War Edwin Stanton on
October 10. "And while I hold him in the front, Sherman will
attack him in the rear."[5] Sherman was unconvinced that the
Confederates would venture into the state. "Hood won't dare
go into Tennessee," he wrote Thomas at Nashville on October

17. "I hope he will. . . . If Hood wants to go into Tennessee . . . let him go, and then we can all turn on him and he cannot escape. The gun-boats can break any bridge he may attempt." Sherman also believed that Hood could not maintain his army north of the river because of his tenuous railroad supply link.[6]

Amazingly, without consulting or informing his superiors, Hood altered his plan in mid-October, veering away from the objectives he had discussed with Davis at Palmetto. He entered northeastern Alabama, targeting the Nashville & Chattanooga Railroad, Sherman's supply line west of Chattanooga and along the Tennessee-Alabama border at Bridgeport and Stevenson, Alabama. To strike this line, he would have to cross the Tennessee River, which hooked down from Chattanooga and cut across upper Alabama. If all went well, he would continue north into Tennessee, hopefully drawing Sherman after him. Still, instead of harassing and destroying Sherman's lifeline to Atlanta, Hood was now essentially abandoning Georgia; his movements already took him well out of the path of any effective action against Sherman, unless the Union commander continued the pursuit.

But there were many advantages to be gained if the Confederates pulled this off. If Hood moved quickly, the presence of a major army on the offensive in Tennessee might influence the upcoming presidential election in the North, perhaps swinging more voters to Democratic candidate George B. McClellan, the former general, whose party favored negotiating a peace with the Confederacy. Moreover, the army was in dire need of a morale boost, and since a large portion of the troops were Tennesseans, a return to their home state would raise their spirits, especially if Hood was successful in reclaiming at least part of it. The Confederates also needed to attract recruits for their depleted ranks, and if this was done, they might drive farther north into Kentucky and to the Ohio River before spearing east to join Lee in Virginia. It was the stuff of unfathomable hope in an already lost cause, but there was little left to scrape from the barrel's bottom.

Hood reached Gadsden, Alabama, on October 20 and was joined there the next day by his superior, Gen. P. G. T. Beauregard, who had days earlier been appointed to head the newly established Military Division of the West, a superficial command with scant control over Hood's decision-making process. With little choice, Beauregard agreed to Hood's new plan, though with some reservations, and stressed that the thrust be made with all possible speed to prevent the Federals from gathering in force and to keep them off balance. The new chain of command caused almost immediate friction between these generals, as Hood realized how little clout Beauregard held over him. Eventually, there would be dust-ups between them about matters as trivial as troop reviews, but Hood did relent to Beauregard's order that the army's cavalry corps, about 6,600 troopers under Joe Wheeler, remain south of the Tennessee to help deal with Sherman. Wheeler had reunited with the army on October 8 after a raid of almost two months in northern Georgia and Tennessee. To leave Wheeler behind meant that Hood had only Brig. Gen. William H. "Red" Jackson's 3,900-man cavalry division when he moved north. Beauregard instructed Forrest and his horsemen to link with Hood at the Tennessee and coordinate with him in the offensive.[7]

Hood initially intended to cross the Tennessee at Gunter's Landing (present-day Guntersville), Alabama, but as the army marched on October 22, he again changed plans, marching northwest, basically parallel to the river, to find another crossing.[8]

By October 19, it appeared to Sherman that he would be unable to catch the enemy army, and he turned his attention to a march from Atlanta to the sea, although he was undecided on his direction and objective. "Hood will escape me. I want to prepare for my big raid," he wrote in a dispatch that day. "I propose to abandon Atlanta and the railroad back to Chattanooga, and sally forth to ruin Georgia and bring up on the seashore." That same day, he wired Thomas, stating that while Hood had evaded him, he was ready to "make a hole in Georgia and

P. G. T. Beauregard.

Alabama that will be hard to mend," no matter whether he struck toward Mobile, Savannah, or Charleston. "I want you to remain in Tennessee and take command of all my division not actually present with me," he wrote Thomas, adding that Hood's army numbered about 40,000. "He [Hood] may follow me or turn against you," Sherman said. "If you can defend the line of the Tennessee [River] in my absence of three months, it is all I ask." By October 20, Sherman had decided to return to Atlanta and slice toward the Georgia coast or possibly Charleston, keeping his other target options open. "To pursue Hood is folly, for he can twist and turn like a fox and wear out any army in pursuit," he wrote Thomas that day.[9]

Grant was not initially enamored of Sherman's proposal and did not consent until Sherman reassured him that he would leave sufficient troops to deal with Hood. Thomas himself did not support Sherman's plan, writing that he hoped the Union cavalry could be loosed on Georgia rather than having Sherman's entire army set off for the coast. The fact that he did not want to be left alone to defend Tennessee with insufficient forces and that he did not want his own Army of the Cumberland further divided also shaded his view. As early as October 18, he had told Sherman that he did not want to oversee Tennessee's defense "unless you and the authorities at Washington deem it necessary." Sherman told him, "I do believe you are the man best qualified to manage the affairs of Tennessee and North Mississippi"—which, along with reinforcements sent to Thomas from Atlanta, had settled matters. There also was the possibility that Thomas would not be defending anything, but would be on the offensive. If Hood went after Sherman when Sherman headed south, Thomas would pursue the Confederates from behind.[10]

Meanwhile, Thomas had requested that his old XIV Corps be sent from Atlanta to assist him in Tennessee. He had organized its first brigade and led the corps on a number of fields, but Sherman turned him down: the XIV was too reliable and too valuable, and Sherman would need it for his mischief in

Georgia. Instead, Sherman assigned Maj. Gen. David S. Stanley's IV Corps to reinforce Thomas. Stanley's 13,000 men moved by rail and foot to Pulaski, Tennessee, about seventy miles south of Nashville. From there, they could keep an eye on Hood in northern Alabama. Days later, the Union XXIII Corps, commanded by Maj. Gen. John M. Schofield—all that was left of the Army of the Ohio after attrition and term expirations—left the Atlanta area for Pulaski. Thomas also was expecting Maj. Gen. Andrew J. Smith and three veteran divisions of the Army of the Tennessee's XVI Corps, which was assigned to his department after duty in Missouri. Thomas would also draw upon a conglomeration of garrison troops from various points as well as units posted to guard the railroads.

By the twenty-sixth, the Confederate army had reached Decatur, Alabama, and spent the better part of two days there while Hood pondered whether he could overpower the Union garrison and cross the Tennessee there. A frustrated Beauregard returned to the army and confronted Hood near Decatur the next day, upset that Hood was not only moving away from the Nashville & Chattanooga Railroad, but also giving the enemy precious time to marshal forces wherever he decided to go. The generals decided Decatur's defenses were too strong, and the army once again headed westward, still looking for a crossing point. Hood's newest objective was Tuscumbia, Alabama, about forty-four miles west of Decatur. The river was narrower there, and he would have a nearby link to supply depots in Mississippi via the Mobile & Ohio and the Memphis & Charleston Railroads. The latter line ran from Corinth to Tuscumbia, but much of it had been destroyed or had deteriorated because of neglect in this vicinity. Still, the rails had been repaired to Cherokee Station, some ten miles west of Tuscumbia, giving Hood access to a few trains bringing much-needed supplies that could then be hauled in by wagons until the railroad was reconnected to Tuscumbia. Hood had not realized the railroad was in such bad shape, but the die had been cast. A bridgehead at Tuscumbia also brought the army closer to a rendezvous with Forrest and his cavalry, who were raiding

Ruins of Hood's twenty-eight-car ammunition train and the
Schofield Rolling Mill, near Atlanta, September 1864.

NATIONAL ARCHIVES

in western Tennessee. Hood also knew the Tuscumbia crossing
put him closer to Nashville, now a formidable Union stronghold brimming with supplies of every kind—his if he could take
the capital city.[11]

By now, however, the Alabama autumn was becoming
harsher: the temperature was dropping and a mix of rain and
snow bedeviled the Confederates. The columns plodded into
Tuscumbia on October 30 after covering about 400 miles—
much of it rugged hill country—since leaving Palmetto almost
a month earlier, and the pace had exacted a toll. "We are now
in a rather bad condition—everything being near exhausted,"
J. A. Tillman of the 24th South Carolina wrote home on
November 1. "We are now 12 miles from where our cars run
and hope soon to be able to obtain necessary articles. The
army is in fine spirits and shortly will be in fine health, I hope,
if permitted to remain stationary a few days."[12]

Hood planned to lay a 1,000-yard pontoon bridge over the
Tennessee at Tuscumbia and continue marching north through

Florence on the north bank and to the Tennessee border. Stephen Lee got three brigades over in small boats on October 30, pushing Union cavalry out of Florence and digging in. The span was completed on November 1, and the rest of Lee's troops went over, constructing defensive works at Florence while the remainder of the army encamped in and around Tuscumbia. Nature quickly bogged down the offensive. Heavy rains began buffeting the region that same day and continued for several days. The deluge hindered any kind of movement, transforming the rural dirt roads into pig wallows. The river rose, partially submerging the bridge. The already negligible repair work on the railroad was slowed even more, meaning that supplies were delayed. The road to Cherokee Station became a long mud pit crowned by wrecked wagons and dead mules. The terrible weather meant that the Army of Tennessee would soak in the downpours and muck for about three cold weeks.

Meanwhile, Forrest was in the midst of one of the most brilliant cavalry raids of the war, hitting the immense Federal supply depot at Johnsonville, Tennessee, some seventy miles west of Nashville. He was wreaking havoc there on October 30 when he received Beauregard's order to report to Hood at Florence. By the time his troopers left Johnsonville on November 4, the destruction was colossal. They destroyed four Union gunboats, eleven steamboats, fifteen barges, and tons of supplies. After a difficult march over muddy roads, Forrest had reached Corinth by November 12, when he wrote to his former commander and friend, Lt. Gen. Richard Taylor, who headed the Department of Alabama and Mississippi: "I know not how long we are to labor for that independence for which we have thus far struggled in vain, but this I do know, that I will never weary in defending our cause, which must ultimately succeed. Faith is the duty of the hour. We will succeed." The coming weeks would severely test Forrest's mettle.[13]

By early November, Thomas had about 31,000 troops on hand—still fewer than Hood—although his ranks were growing daily. One of many problems for him was that he had to spread these men to garrison a dozen or so cities and towns in addition to posting soldiers in blockhouses and outposts strung along the railroads because of the enemy threat. By then, he also was actively engaged in trying to prevent Forrest from taking Johnsonville. Schofield had the main task of trying to slow Hood's advance until Thomas was ready for a confrontation. By November 13, the XXIII Corps had reached Pulaski, with Schofield assuming overall command of his and Stanley's corps—about 22,000 men in all. The Federals also posted a small force at Lawrenceburg, nineteen miles west of Pulaski.[14]

Like Hood, Thomas suffered initially from insufficient cavalry since Sherman kept most of his horsemen to accompany him on his offensive. Furthermore, the Union cavalry was being reorganized around this time. Brig. Gen. James H. Wilson took command of the newly created cavalry corps of the Military Division of the Mississippi on October 24. His force was composed of about 50,000 men in seventy-two regiments, which sounded impressive, but these troopers were widely scattered over several states. Arriving in Tennessee and immediately given the task of trying to block Hood, Wilson found himself with only a division led by Brig. Gen. Edward Hatch and a brigade commanded by Brig. Gen. John T. Croxton—about 4,300 horsemen spread thinly and used primarily to patrol the Tennessee River crossings. Sherman had sent unmounted troopers back to Nashville and Louisville to obtain horses. If remounted, these men would be added to Thomas's force.

CHAPTER 2

"Shot Down like Animals"

With regimental bands playing, the remainder of Hood's army finally crossed the Tennessee amid heavy downpours between November 13 and 20. Forrest's troopers rode into Florence on November 16–17, and Hood assigned Forrest cavalry command of the army. This force consisted of Forrest's own two divisions, led by Brig. Gen. Abraham Buford and Brig. Gen. James R. Chalmers, plus Red Jackson's horsemen— approximately 5,000 troopers in all, according to Forrest. Jackson's command had started from Palmetto with 3,900 troopers but had lost heavily and been spread thin; it had only about 2,000 troopers still with the army. The campaign's rigors had taken a severe toll on the rest of the army's manpower as well. Hood's three corps totaled about 39,400 effective troops, including infantry and artillery, on September 20, days before he began his offensive. As he crossed the Tennessee, the corps had dwindled to some 30,600 troops fit for duty.[1]

Despite Forrest's arrival, the weather and a dearth of supplies prevented the Confederates from moving north. The presidential election in the North was over by then, Lincoln having defeated McClellan in a major blow to any remaining hopes for southern independence. The Confederates had no solid information about Sherman's whereabouts and, at this point, believed that their strategy to draw him north after Hood was working, although their intelligence was as threadbare as the soldiers' uniforms. Beauregard had reports that Sherman was either moving into Tennessee near Chattanooga or was operating in northern Alabama in the vicinity of Decatur or Huntsville. There also was intelligence that Sherman's army was at Pulaski, almost directly in Hood's path if he marched into the central part of the state. A week into November, the Confederates had received information of a "reported division" of Sherman's army as it chased Hood, a move that Jefferson Davis believed would allow Hood to attack and defeat a weakened Sherman. If this could be accomplished, Davis wrote Hood on November 7, Hood could then, "without serious obstruction or danger to the country in your rear, advance to the Ohio River."[2]

Not until November 15 did Beauregard learn that Sherman not only was in Atlanta, but appeared to be ready to leave the city, possibly moving on Savannah or Mobile. In fact, Sherman had torched Atlanta that day, marching out of the flaming ruins with about 62,000 men for the sea—possibly Savannah; the Union base at Port Royal, South Carolina; or Pensacola, Florida. Beauregard and Hood learned this shocking news on the seventeenth, making it all the more imperative for them to strike a blow. Yet with Hood's army now some 300 miles away from Atlanta and with winter descending on the Georgia and Alabama mountains, there was little chance the Army of Tennessee could intercept Sherman. Instead, Beauregard ordered Hood that same day to strike into middle Tennessee, defeat enemy forces that Thomas was believed to have gathered there, and try to lure Sherman back from Georgia through "rapid and vigorous blows." If successful, the move also would "relieve Lee" in Virginia, Beauregard noted.

Hood had all but ignored Beauregard or refused any orders that did not suit him ever since the latter's arrival. Indeed, Beauregard left Tuscumbia for Corinth on the seventeenth, "unable to await any longer the tardy preparations of General Hood for the offensive," one of Beauregard's staff officers wrote. The news about Sherman left Hood with no choice but to spear north as quickly as possible, and the fact that he and Beauregard agreed on the course of action was basically coincidental. Despite the urgency of the moment, the weather again mocked the Confederates, whipping the region with intermittent freezing rain and snow, raising the river level, and delaying Hood a few days more.[3]

Other than hitting enemy communications and supply lines, recruiting, and the expected morale boost for Tennessee troops returning to their native soil, Hood had no stated objectives when he first entered the state, although he seems to have been aiming for Nashville and beyond. As early as November 20, he told Forrest to send parties of cavalry to break the railroad and telegraph lines north of the city so "that the enemy may be prevented from sending away from Nashville any stores they may have accumulated there." On November 18, Hood dispatched a small cavalry force under Brig. Gen. Hylan B. Lyon into Tennessee to try to take Clarksville, northwest of Nashville. Lyon also was to destroy the railroad and telegraph lines to the capital and put in working order all available mills to help sustain the army if and when it reached this region.

In later years, Hood claimed that his goal was to move through Tennessee and into Kentucky, then proceed across the West Virginia mountains into Virginia, where he would join Robert E. Lee and his Army of Northern Virginia and attack the Union besiegers at Petersburg—which would have constituted an amazing feat based on the distance and hardships involved. Jefferson Davis had written to Hood in early November about beating Sherman and then advancing to the Ohio River, where the Confederates could threaten Louisville and possibly Cincinnati. If Nashville was his primary target in the initial phase of his campaign, Hood never stated it in correspondence, writing after the war that he wanted to cut off Union forces opposing him south of the capital and rout them before continuing north. Hood knew there were Federals marshaled to stop him at Pulaski, some forty miles northeast of Florence, but he had scant information about any other enemy troop concentrations in the state, including Thomas's Nashville buildup.[4]

In the continuing rain, the Confederate army began moving north from Florence on November 21, although Stewart's and Lee's corps had marched a few miles the previous day. The troops had less than a week's rations and were poorly shod and uniformed. Nevertheless, Hood had crossed his Rubicon, and as the gray columns swung toward the Tennessee border, he might have reflected on the glory to be won on the road ahead and all he had endured in his relatively young life to reach this career pinnacle.

The son of a prominent physician, John Bell Hood was born in Owingsville, Kentucky, on June 1, 1831. Through the efforts of an uncle, he obtained an appointment to the U.S. Military Academy in 1849, but his time there was dotted by academic and disciplinary issues. Nicknamed "Sam" by fellow cadets, he graduated four years later, ranking forty-fourth out of a class of fifty-two. After service in northern California, Hood was promoted to second lieutenant in 1855 and assigned to the new 2nd Cavalry Regiment, which would become an elite outfit because of its roster of officers who would later significantly shape the course of the Civil War: Albert Sidney Johnston, Robert E. Lee, Earl Van Dorn, William J. Hardee, and a major from Virginia named George H. Thomas. The 2nd spent the next five years battling Indians on the Texas frontier. In a fight at Devil's River in July 1857, Hood's left hand was pierced by an arrow, pinning it to his horse's bridle. He snapped off the point and pulled out the rest of the shaft before riding back into action.

In April 1861, days after the Confederates fired on Fort Sumter to ignite the war, Hood resigned his U.S. Army commission to join the South. Briefly assigned as a cavalry lieutenant in Kentucky before being sent to Virginia and promoted to major, Hood's aggressiveness and leadership began to draw attention. By fall 1861, he was appointed colonel of the 4th Texas Infantry and, by the following March, had risen to brigadier general in the Army of Northern Virginia. A fellow officer described him around this time as "a tall, rawboned country-looking man, with little of the soldierly appearance that West Point often gives its graduates. He looked like a . . . backwoodsman, dressed up in an ill-fitting uniform." Others who wrote of him during this period were more complimentary, mentioning his tall, slender frame, blue eyes, sandy hair,

John Bell Hood.

courteous manner, and soft but powerful voice. Hood fought well enough in the Peninsula campaign, Second Bull Run, and Antietam to be promoted to major general in October 1862 and, soon thereafter, added to his laurels as a division commander at Fredericksburg.[5]

At Gettysburg on July 2, 1863, he was severely wounded in the left arm and hand by artillery shrapnel. Surgeons saved his arm, but it would be useless for the rest of his life; Hood often carried it in a sling. By September, he had recovered enough to accompany his division to Georgia as part of Lt. Gen. James Longstreet's corps sent from Virginia to reinforce the Army of Tennessee, then commanded by Gen. Braxton Bragg. At Chickamauga on September 20, Hood was leading his men against the Federal right flank when he was shot in the right thigh. The bullet fractured his femur, and Hood lost the leg to amputation. During his recovery, soldiers from his old brigade raised more than $3,000 in a single day to buy him an artificial limb. Hood had healed sufficiently by February 1864 to be promoted to lieutenant general and sent to northern Georgia to head a corps in the Army of Tennessee, now led by Joseph Johnston. He wore a boot and spur on his artificial leg and could ride his horse about fifteen miles a day without discomfort, but he needed crutches to walk, leading his soldiers to mutter to each other about "Old Pegleg."[6]

As Sherman advanced toward Atlanta from Chattanooga that summer, Johnston employed a defensive strategy to repel him, but Union forces still edged ever closer to the city. Frustrated with Johnston, Jefferson Davis replaced him on July 17, giving Hood command of the army with a temporary promotion to full general. He was barely thirty-three, but looked older because of the war's ravages, his mustache graying and his body growing gaunt as he struggled to get about. As seemingly always with this army, there was controversy. Hardee had been next in line by seniority, age, and experience to replace Johnston, but Hardee had already had his chance after Bragg's ouster in the winter of 1863. He led the army on an interim basis but refused permanent command, paving the way for Johnston's selection.

Despite all this, Hardee was angered when Hood, his junior in rank, leapfrogged him to relieve Johnston. He claimed that Hood not only was less seasoned but lacked natural ability for such an important post. Hardee headed a corps under Hood as the struggle for Atlanta heightened, but the bad blood between them only worsened.

While he had not sought army command, Hood's pugnaciousness quickly took over. He wrote Sally "Buck" Preston, a beautiful but flirtatious socialite to whom he had been engaged since February, that the Confederates had "left all the good fighting ground behind them, and that an army by constant retreating loses confidence in itself." Hood wasted little time in taking the offensive, launching a massive attack on July 20 at Peachtree Creek and, two days later, against the Federal left east of Atlanta. Neither strike accomplished much except to add to the casualty lists on both sides. On July 23, the *New York Times* told of Johnston's replacement by Hood and carried initial reports of the battles for Atlanta, where the new Confederate commander had apparently been repulsed, despite southern claims of victory. "Ill-starred are the fortunes of all the rebel Generals in the West," the *Times* said, in what would prove to be a prophetic statement about the upcoming Tennessee campaign.[7]

There was still more hard fighting and dying at Ezra Church and Jonesboro, but Sherman could not be stopped, and Hood evacuated Atlanta on the night of September 1. By mid-September, he had shifted his army of about 40,000 to Palmetto on the West Point Railroad about twenty miles southwest of Atlanta, where the army would lick its wounds and decide on a course of action. The tough campaign had left the army with insufficient supplies and equipment, a shortage of officers, ranks thinned by attrition, infighting among its generals, and poor administration. Hood not only had to keep an eye on Sherman, but also had to attend to major rebuilding and reorganization. There had been promotions and transfers to fill officers' ranks, but the troops remained significantly under-equipped and ill-rationed as they left Palmetto in late

Stephen Dill Lee.

September. Such was the basic plight of all Confederate soldiers in late 1864, but the upcoming campaign would only magnify these shortcomings and sufferings for Hood's men.

If the army itself needed an extensive overhaul, its corps commanders all had impressive resumes, despite being in their present positions only a few months. At age thirty-one, Stephen Dill Lee, a distant relative of Robert E. Lee and the other Lees of Virginia, was the youngest lieutenant general in the Confederate army. Lee was a blue blood from South Carolina, born in Charleston, and graduated from West Point in 1854. At the academy, one of his most influential professors had been George Thomas, who instructed him and other cadets in artillery and cavalry. After service in the Seminole Wars and in Texas, Lee resigned his commission to join the Confederacy in early 1861. On Beauregard's staff at Charleston, he had been involved in negotiations for the surrender of Fort Sumter, and his own artillery had opened the bombardment to kindle the war. Lee saw action as a staff officer and artilleryman in the eastern theater, and after his appointment to brigadier general in November 1862, he was sent to command the artillery at Vicksburg. After the city surrendered in July 1863, Lee, having been taken prisoner, was exchanged and promoted to major general in August. He spent less than a year leading the cavalry of the obscure Department of Mississippi, Alabama, West Tennessee, and East Louisiana before he was appointed lieutenant general and assumed command of Hood's old corps in the Army of Tennessee. He and Hood were well acquainted since they had been at West Point together for three years and had served in the Army of Northern Virginia before both came west.[8]

Alexander P. Stewart, forty-three years old, was a Tennessean and 1842 West Point graduate who had resigned from the U.S. Army in 1845 because of poor health. Beginning a new career as an educator, he had served as chair of mathematics and philosophy at Cumberland University and the University of Nashville before the war. Despite being an antisecessionist Whig, he joined the South and was named a brigadier general in November 1861. Nicknamed "Old Straight" by his men,

Benjamin Franklin Cheatham.

Stewart rose to major general in June 1863. A year later, he was appointed lieutenant general and given corps command to replace Lt. Gen. Leonidas Polk, who was killed at Pine Mountain, Georgia.[9]

Benjamin F. Cheatham was newest in corps command, having taken over when Hardee was reassigned in late September. Born in Nashville, Cheatham had turned forty-four while the army was on the march through northeastern Alabama. He had seen action in the Mexican War as a colonel of Tennessee volunteers and later was a major general of state militia as well as a gentleman farmer. Appointed a Confederate brigadier in July 1861 and a major general the following March, he had fought from Shiloh to Atlanta and beyond in all of the Army of Tennessee's campaigns. Recognized as a hard fighter, Cheatham was respected by his men and was especially popular among the Tennesseans, but he was also notorious for his engagements with the bottle, both in combat and in camp.[10]

As his troops prepared to leave Florence, Hood's general orders on November 20 were a mix of bad news and optimism:

> The commanding general announces to the army that on the march we are about commencing there may be a scarcity of the bread ration. He confidently appeals to the officers and men to meet this privation, should it come, in a cheerful, manly spirit with which they have heretofore encountered similar and greater hardships. The privation, at most, will be of short duration, and while it lasts the meat ration can be proportionately increased. The fruitful fields of Tennessee are before us, and as we march to repossess them let us remember that the country we traverse, perhaps with hunger, was a rich and bountiful land till wasted by the enemy, that similar desolation awaits every portion of our country relinquished to the invader, and let the privation be to us not a cause of murmuring, but an incentive and an occasion for the exhibition of a most determined patriotism.[11]

There was a brief respite of agreeable temperatures as the butternut columns entered Tennessee, but this would be a winter to be remembered around warm hearths for years as the cold soon returned with rain and snow. The corps marched north in three columns on roads generally parallel to each other. Forrest's horsemen led the advance, skirmishing with Edward Hatch's and John T. Croxton's Union cavalry, who grudgingly gave ground. Hatch's men were especially troublesome since they were armed with seven-shot Spencer carbines, giving them tremendous firepower. Nevertheless, Hood's men plunged ahead despite short rations, thin uniforms, and bare feet. But spirits soared; the soldiers were eager to be on the offensive and to put behind them the setbacks of the past months that had left the army snake-bitten. At the state line, the passing columns cheered a canvas banner, hung between two trees, which read, "Tennessee—A Grave or a Free Home." "It was as gallant an army as ever any Captain commanded," recalled Capt. W. O. Dodd, one of Forrest's cavalrymen. "The long march from Atlanta had caused the timid and sick to be left behind, and every man remaining was a veteran. Then the long and sad experience of retreating was now reversed, and we were going to redeem Tennessee and Kentucky, and the morale of the army was excellent."[12]

Unknown to Hood, his delay at the Tennessee was giving Thomas valuable time to cobble together his army to meet the threat. There had been no major Union stand at the river because Thomas did not have enough men at the time to fight the Confederates and also guard railroads and other strategic points in the region. The fact that two-thirds of his beloved Army of the Cumberland was with Sherman and by then marching farther south had to be unsettling to Thomas at this critical juncture. Still, the Federals believed Hood would turn and follow Sherman when he learned of the Union foray from Atlanta, but this did not happen. With his cavalry closely watching the Confederates' movements, Thomas was convinced by November 22 that Hood was moving into Tennessee with his entire army. He was still outnumbered, however, and compelled to remain on the defensive. There was cavalry fighting near Lawrenceburg that day in which Hatch held his own before withdrawing toward Pulaski, which Schofield evacuated within hours, fearing that he would be outflanked and cut off.[13]

The cavalry continued to spar as Schofield back-pedaled in the face of Hood's advance, retreating north of the Duck River at Columbia on the night of November 27. Movements of both sides during this period were complicated by the cold weather, sleet, rain, and snow; the roads were clogged with mud and frozen ruts. Schofield sent Stanley's 2nd Division, commanded by Brig. Gen. George D. Wagner, to the village of Spring Hill on the Columbia Turnpike about twelve miles north of Columbia. Unsure of what Hood was planning, Schofield wanted to secure his escape route to that point and then withdraw to Franklin, twenty miles south of Nashville. While Stanley moved toward Spring Hill, Schofield's corps occupied its new position north of the Duck, near Columbia. Hood was indeed up to something. He wanted to outflank the enemy, reach the turnpike behind him, and trap or destroy Schofield's little army— or at least keep Schofield from reaching Nashville before the Confederates. By this time, Hood had decided to strike the capital, telling chaplain Charles T. Quintard of the 1st Tennessee Infantry about his plans to take Nashville. Even so, Hood seemed to be unaware of Thomas's ever-increasing troop strength there and perhaps believed Schofield's force was all that stood in the way of the city's capture.[14]

Forrest and most of his riders crossed the Duck late on November 28, making for Spring Hill. Leaving a portion of Lee's Corps in front of the Union positions at the river, the rest of Hood's infantry followed the cavalry on the morning of the twenty-ninth. Forrest brushed aside bluecoat cavalry and collided with Stanley's infantry near Spring Hill, but he could not penetrate the Union lines since they had artillery and more men. By late afternoon, however, elements of Cheatham's Corps, primarily Cleburne's Division, had reached the scene, sparking hard fighting before sundown. The gathering darkness would come to symbolize the most critical lost opportunity of Hood's campaign and ignite a controversy still debated.

Apparently believing that Cheatham had secured the road behind Schofield, Hood bivouacked for the night. But the turnpike remained in Union hands, and overnight on November 29–30, all of Schofield's troops withdrew north through this still-open door, easily within earshot and sight of the Confederates huddled around their campfires. A communications breakdown, not negligence, seems to have caused the problem, but to the end of his life, Hood blamed Cheatham for not closing the trap. "From Palmetto to Spring Hill, the campaign was all that I could have desired," Hood wrote in February 1865. "The fruits ought to have been gathered at that point." After the war, Hood described his maneuver to get behind Schofield at Spring Hill as "the best move in my career as a soldier" but one that he was "destined to behold come to naught." It also deepened his doubts about his troops' willingness to fight unless shielded by defenses, a flaw he blamed on Joe Johnston's lack of aggression. The army seemed to be "unwilling to accept battle unless under the protection of breastworks," which worried him greatly. "In my inmost heart, I questioned whether or not I would ever succeed in eradicating this evil. It seemed to me I had exhausted every means in the power of one man to remove this stumbling block to the Army of Tennessee." The war of words and accusations would last for years after the conflict. By then, the thousands of Confederate soldiers who fell in Hood's Tennessee offensive and during the hellish retreat that followed would not have a say in the outcome.[15]

If the mistakes at Spring Hill troubled Hood to the grave, the nightmare of Franklin, less than a day later, would be torment for the ages. Hood was enraged on the morning of November 30 when he realized that Schofield had escaped. He ordered the advance of Cheatham's and Stewart's corps, unwilling to wait for Lee's troops, who were coming up from Columbia but were still well to the rear. Schofield reached Franklin that morning and expected to continue his withdrawal through the town and across the Big Harpeth River, but both the turnpike bridge and the railroad span needed work before the army could pass. Because of this delay, Schofield hustled his men into previously prepared earthworks south of town.

Nearing Franklin that afternoon, Hood surveyed the Federals entrenched in the distance and, despite objections from Forrest and others, ordered an immediate attack. The army that had forgotten how to fight in the open was about to relearn smash-mouth combat with the enemy—at least in Hood's view, his bloody and fruitless offensives at Atlanta the previous July now an apparently distant memory. By about 4 P.M., Stewart's and Cheatham's soldiers were formed in battle lines, 20,000 men ready to make an assault that would eclipse Pickett's Charge at Gettysburg in numbers. This would be one of the grandest and most terrible spectacles of the war. Marching over mostly level, open fields, the massed Confederates soon came under fire. Union artillery shredded gaps in the gray lines; infantry unleashed a tornado of lead.

The Confederates were repelled, but regrouped and came on again and again, despite ghastly casualties. There was brutal hand-to-hand fighting until the battle flickered out around 9 P.M., but Schofield's defenses were never seriously breached. Echoes of gunfire faded in the cold darkness, only to be replaced by the shrieks, prayers, and moans of thousands of wounded. The Confederate dead lay in contorted heaps, five of Hood's generals among them, including the irreplaceable Patrick Cleburne and one of his brigadiers, Hiram Granbury. Maj. Gen. John C. Brown's division of Cheatham's Corps was particularly hard hit: Brig. Gen. John Adams, Brig. Gen. States Rights Gist, and Brig. Gen. Otho F. Strahl were killed, while John C. Carter was mortally wounded. Brown himself was injured, one of six of Hood's generals wounded or captured at Franklin. Hood reported casualties of 4,500, but they were actually about 7,700, including approximately 1,750 dead. Union losses were considerably less, about 2,300. In addition to his generals, Hood also lost severely among other officers at every level, including fifty-four regimental commanders killed,

John M. Schofield.

wounded, or captured. What was left of the Army of Tennessee held its ground.

Leaving his dead and wounded to the care of the enemy, Schofield evacuated Franklin that night, and by the morning of December 1, he had his troops safely within Nashville's defenses. These fortifications were growing stronger by the hour thanks to "constant and severe labor," according to a Federal officer, and Thomas's forces were further bolstered by the arrival from Missouri of Maj. Gen. Andrew J. Smith's three divisions from the XVI Corps. Also reaching Nashville was a mishmash of some 5,000 men who came in from Chattanooga, described by Capt. Henry Stone of Thomas's staff as "chiefly sluggards of General Sherman's army, too late for their proper commands." These soldiers were organized into a division called the Provisional Detachment (District of the Etowah) under Maj. Gen. James B. Steedman; the detachment also included several regiments of U.S. Colored Troops that had been on railroad guard duty. Adding in Wilson's cavalry, Thomas by now had about 72,000 troops, including garrison and reserve units, to face Hood, but it was far from a cohesive fighting force. "It was an ill-assorted and heterogeneous mass," Stone stated, "not yet welded into an army, and lacking a great proportion of the outfit with which to undertake an aggressive campaign. Horses, wagons, mules, pontoons, everything needed to mobilize an army, had to be obtained. At that time, they did not exist at Nashville." The shortage of pontoons would figure prominently in the near future.[16]

While ambulances and burial details scuttled about the Franklin battlefield on December 1, Hood faced monumental decisions. While he claimed victory, his army had been mauled, the already tough winter was deepening, and he was a long distance from his Mississippi supply depots. His command structure was seriously chewed up and had to be addressed immediately. The enemy not only knew of Hood's situation, but was poised with at least a substantial, if not overwhelming, force in one of the most strongly fortified cities on the planet. Riding over the horrible field that morning, Hood is said to have wept openly and later wrote that he "could but indulge in sad and painful thought, as I beheld so many brave soldiers stricken down by the enemy whom, a few hours previous, at Spring Hill, we had held within the palm of our hands." Despite the harsh reality, he still had options. From Franklin, he could easily march the thirty-five miles southeast to Murfreesboro, where he could likely overpower the Union garrison and slice its rail link to Chattanooga, or he could cross the Cumberland River east or west of Nashville and disrupt communications and supply lines. Hood's other choices were more direct: he could retreat, basically admitting defeat and the failure of his campaign, or he could resume his drive toward Nashville.[17]

As was his nature, Hood did not hesitate: he would march on Nashville. While occupying the capital would be a significant step in helping the Confederates reclaim the state, just as important at this stage of the war was the fact that the city was the Union military's communications and transportation hub in central Tennessee. Located mainly on the south bank of the serpentine Cumberland River, the city held a vast stockpile of supplies for the western U.S. armies and had been occupied by Federal troops since February 1862. Since then, Union forces had constructed a formidable defensive complex of two lines around the city, anchored by three strongholds, Forts Negley, Morton, and Houston. When Hood entered Tennessee, thousands of Union soldiers and laborers had started to further strengthen the defensive lines, which stretched in a jagged crescent of about twenty miles, generally facing south.

The missed chance at Spring Hill and the slaughter of Franklin haunted many of the Confederates who trudged toward Nashville. Capt. W. O. Dodd of Chalmers's cavalry recalled the acres of Confederate dead at Franklin:

> I could not but feel that the lives of these men were a useless sacrifice. It seemed to me to be a rashness occasioned by the blunder of the day before. It was an attempt to make good by reckless daring the blunder which incapacity had occasioned the previous day [at

Fortified railroad bridge across the Cumberland River at Nashville, 1864. LIBRARY OF CONGRESS

Spring Hill]. . . . The next morning we should have buried our dead, and those of the enemy, and retired from the State. While we held the battle-field . . . we were disheartened and demoralized. We had witnessed on one day a brilliant flank movement terminate by lying down by the roadside in order to let the enemy pass by, and on the next day saw the army led out in a slaughter-pen to be shot down like animals. Soldiers are quick to perceive blunders.

Dodd added that while most of the soldiers believed Cheatham was to blame for Spring Hill, Hood was also at fault: "And when at Franklin, the attempt was made to do by storm against an entrenched and reinforced foe, what strategy failed to do the day before, the morale of the army was destroyed."[18]

The Confederates' failure to snag Schofield at Spring Hill and its effect on what transpired at Franklin hours later was not lost on the Federals. Captain Stone of Thomas's staff later wrote that November 29 "may well be set down in the calendar of lost opportunities. The heroic valor of those same [Confederate] troops the next day, and their frightful losses, as they attempted to retrieve their mistake, show what might have been."[19]

Reaching Nashville on December 2, Hood now had about 23,000 men, including 18,700 effective infantry, left to try to invest the city. His 5,000 or so cavalry were scattered in various assignments. Dodd wrote that "instead of retreating at once [after Franklin] and saving the remnant of a magnificent army, we moved up and formed around Nashville. Our little army . . . was stretched for miles around the city." Gleaming at them from about two miles away, the Confederates could see the state house on its hill, the Stars and Stripes fluttering from the dome. Bugle calls and the music of Union regimental bands floated on the wintry air. Tennesseans in the ranks were surprised to see the fine building so clearly, but the once tree-covered hills around it were now bare, the thousands of logs now part of the seemingly endless Union defenses. "The Rebs might as well butt their brains against the Rocky Mountains as attempt to take it," a Union colonel wrote of Nashville.[20]

The unpredictable weather lulled the Confederates from December 2 through December 8 with fair skies and mild temperatures. They used this time to dig in on the high ground. Hood established his headquarters at Travellers Rest, the home of the John Overton family, about six miles from Nashville amid the outlying heights of the Brentwood (also known as the Overton) Hills, a rugged range of ridges overlooking the Franklin Pike and the Granny White Pike. From there, he issued orders for the army's deployment. Not strong enough to take the city by assault, Hood established a five-mile-long ribbon of defenses southeast of the city and facing north. His position closed two railroads going into the city—the Nashville & Chattanooga and the Nashville & Decatur—as well

Railroad yard and depot at Nashville. The capitol building is in the distance. LIBRARY OF CONGRESS

as four major roads from the south, but this was not nearly enough to prevent the Federals from moving freely elsewhere. There were at least five other open turnpikes and two railroads by which Union forces could be supplied and reinforced or could maneuver on the offensive. The Cumberland River, which wound through Nashville, primarily to the north, was also open to Thomas and was prowled by Union gunboats. Stewart's Corps anchored Hood's right, his troops astride the Granny White Pike and about a mile to the west bending to the southwest to cover the Hillsboro Pike. Lee's Corps held the Confederate center, his line on both sides of the Franklin Pike, while Cheatham's Corps formed the right near the Nolensville Pike and blocked the Nashville & Chattanooga. The cavalry operated on both flanks. Cheatham had been especially decimated by the loss of officers at Franklin. "Where were our generals?" the infantryman Sam Watkins lamented. "Nearly all our captains and colonels were gone. Companies mingled with companies, regiments with regiments, and brigades with brigades."[21]

The gray army still was not remotely outfitted for the rigors of a winter campaign; the wear of months of hard activity in the field, the long marches, and the bloody battles had exacted an awful price with each passing day. Hood's supply and communications lines were stretched razor thin, and ever-increasing numbers of his men needed hats, shoes, blankets, and other equipment. Occasional trains from Decatur, which the Federals evacuated on November 23 to consolidate their forces against Hood, brought in some provisions and clothing items. There were few tents and a good portion of the soldiers slept in the newly dug trenches, sheltered with blankets and oil-cloths. The butchering of a cattle soon became a main event since it meant not only meat for the troops, but rawhides that some of the men cut up and wrapped around their feet for makeshift shoes.[22]

As his men entrenched on December 2, Hood was bothered by the fact that a Union force still held Murfreesboro, which lay on the Nashville & Chattanooga Railroad about thirty miles southeast of the capital. Chattanooga and Knoxville were also very much in Federal hands. "It was apparent that he [the enemy] would soon have to take the offensive to relieve his garrisons at those points or cause them to be evacuated," Hood later wrote. Maj. Gen. William B. Bate's infantry division was nearing Nashville that morning when Bate received orders from Hood to destroy the railroad between the capital and Murfreesboro.

On December 4, Hood ordered Forrest and most of the cavalry to Murfreesboro to determine if the town could be taken. With the divisions of Buford and Jackson, Forrest moved out the next morning and soon linked up with Bate's infantry, with Forrest assuming overall command of the combined force. The Confederates soon realized that the Murfreesboro garrison, commanded by Union major general Lovell H. Rousseau, was considerably stronger than they realized. Hood had

Nashville as seen from the capitol building, 1864. NATIONAL ARCHIVES

believed that about 5,000 Federals held the place, but reinforcements had more than doubled that total. Forrest was reinforced on December 6 with the arrival of two small infantry
brigades, Sears's and Palmer's, but still was not strong enough
to launch an attack. The Federals seized the initiative the next
day, springing an assault of about 3,500 men and routing most
of Bate's men. A furious Forrest tried to rally the troops; at least
one account stated that he shot a fleeing color bearer, grabbing
the flag in a vain attempt to stop this "shameful retreat," as he
described it. Bate also failed to halt the exodus, and Forrest had
to bring up cavalry to help quell this threat. Nine days later,
Bate's soldiers would again be put to the test, this time with the
fate of Hood's army hanging in the balance.[23]

Despite the setback at Murfreesboro, Hood's confidence
grew daily as his siege lines were strengthened. The keystones
of his perimeter would be five earthen redoubts constructed to
protect the Hillsboro Pike as well as the army's left flank. These
forts were identified as Redoubt No. 1 through 5, each generally facing west and armed with a few artillery pieces and some
riflemen. "Should he [Thomas] attack me in position, I felt

that I could defeat him, and thus gain possession of Nashville with abundant supplies for the army," Hood later reflected. "This would give me possession of Tennessee." In later years, Hood claimed that he knew he was vastly outnumbered by Thomas, but this does not appear to be true since he had dispatched a substantial portion of his force to assail Murfreesboro, leaving him with only 15,000 infantry. He also continued his quest to draw reinforcements from other quarters, even sending a letter to Thomas under a truce flag on December 5 asking for an exchange of prisoners. Thomas replied promptly that all of his prisoners of war had already been sent north. With Forrest's departure, Hood left himself with only one cavalry division—Chalmers's—which he posted between the Hillsboro Pike and the Cumberland River on the left.[24]

The weather continued to be sunny and mild until about noon on December 7, when wind-whipped rain arrived with colder temperatures. Conditions worsened the next day as the ground froze and the mercury continued to plummet. A winter storm rolled in that night, attacking both armies, with temperatures of about twelve degrees and rain turning to sleet. A mix of ice and snow glazed the countryside in silvery sheets by the morning of the ninth. The ground was now brick-like to the shivering Confederates who tried to dig their fortifications or burrow into foxholes with little more than thin blankets for protection. The freezing and muddy conditions all but paralyzed Hood's wagon supply line between the army and Franklin. Work on Redoubts No. 4 and No. 5 was slowed not only by a lack of entrenching tools, but also by the granite-like ground.[25]

The winter had quickly devolved into what would be one of the worst in Tennessee history, and the tattered besiegers suffered substantially more in the teeth-rattling frigidity than did Thomas's well-fed, well-clothed troops hunkered in and around the city. "Being in range of the Federal guns from Fort Negley, we were not allowed to have fires at night, and our thin and ragged blankets were but poor protection against the cold, raw blasts," Sam Watkins recalled. "The cold stars seem to twinkle with unusual brilliancy, and the pale moon seems to be but one vast heap of frozen snow, which glimmers in the cold gray sky, and the air gets colder by its coming." Another Confederate remembered the freezing rain leaving two- to three-inch icicles dangling on soldiers' coattails.[26]

By December 10, the Confederates' fuel supply was so depleted that Hood ordered Lee's and Stewart's corps back from their lines a short distance to cut wood. The next day, the temperature dipped to about ten below zero, and three inches of ice and snow covered the ground, while brutal wind gusts howled over all. Rugs and carpets disappeared from houses in the area as the Confederates cut them into blankets. Union patrols reported seeing the bodies of men who had frozen to death. "We bivouac on the cold and hard-frozen ground, and when we walk about, the echo of our footsteps sound like the echo of a tombstone," Watkins noted. "The earth is crusted with snow, and the wind from the northwest is piercing our very bones. We can see our ragged soldiers, with sunken cheeks and famine-glistening eyes. . . . A few raw-boned horses stood shivering under the ice-covered trees, nibbling the short, scanty grass." Still, the sufferings were not universal. An Alabama artillerist in Stewart's command wrote his sister in mid-December, "We had chimneys to our tents and were doing finely."[27]

While the sub-freezing temperatures lingered, Hood recalled Bate and his division from Murfreesboro on December 9, later telling Beauregard that "our infantry behaved badly." As a replacement, Hood sent Smith's Brigade, commanded by Col. Charles H. Olmstead, to Forrest. Meanwhile, the cavalry chief was busy prying up sections of the railroad, burning blockhouses, and trying to prevent the Murfreesboro garrison from launching any other offensive strikes. "I hoped thus to isolate the enemy's force . . . and prevent them from foraging on the country or obtaining fuel, and if they should attempt to leave the place to have attacked them on their march," Hood later said of Forrest's operations.[28]

Nine days after reaching Nashville, Hood remained confident, at least outwardly, that his army was in good shape overall, despite the cold and the incompleteness of his defenses. The

Tennessee & Alabama Railroad was operational and open to the Confederates south to Pulaski, and they had captured two engines and three cars to use on this line, but the railroad farther south to Decatur needed to be repaired to bring up ordnance and other supplies on a regular basis. Hood also requested that the Memphis & Charleston be repaired between Cherokee Station and Decatur, further lengthening his supply route. "Our line is strongly intrenched, and all the available positions upon our flanks and in rear of them are now being fortified with strong, self-supporting, detached works, so that they may easily be defended should the enemy move out upon us," Hood wrote to Secretary of War James A. Seddon on December 11. "I think the position of this army is now such as to force the enemy to take the initiative."

Hood also was set to organize a conscription system to bring into the army men of military age. His spies within the city also had brought word of Smith's Union troops coming in from the trans-Mississippi region. "I hope this will enable us to obtain some of our troops from that side in time for the spring campaign, if not sooner," he told Seddon.[29]

Seddon and Beauregard requested reinforcements for Hood—or at least some diversion to draw Federal forces away from him—from Gen. Edmund Kirby Smith, commander of the Trans-Mississippi Department. But Smith did not learn of the request until December 20, too late to assist Hood. The Confederates also held out the remote hope that troops would be sent to Tennessee from Texas. The effort to fill the army's ranks with new recruits had been greatly disappointing, with only 164 men joining the Confederates from the point they entered Tennessee until December 13.[30]

With his troops suffering in the unmerciful cold, Hood on December 13 learned that fifty bales of blankets belonging to his army were at Augusta, Georgia, and asked Beauregard to have them shipped immediately. "The weather is severe, the ground covered with snow, and the men stand much in need of them," he wrote, also requesting 10,000 "suits of clothing" and all additional blankets that could be spared. While many

Edmund Kirby Smith.

of his soldiers froze, Hood appears to have suffered very little in his well-appointed headquarters tents near the Overton house. There was plenty of good food and a barrel of whiskey for the staff.[31]

Amid all his preparations, Hood received word about this time that General Carter had died on the night of December 10 from his Franklin wound. He was nine days short of his twenty-seventh birthday.

CHAPTER 3

A Much-Doubted Thomas

As the Confederate legions fanned out before Nashville in December's frosty first week, George Thomas was feeling uncomfortable heat from the Union brass. They were impatient for him to strike the enemy, weather be damned. "From the time of Hood's arrival . . . the President and Secretary of War [Edwin Stanton] became very urgent in their desire that Thomas should at once assume the aggressive," wrote Gen. Jacob Cox. Based on their suggestions, Grant sent word to Thomas on December 2 to attack Hood at once. "Probably no commander ever underwent two weeks of greater anxiety and distress of mind than General Thomas" between Hood's arrival and the climactic battle, recalled Henry Stone of Thomas's staff. Grant "did not cease, day or night, to send him . . . most urgent and often most uncalled-for orders in regard to his operations."[1]

To understand the tension sizzling between Nashville and Washington, it is essential to know the general in the crosshairs. One observer who saw Thomas that winter described him as standing about five feet, eleven inches, and weighing 200 pounds, "a fine specimen of the physical man, graceful, easy and deliberate in all his actions, a splendid rider, thoroughly informed, and exceedingly courteous with all men high and low. . . . His head is very well shaped, hair light and sprinkled with gray, gray whiskers and beard, full, square face, fine forehead, full blue eyes expressive of kindness and at times twinkling with ill restrained humor." Thomas had earned a variety of nicknames prior to Nashville. While the Northern press crowned him the "Rock of Chickamauga" after his legendary stand there, his contemporaries had called him "Old Tom" as a West Point cadet. Later classes on the Hudson dubbed him "Slow Trot" or "Old Slow Trot" when he was an instructor at the military academy. The boys in his beloved Army of the Cumberland mostly called him "Pap" or "Old Pap."[2]

George Henry Thomas was born in Southampton County, Virginia, on July 31, 1816. He and his family, consisting of a widowed mother and two sisters, were in the eye of a historic hurricane in 1831 when Nat Turner's slave rebellion erupted in the county, forcing the Thomases to flee and hide in the woods. Appointed to West Point in 1836, he graduated in 1840, ranked twelfth behind classmate William Tecumseh Sherman (sixth) and top-ranking Paul O. Hebert from Louisiana. Hebert went on to become a little-known Confederate brigadier while Thomas and Sherman constituted, with Grant, the "triumvirate who won the war for the Union," according to historian Ezra Warner. After graduation, Thomas was an artilleryman for fifteen years, serving in several coastal forts and seeing combat against the Seminoles in Florida and in the Mexican War, during which he earned brevets for gallantry at Monterey and Buena Vista. Thomas instructed at West Point in 1853 while Hood and Schofield were cadets there. It also was about this time that he began courting and then married Frances Kellogg of Troy, New York, whom he met when she came to the academy to visit a relative.[3]

When the 2nd U.S. Cavalry was organized in 1855, Thomas was one of its first majors, gaining more invaluable experience in the regiment's five years of hard campaigns in Texas. During much of this period, Thomas served under Col. Albert Sidney Johnston, Lt. Col. Robert E. Lee, and Maj. William J. Hardee. Amid the looming secession threat, Thomas applied for the position of commandant of cadets at the Virginia Military Institute in January 1861. Believed by many to be pro-Confederate because of this, Thomas showed his Union allegiance in March when he rejected Virginia governor John Letcher's offer to become the state's chief of ordnance. His decision infuriated his Virginia relatives, who disowned him, turning his picture to

George H. Thomas.

the wall, destroying his old letters, and telling him that he should change his name.[4]

After hostilities flared, Thomas led a brigade in Brig. Gen. Robert Patterson's Shenandoah Valley operations in 1861 and was promoted to brigadier general of volunteers in August. Transferred to the western theater, his first victory as a commander came at Mill Springs, Kentucky, in January 1862. Seeing action at Shiloh, Thomas was promoted to major general of volunteers in April and led the Army of the Tennessee in the siege of Corinth that month.

Thomas was to assume command of the Army of the Ohio in September 1862 to replace Maj. Gen. Don Carlos Buell, but Thomas backed Buell, essentially refusing the promotion, and the order was suspended. When Buell was relieved in late October after the Battle of Perryville, Thomas's earlier reluctance resulted in his being bypassed in favor of William S. Rosecrans, who would command the newly established Army of the Cumberland. At Stones River, Thomas led Rosecrans's center wing, composed of almost 30,000 troops, and days after the battle, he was assigned to lead the army's XIV Corps after yet another reorganization.[5]

Thomas's legend was forged on the slopes of Snodgrass Hill, also known as Horseshoe Ridge, at Chickamauga on September 20, 1863. With most of the Union army in retreat, he had held the height with a patchwork defense against repeated Confederate assaults for several hours before withdrawing. Promoted to brigadier general in the Regular army a few weeks later, Thomas was given command of the Army of the Cumberland. He performed admirably in the defense of Chattanooga and the subsequent defeat of Bragg's besieging army at Missionary Ridge, which overlooked the city. In the Atlanta campaign, Thomas's army had composed more than half of Sherman's force. Still, Thomas had a reputation for being deliberate, if efficient; Sherman called him "true as steel."[6]

An increasingly impatient Grant, however, expressed his uncertainty about Thomas in a December 3 note to Sherman: "Thomas has got back into the defenses of Nashville, with

Gen. George Thomas and a group of officers at a council of war near Ringgold, Georgia, May 5, 1864. NATIONAL ARCHIVES

Hood close upon him. . . . Part of this falling back was undoubtedly necessary, and all of it may have been. It did not look so, however, to me. In my opinion, Thomas far outnumbers Hood in infantry. In cavalry Hood has the advantage in morale and numbers. I hope yet that Hood will be badly crippled, if not destroyed." In a dispatch the same day, Thomas explained his reasons for pulling his forces back to Nashville after the Franklin battle: "My force of cavalry and infantry at Franklin being so much less than that of the enemy, I determined to fall back to this place to concentrate my infantry and give time to General Wilson to arm and equip sufficient cavalry to meet Forrest," he wrote. "I have here now nearly as much infantry as Hood, and in a few days hope to have cavalry enough to enable me to assume the offensive."[7]

The Union cavalry that had faced Hood needed rest and had lost a great many horses, but Wilson went about the organization of his new corps with great vigor and enthusiasm. His troopers had confiscated mounts during the retreat to

Nashville and this impressment continued in and around the city and surrounding countryside and into Kentucky. "The cavalry officers did their duty well and rapidly," Wilson noted, "sparing no man's horses provided they were fit for cavalry service." These included animals belonging to Andrew Johnson, military governor of Tennessee and vice president–elect after Lincoln's reelection, as well as to farmers, street car companies, hospitals, and circuses. Troopers also were coming in from various quarters, and there was a wholesale hubbub in the cavalry camps at Edgefield on the city's northern outskirts as the horses were shod and the men equipped. In little more than a week, Wilson had a command totaling 12,000 cavalry ready for action, not including about 3,000 other men for whom mounts were unavailable but who were ready to fight as infantry. Many of the mounted troopers were issued the new seven-shot Spencer repeating carbine, which gave them an immense advantage in firepower, but there was not enough time to rearm the entire command, which had a mix of Maynard and Sharps carbines and Spencer multishot rifles.[8]

Wilson was serving in western Virginia with Maj. Gen. Philip H. Sheridan's Army of the Shenandoah when he celebrated his twenty-seventh birthday on September 2, 1864, even as Sherman entered Atlanta. Born and raised on the family farm near Shawneetown, Illinois, he had Virginia roots. His father was a native of that state and related to the prominent Harrison family from the James River region. Wilson spent a year at McKendree College in Lebanon, Illinois, before entering West Point in 1855. He completed the five-year course in 1860, ranking sixth in his class, which also included Wesley Merritt and Stephen Ramseur. All three would rise to the rank of major general in the coming war, and Ramseur would fight and die for the South.

Upon graduation, Wilson was sent to the Pacific Northwest, where he served as assistant topographical engineer for the Department of Oregon and was posted at Fort Vancouver. When the war came, he was chief topographical engineer for the Port Royal Expedition during the winter of 1861–62 and held the same assignment for the U.S. Department of the South, participating in the siege and reduction of Fort Pulaski near Savannah, Georgia. As an aide-de-camp to Gen. George McClellan, Wilson saw action during the Maryland campaign in 1862 and also served on Grant's staff in the western theater, primarily as an engineer. During the Vicksburg campaign, he was inspector general of the Army of the Tennessee, and in late October 1863, he was promoted to brigadier general of volunteers.

His advancement, however, did not jumpstart his mundane career, at least not at this point. Wilson remained on staff duty at the Battle of Chattanooga and was chief engineer for Sherman's force sent to relieve Knoxville in late 1863. He was named chief of the newly established Cavalry Bureau in February 1864, although he basically had no cavalry experience. In this capacity, amid the Washington bureaucracy, he showed his vast talent for organization and administration, "which, coupled with the tactical sense he was later to demonstrate, made him one of the war's foremost figures," wrote historian Ezra Warner. In the Richmond campaign of 1864, Grant assigned Wilson to lead one of Sheridan's cavalry divisions, and he was in combat from the runup to Petersburg to the clashes in the Shenandoah. In late September, he was assigned as chief of cavalry for Sherman's Military Division of the Mississippi; Sheridan called him "the best man for the position." Grant added his own praise, telling Sherman that the tireless Wilson's personal activity would increase the effect of the cavalry by "fifty percent." When Wilson first arrived in late October, Sherman initially wanted him to organize the cavalry into a corps composed of three small divisions. Based on Wilson's advice and the poor condition of the horses, Sherman retained only one division, led by Judson Kilpatrick, and sent Wilson on to Nashville to aid Thomas.[9]

Even as Thomas's army came together, Grant remained antsy and again aired his frustration with Thomas in a December 6 message to Sherman: "I have said all I can to force him to attack, without giving the positive order until today. Today,

James H. Wilson.

however, I could stand it no longer, and gave the order without any reserve. I think the battle will take place tomorrow."[10] Other heavyweights were also urging action. "Thomas seems unwilling to attack because it is hazardous, as if all war was anything but hazardous," Secretary of War Stanton wrote to Grant on the morning of December 7. "If he waits for Wilson to get ready, Gabriel will be blowing his last horn." From his headquarters at City Point, Virginia, a few hours later, Grant replied, "You probably saw my order to Thomas to attack. If he does not do it promptly, I would recommend superseding him by Schofield, leaving Thomas subordinate."

Grant's criticism was not wholly unexpected by Thomas, since they were not on the best of terms. There had been friction between them during the siege of Corinth in 1862, and Thomas also believed Grant had been given credit that he himself deserved for the Missionary Ridge victory. Furthermore, when Grant had been elevated to commander in chief of the armies, he had chosen his close friend Sherman, Thomas's junior in rank, for promotion to major general in the Regular army. Thomas was quietly resentful of all this, as the telegraph clicked daily with more acid words from his superiors. While enduring Grant's verbal barrage, Thomas focused on the real enemy, stretched amid the silent ridges to the south. He knew Hood from West Point as a student who had ranked near the bottom in artillery and cavalry proficiency. He also remembered their days in the 2nd Cavalry when he was Hood's senior officer.[11]

Despite these distractions and sideshows, Thomas had a detailed battle plan ready to implement and issued orders to his corps commanders for an attack at daybreak on December 10. But the ice and snow storm of the eighth and ninth forced him to delay his offensive, the soldiers turning to the ax rather than the musket. The Federals received wood supplies by train and river transport, especially for the hospitals, but the men in the outlying defenses felled trees for their campfires. With the enemy doing the same, thousands of cord were chopped daily. A Union officer who had enjoyed the beauty of the city's groves and forests remarked that if the weather persisted and the Confederates stuck to their trenches, there would not be a tree standing within five miles of Nashville before the end of December.[12]

In the Union works, the Federals, like the Confederates across the way, also dealt with the cruel temperatures and conditions. Captain Stone of Thomas's staff wrote that "the ground was covered with a glare of ice which made all the fields and hillsides impassible for horses and scarcely passable for foot-men. The natives declared that the Yankees brought their weather as well as their army with them. Every corps commander in the army protested that a movement under such conditions would be little short of madness, and certain to result in disaster." The weather was "excessively cold for this latitude," a Union surgeon wrote, the result being "much suffering on the part of the troops." A number of the already much-fatigued men who had retreated from the Alabama border to Nashville and then had been put to work on the defenses began to show up on hospital rolls. "Many, too, who had without detriment to their health undergone all the hardships of the summer and fall campaign, now yielded to the effects of the bitter cold," pulmonary and rheumatic problems becoming "quite prevalent," the physician noted.[13]

Even as the winter storm raged, the drumbeat against Thomas was unrelenting. "If Thomas has not struck yet, he ought to be ordered to hand over his command to Schofield," Grant wired Maj. Gen. Henry W. Halleck, the army's chief of staff, on the eighth. "There is no better man to repel an attack than Thomas, but I fear he is too cautious to ever take the initiative." When Halleck offered only lukewarm support for the change, stating that Grant himself should issue the order and accept sole responsibility for it, Grant backed off somewhat. "I want General Thomas reminded of the importance of immediate action," he answered Halleck that night. "I would not say relieve him until I hear further from him."[14]

The situation at Nashville had evolved into a battle of wills pitting Grant and, to a lesser degree, Lincoln and Stanton

Ulysses S. Grant.

against Thomas. Right or wrong, Thomas was as immovable as he had been at Chickamauga, and with these superiors hundreds of miles away, he proceeded with his meticulous plans to destroy Hood when his own army was ready and the weather looked promising for a successful offensive. On the morning of December 9, Halleck sent this message to Thomas: "Lieutenant-General Grant expresses much dissatisfaction at your delay in attacking the enemy." Thomas received the dispatch a few hours later and penned a reply that afternoon. Freezing rain had bombarded Nashville and its environs since daybreak and would continue into the next day. "I feel conscious I have done everything in my power, and that the troops could not have gotten ready before this," he wrote Halleck. "If General Grant should order me to be relieved, I will submit without a murmur." Unknown to Thomas at the time—although he sensed it was in the works—the paperwork to replace him with Schofield already had been filed that very day. The order, however, was never sent to Thomas; Grant had a change of heart, at least temporarily.[15]

Despite these weighty distractions, Thomas continued to gird for his assault on Hood. He sent word to his generals on the ninth that the next day's offensive was postponed but that they should be ready to strike as soon as the storm eased. "With the threat hanging over him; with the utter impossibility, in that weather, of making any movement; with the prospect that the labors of his whole life were about to end in disappointment, if not disaster—he never, for an instant, abated his energy or his work of preparation," Stone related. Thomas did not share the content of the ominous telegrams with his staff, but "it was very evident that something greatly troubled him," according to Stone. "While the rain was falling and the fields and roads were ice-bound, he would sometimes sit by the window for an hour or more, not speaking a word, gazing steadily out upon the forbidding prospect, as if he were trying to will the storm away."

The army's leadership was retooled during the frosty lull. Maj. Gen. David S. Stanley, commander of the IV Corps, was unable to continue because of a wound sustained at Franklin and was replaced by Brig. Gen. Thomas J. Wood. Darius Couch, a veteran of the Army of the Potomac, succeeded Brevet Maj. Gen. Thomas Ruger, disabled by illness, to lead a division in Schofield's corps. Brig. Gen. George D. Wagner was relieved, and command of his division in the IV Corps went to Brig. Gen. Washington L. Elliott, Thomas's chief of cavalry in the Atlanta campaign. Brig. Gen. Kenner Garrard, who had been in combat from Fredericksburg to Gettysburg before coming west to lead a cavalry division in the Atlanta fighting, was to head an infantry division in Smith's corps. In each of these cases, other than Wood's, "the newly assigned officers were entire strangers to the troops over whom they were placed."[16]

The unknown Confederate soldier who wounded Stanley at Franklin had indirectly thrust the forty-one-year-old Wood into a role of destiny in the upcoming weeks. A native of Munfordville, Kentucky, and a second cousin of Confederate general Benjamin H. Helm, Wood was an 1845 graduate of West Point, where his first roommate had been Ulysses Grant. He had served in the Mexican War and was breveted for gallantry at Buena Vista. Commissioned as a topographical engineer, he transferred to the cavalry in 1846 and saw action in the Indian campaigns on the frontier and in the Kansas-Missouri border clashes. Promoted to brigadier general of volunteers in 1861, he led a division at Shiloh, Perryville, and Murfreesboro, especially distinguishing himself at the last battle, where he was wounded and refused to leave the field.

It was at Chickamauga that Wood shared the stage with Thomas, playing a key, but involuntary, role that resulted in the Union defeat. Bad communications among the Federals during the battle led to the misconception that a gap existed in the line on the Union right. Rosecrans, who commanded the Army of the Cumberland at the time, ordered Wood's division north to plug this hole. When Wood pulled his men out of position to comply, the movement left a real opening. Six Confederate divisions poured through it, rolling up Federal units on either side, and soon much of Rosecrans's army was retreating in disorder. Only Thomas's stand on Horseshoe Ridge saved the

Thomas J. Wood.

army from complete disaster. Rosecrans was relieved less than a month later, but Wood was not blamed for what happened and had excelled in action since then. His soldiers were first to breach the enemy's defenses in the Union victory at Missionary Ridge in November. During the Atlanta campaign, Wood saw combat from Dalton to Jonesboro and was seriously wounded in the leg in fighting at Lovejoy Station on September 2, 1864. Three months later, he had recovered sufficiently to assume command of the IV Corps. James Wilson described him as "a soldier of great experience and unfaltering courage."[17]

The units of the IV Corps had been bloodied on many western battlefields, including Stones River, Chickamauga, Atlanta, and now Franklin. The corps had been organized from a consolidation of the XX and XXI Corps in September 1863. Of the western regiments sustaining the highest battle losses, more casualties were in this corps than in any other. These veterans were more than ready for whatever challenges lay ahead of them.[18]

Thomas met with his corps commanders again on the night of December 10, asking Wilson to remain after the others departed. "Wilson, they treat me as though I were a boy and incapable of planning a campaign or fighting a battle," Thomas confided about the Union brass, according to the cavalryman's account. "If they will let me alone, I will fight this battle just as soon as it can be done and will surely win it; but I will not throw the victory away nor sacrifice the brave men of this army by moving till the thaw begins."[19]

With the terrible weather limiting offensive action, Thomas delved into other matters when army duties allowed: a city delegation needed to discuss a municipal regulation; someone's horse had been taken for the cavalry; a citizens' committee requested firewood for needy families. He spent many evenings with Andrew Johnson, the military governor who was vehement and repetitive in his opinions about secession and the expected reconstruction once the Confederacy was shattered. Thomas surprised the governor with his knowledge of constitutional and international law. "To all, he [Thomas] gave a patient and kindly hearing," Captain Stone wrote. "But underneath all, it was plain to see that General Grant's dissatisfaction keenly affected him, and that only by the proof which a successful battle would furnish could he hope to regain the confidence of the general-in-chief."[20]

Grant was not done, wiring Thomas on the afternoon of December 11 that he should launch an immediate offensive, regardless of the weather. "If you delay attack longer, the mortifying spectacle will be witnessed of a rebel army moving for the Ohio River, and you will be forced to act, accepting such weather as you find," Grant stated. "Let there be no further delay. Hood cannot stand even a drawn battle so far from his supplies of ordnance stores. If he retreats and you follow, he must lose his material and much of his army." Thomas responded that night, telling Grant that he would assail Hood as soon as possible but that his assault plan for the tenth had been thwarted by the storm and that the "whole country is covered with a perfect sheet of ice and sleet." Under this kinetic stress, even the stoic Thomas could not suppress his feelings, especially after how he had been treated by his superior officers in the past few weeks. He was heard to complain that Sherman had taken the pick of his army for his march—during which he would face a much weaker enemy force in Georgia—while Grant and his 100,000 men had been unable to uproot Lee in seven months of operations. Thomas also declared that he felt like wiring Grant, "If you want me to go out at Hood with inferior forces, why don't you go in at Lee with superior forces?"[21]

Finally, the weather eased somewhat, with a thaw beginning on the afternoon of December 13, giving Thomas a window of opportunity to strike. Gathering his generals the next afternoon, he gave each of them written orders containing detailed battle plans. It had been a teeth-grinding wait but now his troops, spurred by a promising forecast, were readied for action on December 15. "Never had a commander a more loyal corps of subordinates or a more devoted army," Stone recorded. "The feeling in the ranks was one of absolute and enthusiastic confidence in their general. Some had served with him since his opening triumph at Mill Springs; some had never seen his face till two weeks before. But there was that in his bearing, as well as in the proud security of his old soldiers, which inspired the new-comers with as absolute a sense of reliance upon him as was felt by the oldest of his veterans."[22]

With Thomas prepared to attack, Wilson's cavalry—now about 15,000 troopers organized in remarkable time—was weakened somewhat on the fourteenth to meet the threat of Lyon's raiders, whom Hood had sent toward Clarksville. Lyon had only about 800 mostly inexperienced and ill-organized Kentuckians, but he had to be dealt with, so Wilson sent two cavalry brigades—about 3,000 men—of Brig. Gen. Edward M. McCook's 1st Division, to chase Lyon. McCook's 3rd Brigade, commanded by John Croxton, remained to assist in Nashville's defense. This left Wilson with 12,000 cavalry—some 9,000 horsemen and another 3,000 dismounted and organized as infantry.[23]

Around 8 P.M. on the fourteenth, Thomas telegraphed Halleck: "The ice having melted away today, the enemy will be attacked tomorrow morning." Stone noted that the strain of the past twelve days seemed to have lifted from Thomas now that action appeared imminent. He "showed again something of his natural buoyancy and cheerfulness. He moved about more briskly." Thomas went to bed after instructing his staff to be ready at 5 A.M. Yet even on the eve of battle, his army command remained beyond precarious. As Thomas met with his officers, Maj. Gen. John A. "Black Jack" Logan was making his way to Nashville to relieve him and take the army's reins, based on Grant's order. Thomas was to be replaced if he had not attacked by the time Logan arrived in Louisville. Logan had led the XV Corps in the Army of the Tennessee, but had been recuperating from a wound sustained in the Atlanta campaign. He was healed enough to replace Thomas, but when Logan reached Louisville three days later, there would be no need for him to go any farther.[24]

CHAPTER 4

The Battle of Nashville

Heavy fog crowned the dawn, concealing the early dispositions of Thomas's army as it readied to attack on Thursday, December 15, 1864. Martial music from bands hidden in
the mists danced in the wintry air, a preamble for one of the
war's decisive battles. The welcome warmth had transformed
the ice into slushy mud for the most part, making every movement, from individual soldier to artillery caisson, an exercise in
laborious slow motion. Thomas left his hotel around 5 A.M. and
headed three miles to the front, setting up his field headquarters on Lawrence Hill, east of the Hillsboro Pike. In and about
the city, civilians crowded rooftops and any other elevation to
watch the show, most of them quietly hoping for a Southern
victory.[1]

Thomas's battle plan called for Steedman to make a
diversionary attack against the Confederate right, held by
Cheatham, hopefully drawing enemy troops to that sector.
Wood and Schofield would assail the center of Hood's positions while, in the main assault, Wilson's cavalry and Smith's
infantry would strike the enemy's left flank, held by Stewart.
Wilson and Smith were to make a "turning movement" that
would overlap Stewart's lines paralleling the Hillsboro Pike and
allow the Federals to get behind Stewart and close off that
route. Schofield's men were to support Smith. Erroneously
believing that Hood had 40,000 men, Thomas was committing
about 55,000 to his offensive, with the rest remaining in the
city's defenses. Thomas's initial plan had called for Steedman
to guard the city's interior lines but had been changed that
morning, resulting in some confusion as the troops marched
through the fog to reach their new assembly points. The Union

soldiers had been up since four that morning in preparation to move at six, but the fog, aggravated by clouds and smoke from hundreds of campfires, held up everything. Finally, the soup began to lift around eight, but problems persisted. Wilson prepared to move then, but was frustrated to find that some of Smith's units blocked his way. His troopers would not move for another two hours when the infantry cleared his front.[2]

While Wilson fumed, Steedman's brigades on the Federals' left moved forward into the thinning mist around eight, accompanied by a heavy bombardment from Union artillery and gunboats on the Cumberland. Col. Thomas J. Morgan's brigade of U.S. Colored Troops attacked the end of the Confederate line where it was bisected by the Nashville & Chattanooga Railroad. Morgan's troops met with initial success, overrunning some outer rifle pits, before they reached the enemy's main defenses, the focal point being a lunette with four guns supported by about 500 infantry of Granbury's Brigade. A deep railroad cut also blocked their way, and the stalled Federals—some within thirty yards of the enemy—quickly came under a devastating blaze of canister and small-arms fire. A number of Union men jumped to the railroad bed below to try to escape, but this soon became a deathtrap as Confederates hustled to the mouth of the cut and blazed away at the blue mass. Union reinforcements rushed up, trying to reach the lunette, but their effort did little more than to add to the bloodshed. By noon, Morgan had withdrawn, and Steedman was apparently satisfied that his diversion was successful and content to duel with Confederate skirmishers at long range for the rest of the day. Seven colored regiments had participated in Steedman's attack—one of the largest concentrations of black soldiers in the war—but that fact was lost for the moment as the larger battle unfolded.

Steedman's ruse occupied Cheatham until about midday—long enough, despite the hours of delay and confused movements, for Thomas to ready his hammer for the anvil blow aimed at Stewart on the Confederate left flank. Smith, Wilson, and Wood commenced their massive wheeling movement

James B. Steedman.

around 10 A.M., with Wood's position near the Hillsboro Pike
serving as the pivot. Smith's corps was soon south of the Hard-
ing Pike, generally parallel to it, and was advancing toward the
Confederate defenses along the Hillsboro Pike. Most of Wilson's troopers—two divisions—were farther to the south: in all,
more than 20,000 men (more than 30,000, if Wood's troops
were added in—basically doubling the number of Confederate
troops who had participated in Pickett's Charge at Gettysburg).

As Steedman's bloodied units pulled back, Wilson and
Smith posted artillery, sixteen guns total, to blast Redoubts No.
3, No. 4, and No. 5. This cannonade lasted until about 1 P.M.,
when Smith and Wilson ignited their attack and long waves of
shouting soldiers swept toward the enemy trenches and breastworks. Canister spat from the redoubts, and Confederate musketry ripped the blue ranks, but still they charged on. Smith by
now had linked with Wood's corps, which simultaneously was
assailing the Confederates from the north, concentrating on
Montgomery Hill and Redoubt No. 1, near the point where
Stewart's defenses bent southward along the pike. As the foggy
veil lifted that morning, the Federals had opened a heavy bombardment, much of it in this sector aimed at Montgomery Hill.
This appeared to be a formidable stronghold, but unknown to
Union forces, it was occupied by only a few troops since Hood
had pulled most of the defenders back to the main line on
December 10 when it was deemed to be too close to the Union
works. Wood's men clambered up the slopes of Montgomery
Hill, seizing it with little trouble.

Meanwhile, Wilson and Smith were temporarily held up by
stiff fire from Redoubts No. 3 and No. 4, but Redoubt No. 5,
exposed on Stewart's far left, was attacked from the front and
flank and overrun fairly quickly by a brigade of dismounted
cavalry and one of Smith's brigades. These forces soon turned
the fort's four guns against Redoubt No. 4, just to the north,
which was still being pummeled by the Union field artillery.
The Alabamians occupying this redoubt held on until about 3
P.M., when they were overpowered. The Union gunners then
rumbled to other positions to batter a long stone wall east of

the pike, behind which the Confederate division of Maj. Gen. Edward C. Walthall was hunkered.[3]

Watching the blue columns deploying that morning, Stewart had requested reinforcements from Hood, who, around noon, dispatched two brigades from Maj. Gen. Edward "Old Allegheny" Johnson's division of Lee's Corps in the Confederate center. Shortly afterward, Hood informed Stewart that two of Cheatham's divisions on the extreme right would be sent over to buttress the left flank. Johnson's two brigades, commanded by Arthur Manigault and Zachariah Deas, did not reach Stewart until after Redoubts No. 4 and No. 5 had fallen. They were placed in line just to the south of Walthall and also east of the pike. By now, however, most of the Confederates in this area were not only being battered by heavy artillery fire but were under attack by Smith's infantry, primarily Brig. Gen. John McArthur's division.

Not long after going into position, Manigault's and Deas's troops broke under this pressure, leaving Walthall's left flank exposed. Johnson's other two brigades came up, but were of little use. Elements of Schofield's corps, which had been ordered to fill in on Smith's right, were on the scene by now, and the Federals had a firm foothold east of the Hillsboro Pike. Walthall held as long as he could before ordering a retreat around 4:30 P.M. With Union forces also threatening to overrun his other division, commanded by Maj. Gen. William W. Loring, from behind, Stewart ordered Loring to pull back as well. Stewart's men scampered to the rear, most of them heading toward the Granny White Pike and the safety of the rest of the army toward the southeast.[4]

Less than a mile to the north, Wood's Union IV Corps had done little that afternoon since seizing Montgomery Hill, other than bringing up guns to pound Redoubt No. 1 and the parts of Stewart's line that were in the vicinity. Around 4 P.M., Wood ordered Washington Elliott's division to attack. When Elliott hesitated, Wood did not, instructing the division of Brig. Gen. Nathan Kimball to make the assault instead. Kimball did not wait, his boys plowing across a muddy cornfield to reach the enemy defenses held by Loring's division. Most of Loring's soldiers had retreated by then, but there was brief hand-to-hand fighting before Redoubt No. 1 fell, leaving the Federals with several guns.

Meanwhile, McArthur's troops had captured Redoubt No. 3, despite a vicious crossfire from enemy artillery, and Redoubt No. 2, cementing the collapse of the Confederates' left flank, sending soldiers in gray to the rear in a "full stampede," according to one Confederate. With no more action from Steedman's Federals on his right, Hood had sent word to Cheatham around 3 P.M. to send reinforcements to the embattled Stewart, but they did not arrive in time to make much impact before the winter sun set around five. Bate's Division did get into action, but was driven back by Maj. Gen. Darius Couch's division of Schofield's corps. The fighting soon flickered out, and a damp cold claimed the hazy battlefield, mercifully obscuring the battered Confederate army from even worse defeat. Penning his war memoir years later, Hood devoted all of one sentence to the first day of Nashville, the battle that wrecked his career: "Throughout that day, they were repulsed at all points of the general line with heavy loss and only succeeded towards evening in capturing the infantry outposts on our left, and with them the small force together with the artillery posted in these unfinished works [the five redoubts]."[5]

Near Murfreesboro, Forrest had received word that afternoon that the climatic struggle for Nashville had begun. Hood told him to be "in readiness to move at any moment." As always, Forrest had been up to his usual destructive ways. Red Jackson's troopers, operating south of the town on December 13, stopped and captured a supply train of seventeen cars, which included 200 soldiers of the 61st Illinois. Bound for Murfreesboro from Stevenson, Alabama, the train also contained 60,000 rations, "all of which were consumed by fire," Forrest noted, before the Union prisoners were taken to the rear. On the fifteenth, Brig. Gen. Lawrence S. Ross's cavalry of Jackson's command attacked another inbound train a few miles south of Murfreesboro. Union infantry guarding the

Spectators watch the fight between Hood and Thomas at
Nashville, December 15, 1864. LIBRARY OF CONGRESS

train fought from a railroad cut for about an hour before a
charge by the 6th Texas overran them. The train was torched,
along with some 200,000 rations, sugar, coffee, hard bread, and
bacon. These successes were heartening, but the latest news
from Nashville was foreboding. Forrest's "sound military judgment told him that the contest between the greatly superior
army of Thomas and the troops under General Hood would
end in the overthrow of the latter," according to Forrest's biog-
rapher John Allan Wyeth, who also fought under him. "He
knew full well that the battle of Franklin had broken the spirit
of this army." Hood's soldiers "had lost heart and hope, and
were practically beaten before a gun was fired in the battle."[6]

Even as John Logan made his way toward Tennessee that
day, Grant arrived in Washington from City Point in the afternoon. His annoyance with Thomas now pushed to the limit,

he was preparing to go to Nashville himself and assume command of operations. Either way, Thomas would be relieved. Grant learned that telegraph communications from Nashville had been down for the past twenty-four hours, with no word from Thomas, and this roiled his anxiety. He feared that Hood would slip past Thomas and set up a race between the armies to reach the Ohio River. Grant also was worried about Forrest's whereabouts, knowing the lethal prowess of the cavalryman. Unaware of the battle's result, much less that Thomas had finally taken the offensive, Grant conferred with Lincoln, Stanton, and Halleck about his intent to go to Nashville and wrote an order for Schofield to relieve Thomas until Grant could reach the scene. This order was intentionally delayed for telegraph transmission by a staff officer, Maj. Thomas Eckert, until there was some word from Nashville. Finally, telegraph service was restored, and Thomas's 8 P.M. message from December 14—"The enemy will be attacked tomorrow morning"—reached Washington.[7]

A newspaperman who observed Thomas during the battle stated the general "sits his steed like a grim old warrior whom neither disaster nor success can move." By nightfall, the stolid fighter was ecstatic—in his understated demeanor—about the day's results. Riding back to his headquarters in the city, Thomas remarked to an officer, "So far I think we have done pretty well." Along the way, he was hailed by a group of Confederate prisoners from South Carolina who shouted to him that they would rather die than suffer the humiliation of being taken into Nashville by their guard of black troops. "Well, you may say your prayers and get ready to die, for these are the only soldiers I can spare," he yelled in reply.

At 9 P.M., Thomas sent a message to Halleck with news of his success, stating that he had captured between 800 and 1,000 prisoners, sixteen artillery pieces, and a number of wagons, including Brig. Gen. James Chalmers's baggage train, which had been burned. "The troops behaved splendidly, all taking their share in assaulting and carrying the enemy's breastworks," he wrote. "I shall attack . . . again tomorrow, if he stands to fight, and, if he retreats during the night, will pursue him, throwing a heavy cavalry force in his rear, to destroy his trains, if possible." He also sent a brief note to his wife, Frances, who was staying in New York: "We have whipped the enemy, taken many prisoners and considerable artillery."[8]

The telegraph clicked the great news to Washington, but Grant's initial reaction was a diluted congratulation, much like a teacher would give a student who needed careful guidance. "I was just on my way to Nashville, but receiving a dispatch . . . detailing your splendid success of to-day, I shall go no farther," Grant stated in a telegram at 11:30 P.M. "Push the enemy now, and give him no rest until he is entirely destroyed. Your army will cheerfully suffer many privations to break up Hood's army and render it useless for future operations. Do not stop for trains or supplies, but take them from the country, as the enemy have done. Much is now expected." Fifteen minutes later, Grant sent another telegram: "I congratulate you and the army under your command for to-day's operations, and feel a conviction that to-morrow will add more fruits to your victory."[9]

Amid the windy night, Hood tried to pull his roughed-up army together and withdrew to a new and more compact position about two miles to the south, still astride the Franklin and Granny White Pikes. His exhausted soldiers dug in along a three-mile front as best they could, expecting the Federals to renew their onslaught early on Friday, December 16. Shielded by the darkness, needy Confederates slipped out to strip Union corpses of their shoes, clothing, and other belongings.

Hood shifted Cheatham's Corps to the left to replace Stewart's jumbled brigades. Cheatham's position extended west of the Granny White Pike to Compton's Hill and then bent south, with some of his units facing west and south to try to guard against further flanking movements. Chalmers's cavalry division, which had rejoined the army after dark, was posted along the Granny White to help guard this vulnerable sector. Stewart held the center of the new line, and most of his men hunkered along a stone fence on the J. M. Lea farm, facing north. Lee's Corps occupied the right, his line extending to Peach Orchard

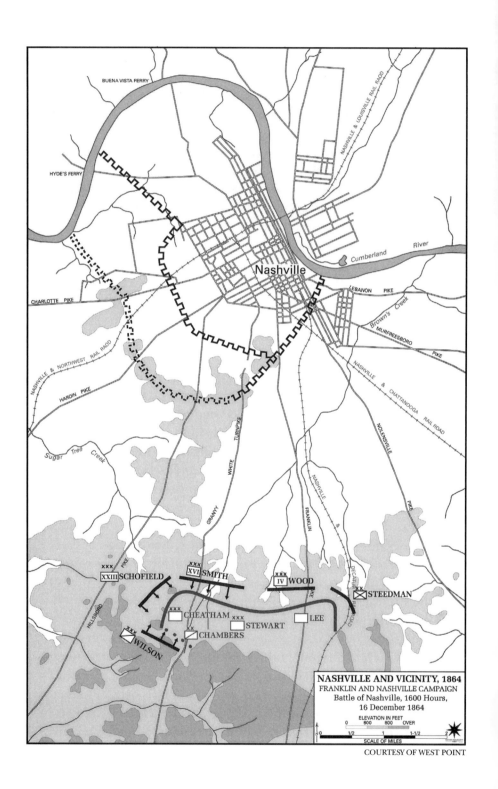

NASHVILLE AND VICINITY, 1864

FRANKLIN AND NASHVILLE CAMPAIGN
Battle of Nashville, 1600 Hours,
16 December 1864

ELEVATION IN FEET

SCALE OF MILES

COURTESY OF WEST POINT

Hill (also known as Overton's Hill), east of the Franklin Pike. Hood's control of the two turnpikes south gave him two avenues of retreat if matters worsened. Unknown to him, however, the Granny White was in danger of being cut by Wilson's squadrons by Friday morning.

The weakest point in the Confederates' new line was Cheatham's Compton's Hill angle. At the time, Cheatham did not know that there were Union forces on three sides of his position—Schofield's XXIII Corps to the west on a ridge overlooking Sugartree Creek, Smith's XVI Corps poised to attack from the north, and Wilson's squadrons to the south. Aiming south, Smith's units straddled the Granny White—some within 300 yards of Compton's Hill—and also were in line against Stewart's men. Wood's IV Corps, the largest in Thomas's army with about 13,500 effective infantry, was eye to eye with Lee along the Franklin Pike, and Steedman's troops anchored the Union left along the Nashville & Decatur Railroad after moving forward from their positions of the fifteenth. Thomas had a simple plan: if the enemy was present at daylight, there was to be a general attack; if the Confederates had fled, his troops would pursue.[10]

Hood was uncertain whether he could hold this new line, especially in light of what had happened the previous day. In fact, as the battle progressed on Thursday afternoon, he had started his wagon trains south to Franklin. From his headquarters at the Lea farm, at about 8 A.M. on the sixteenth, he sent a dispatch to Stewart with orders on what to do "should any disaster happen to us today." In such case, Stewart was to retreat on the Franklin Pike while Lee's Corps acted as rear guard. After passing Brentwood, about four miles to the south, Stewart was to reform his troops for battle, possibly in some narrow gorges along the road, and "let the whole army pass through you. At all times the road must be left open for artillery and wagons, the men marching through the fields and woods." Based on these orders, Stewart dispatched an engineer officer to examine the terrain beyond Brentwood and determine where a stand might be made. Cheatham was to retreat on the

Granny White Pike, not yet realizing the presence of the Union cavalry behind him.[11]

If Hood was unsettled about what was to come, not all of his troops shared the same opinion. "I have never indulged as high hopes of the results of a coming battle, because I was confident the Army of Tennessee had never had so good an opportunity for a great victory," one Confederate wrote a few weeks later. "I had seen the Army . . . encounter and whip the enemy with even greater disparity of numbers in the open field, and I did not believe it possible for three times our numbers to attack us in front and drive us from our fortifications."[12]

The armies awoke to more fog, less dense than the previous morning, and it burned off by about 8:30. By then, A. J. Smith's Union veterans already were on the move, closing with Cheatham's Confederates and enduring enemy artillery fire. Smith made his advance with two divisions, including McArthur's; his 3rd Division had been sent to reinforce the army's right during the night. Wood and Steedman also were on the march by first light, probing the enemy positions. Wood's infantry struck east, scuffling with enemy skirmishers, and by about 8 A.M., they had occupied the Franklin Pike. Elements of Wilson's cavalry also began pushing against Cheatham from the south, along the Granny White; most of the troopers fought dismounted because of the difficult terrain.

Despite all this, an air of cautiousness seemed to permeate the decisions of Thomas's generals that morning—all of them took longer than expected to get into attack positions. Nevertheless, the Federals' movements were accompanied by an artillery bombardment of the entire enemy line, with a concentration of fire on the salients of Compton's Hill and Peach Orchard Hill. Some Confederate veterans later claimed it was the most furious—and accurate—bombardment they ever witnessed, with scarcely a shell failing to explode in their defenses. About midday, the weather shifted again as mild temperatures surrendered to a cold rain, and the battle built toward its climax.[13]

After conferring with Thomas around noon, Wood coordinated with Steedman for an attack against Peach Orchard Hill. Thomas wanted this done so that the tactics of the previous day—outflanking and turning the Confederates' left flank—could be resumed, Wood noted. The steep-sided, 300-foot hill bristled with Confederate cannon and infantry, but if the assault was successful, the Franklin Pike could be sealed off to Hood. Concerned about this enemy activity on his right, Hood shifted two brigades of Cleburne's old division, now led by Brig. Gen. James A. Smith, away from Cheatham's position to buttress Lee's defenses. Hood had unwittingly weakened his left even as Thomas coiled for a knockout punch there.[14]

The Union attack against Peach Orchard Hill was launched around 3 P.M.. Three brigades—two of Steedman's and one of Wood's—tried to reach the rain-slick slope only to be blasted by grape, canister, and musketry from the height above. The assaulting soldiers pulled back, leaving their dead and wounded on the hillside. "The troops of my entire line were in fine spirits and confident of success," Lee reported, "so much so that the men could scarcely be prevented from leaving their trenches to follow the [retreating] enemy on and near the Franklin pike." Thomas sustained more than 1,000 casualties in this attack. The 13th U.S. Colored Troops alone lost 220 officers and men and had 5 successive color bearers shot down in its baptism of fire. With its 40 percent casualty rate, no regiment on either side lost more than the 13th at Nashville.[15]

The situation for the Confederates was not going as well on Hood's left flank, where Wilson's dismounted cavalry and the infantry were finally pressuring the gray line, already stretched thin by the departure of James Smith's brigades. Despite some delays by Wilson and Schofield throughout the morning, the massive Union attack against Hood's left was finally beginning to take shape. The Confederate defenders on Compton's Hill—some of Bate's troops—were pinned down by continuous artillery blasts and Union sharpshooters. By noon, Wilson had about 4,000 troopers menacing the rear of Cheatham's and Stewart's defenses and had sliced across the

Granny White Pike where it cut through the Brentwood Hills behind Hood's army. This left Hood with only one escape route, the Franklin Pike.

With Forrest away at Murfreesboro, Hood had only Chalmers's cavalry division of two brigades assigned to the main army, Col. Jacob B. Biffle's brigade on Hood's right flank and Col. Edmund W. Rucker's on the left. Chalmers was with Rucker's Brigade on the sixteenth and had not been seriously engaged during much of the day, but this was about to change. In the afternoon, Chalmers had withdrawn east from the Hillsboro Pike to the Granny White Pike to protect wagons and ambulances concentrated near Brentwood. This move put Rucker's troopers in the rear (south) of Wilson's horsemen, who were pressing Cheatham. The presence of Rucker's troopers on the Granny White would prove critical shortly afterward.

By about 3:30 P.M., it appeared, at least to the Confederates, that the fighting on this miserably gloomy day was waning with the muted sunlight. The day's success to this point heartened the Southerners, who had had little to cheer about for a long time. Having repulsed the Union thrusts, some of the Confederates waved their flags in defiance toward the Union positions, shouting for the Federals to "Come on! Come on!" Hood later claimed he already was finalizing preparations for his operations the next day, planning a surprise assault against the exposed Union right flank. Knowing that these Federals appeared to be unsupported and were strung out about six miles from the city, Hood would withdraw his entire army overnight, skirt them, and attack from behind in the morning. "I could safely have done so, as I still had open a line of retreat," he stated. To ask this of an already decimated, outnumbered army that had fought a battle, retreated to a new position, and entrenched overnight would have been an amazing feat, considering all that these troops had endured in the campaign. To do this, Hood would have had to march his men into the teeth of Wilson's cavalry and then tangle with the veterans of Schofield's and Smith's corps—an imposing task, to say the least.[16]

James R. Chalmers.

Within thirty minutes, his plans were forgotten, lost forever in what would have been the Army of Tennessee's last offensive. Hood would never have the chance to make his bold flanking stroke, but the Rock of Chickamauga was about to earn yet another nickname.

CHAPTER 5

"The Scene of Disaster"

The cold drizzle was still falling about 4 P.M. when a heightening cacophony of yells, cannon fire, and musketry rumbled up through the stark woods and ridges from the Confederate left flank in the vicinity of Compton's Hill, drawing the attention of much of the rest of Hood's army.

As Steedman's and Wood's bloodied troops fell back, the Union sledgehammer blow finally fell on Cheatham. The XXIII Corps poured across Sugartree Creek from the west while the XVI Corps assailed the Confederates from the north. Wilson's cavalry—primarily two divisions fighting dismounted—pressed forward from the south. The massive three-pronged offensive was too much for the Confederates, and the battle lasted only a few minutes longer. On Compton's Hill, elements of Bate's Division were overrun. A gallant but brief stand by a mixed command of Tennesseans under Lt. Col. William Shy was overwhelmed by the blue tide as Shy was killed by a bullet to the head. The remainder of Cheatham's units collapsed in amazingly short order. Some of the routed men streamed toward the Granny White Pike, but when they found the road blocked by Wilson's men, their exodus shifted to the Franklin Pike. Disorder and panic grew by the second. Crashing and slogging through the cheerless woods and cornfields and across the hilly terrain, hundreds of the Confederates tossed aside muskets, packs, and any other accoutrements that impeded their flight. Others surrendered, too tired or dispirited to do anything more. Among the hundreds of prisoners in this sector were two of Bate's brigadiers, Thomas B. Smith and Henry R. Jackson.

Cheatham's sudden undoing had a chain-reaction effect on Stewart's Corps, which was still reeling from its debacle the previous day. The blue tsunami surged over their outflanked trenches, seizing guns, flags, and prisoners. The Arkansans of Brig. Gen. Daniel H. Reynolds's brigade briefly clung to their ground, but the onslaught was too much, and Stewart's command disintegrated as well, its fugitives joining Cheatham's in the escape. "Soon the whole army had caught the infection, had broken, and were running in every direction," related the Tennessee infantryman Sam Watkins. "Such a scene I never saw. The army was panic-stricken."[1]

In the saddle a short distance to the rear, Hood was conferring with Stewart when a staff officer informed them of the break on the left, even as the contagious defeat began to infect the rest of his army. Hood watched in disbelieving horror as his divisions dissolved "and soon discovered that all hope to rally the troops was in vain. . . . Our line, thus pierced, gave way. Soon thereafter it broke at all points, and I beheld for the first and only time a Confederate army abandon the field in confusion." In one of his battle reports, he noted, "In a few moments our entire line was broken, our troops retreating rapidly down the pike in the direction of Franklin, most of them, I regret to say, in great confusion, and all efforts to reform them were fruitless."[2]

"The infantry ran like cowards," related E. T. Eggleston, a Mississippi artillerist, "and the miserable wretches who were to have supported us refused to fight and ran like a herd of stampeded cattle. I blush for my countrymen and despair for the independence of the Confederacy if her reliance is placed in the army [sic] of Tennessee to accomplish it." From their rifle pits straddling the Franklin Pike and the hills well east of Cheatham's position, Lee's infantrymen, who had borne most of the action all day, were surprised to see an ever-increasing number of Confederates to their left scampering away from their trenches. "Suddenly all eyes were turned to the center of our line of battle near the Granny White Pike, where it was evident the enemy had made an entrance, although but little firing had been heard in that direction," Lee related. In minutes, the gray line toppled like dominos, "Our men . . . flying to the rear in the wildest confusion, and the enemy following with enthusiastic cheers," Lee said of Cheatham's and Stewart's troops. Lee's first domino, his left division, led by Old Allegheny Johnson, was quickly in trouble, with waves of Union soldiers appearing in its rear. Johnson tried frantically to form his troops in a hollow square, but he was outflanked and outnumbered. He held briefly before the ranks crumbled; men either surrendered or scrambled out of their rifle pits and joined the exodus. "The ground was very muddy, and not a good race track, though we made very good time," one of Johnson's Tennesseans related, adding that when the break occurred, the men "stood up in the ditches, adjusted their accouterments, and prepared for the race before them."[3]

Next to Johnson, the Confederates of Carter Stevenson's division in Lee's Corps, had been hugging the wet ground, enduring the Federals' thunderous artillery barrage, when hell got hotter. These troops were "keeping closely in the trenches and perfectly cool and confident" when Stevenson received a late-afternoon dispatch from Lee that things were not going well on the army's left. This was a surprise to Stevenson since the mist and rain had prevented him from observing anything beyond his own line since about midday. Lee told him that he might have to retreat during the coming night, and Stevenson ordered up his artillery horses, which had been sent to the rear much earlier in the day because of the brutally efficient enemy shelling. Minutes after sending for these teams, the army to Stevenson's left, including Johnson's Division, seemed to shatter into splinters of thousands of men running away.[4]

Next to Stevenson's position, on the extreme right of Hood's line, Henry Clayton's division of Lee's Corps also was initially unaware of what was happening on the army's left and center and had repulsed Union infantry assaults and outlasted the awesome cannonading through much of the day. The men still were "in the highest state of enthusiasm" around 4 P.M. when Clayton received a baffling dispatch from Lee, stating that he expected the division to pull back in order. Clayton was puzzled since the battle seemed to be going well in his sector.

Edward "Old Allegheny" Johnson.

He tried to find out what was happening on the left, but got no immediate information. Nevertheless, he ordered nearby batteries to limber up or make preparations to do so and be ready to move. Shortly thereafter, Clayton saw "the troops on my left flying in disorder." Thirty-seven years old, Clayton was a battle-wise veteran, a Georgian by birth who had been a lawyer and state legislator in Alabama before the war. Seriously wounded in the right shoulder at Stones River, he also had seen action in Braxton Bragg's Kentucky campaign, at Chickamauga, and in the Atlanta battles, leading A. P. Stewart's old division in the latter. Still, his combat resume did not include anything like what was about to envelop him and his soldiers.[5]

By now, most of Hood's army had devolved into an undisciplined mass of men struggling to get away from the enemy onslaught, rolled up from the west like a gray carpet. Only Lee's Corps held together somewhat. The fact that Lee had not reached the field at Franklin until after Hood's main attack—thus being spared much of the decimation of officers and men—that he had not been greatly tested on December 15, and that his position was on the other end of the line from the breakthrough certainly had much to do with Lee's maintaining his basic organization.

The same could not be said for the rest of the Confederate army in the dimming light. "The woods everywhere were full of running soldiers," remembered Watkins, who had been wounded in the thigh and hand. "Our officers were crying, 'Halt! Halt!' and trying to rally and re-form their broken ranks. The Federals would dash their cavalry in amongst us, and even their cannon joined in the charge. One piece of Yankee artillery galloped past me . . . unlimbered their gun, fired a few shots, and galloped ahead again." Meanwhile, Hood, Cheatham, and other officers tried to stem the flood on the Franklin Pike, but with little success. One of Bate's Georgians watched the procession of "demoralization in the extreme," one soldier ducking under Cheatham's horse to continue his flight as the general attempted to rally the fugitives. In another instance, a young officer tried to stop some troops, pointing toward the battlefield and shouting, "Halt, there is no danger there!" A grizzled soldier, his face a mask of gunpowder, eyed the officer and growled, "You go to hell. I've been there."[6]

All along the works, Confederate cannoneers frantically tried to withdraw their guns, but the break was too sudden for many of them. Artillery horses had been killed or taken to the rear to keep them from being exposed to enemy fire and so could not be returned and hitched in time. Now the desperate Confederates tried to manhandle the pieces to safety, but the mud was too deep and the onrushing bluecoats too near. Watching the catastrophe unfold, Clayton quickly sent word to his brigade commanders and batteries to pull back. Clayton later stated that at that time, the entire army—other than his division, Brig. Gen. Edmund W. Pettus's brigade of Stevenson's Division, and the 39th Georgia of Cumming's Brigade (also under Stevenson)—"was then in complete rout." The 39th had been sent to Clayton shortly before as a support unit and was in reserve.

Stevenson was struggling to hold the rest of his division together before pulling back. "When the true situation of affairs became apparent, and it was evident that the whole army, with the exception of my division and Clayton's, had been broken and scattered, the order for their withdrawal was given," Stevenson recalled. He tried to post skirmishers to cover his retreat, but the Federals seemed to be everywhere, pouring in fire from front and flanks. The rout happened so quickly that many of Stevenson's men were unable to climb out of their trenches before they were overrun and captured. His dilemma was further complicated since his brigade and regimental officers also had sent their horses to the rear and could not retrieve them in time to reform their units amid the expanding chaos. While these Confederates maintained their composure for the most part, the army's collapse was epidemic. Clayton admitted that "some confusion existed even in these commands," though Brig. Gen. Marcellus A. Stovall's brigade and the 39th Georgia were the coolest under fire.[7]

These Confederates would not be nearly enough to stem the Federal high tide, but Lee seemed to be everywhere at once, trying to keep the army from falling apart. He had been sitting on his horse behind Clayton's line when the break occurred, and he immediately rode toward the left, where Johnson's Division was faltering. Lee rode hard, leaping the stone fences on each side of the pike, and was followed by Maj. J. W. Ratchford of his staff and two members of his escort, Pvt. Robert Howard and Pvt. Louis F. Garrard.

Reaching the rear of Stevenson's defenses west of the pike, Lee found himself amid a growing flood of disorganized soldiers being pressed by yelling, charging soldiers in blue. Grabbing a flag from a color bearer, he rode among the Confederates, shouting, "Rally, men, rally! For God's sake rally! This is the place for brave men to die!" His calm and courage caused knots of Confederates to stop and form, and soon Lee had three or four other stands of colors gathered around him in the deepening gloom. "His example was inspiring," Garrard remembered. "He looked like a very god of war." Some of the attacking Union men were led by a mounted officer who himself carried a flag. The officer went down, and Garrard was unsure of his fate: "If he was not killed [or wounded], it was not because he was not shot at often enough." This resistance was short-lived because of the fractured Confederate lines, but the oncoming Federals hesitated just long enough for other elements of Lee's Corps, primarily Clayton's men, to regroup farther south along the pike and try to make a piecemeal defense. "My troops left their line in some disorder," Lee wrote of the initial shock, "but were soon rallied and presented a good front to the enemy."[8]

Meanwhile, Clayton had retreated about a half mile when he came upon Lt. W. J. McKenzie's battery of the Eufaula Light Artillery, which was halted but about to resume its flight. Clayton likely saw some familiar faces among McKenzie's Alabamians since he had studied law in Eufaula and was an attorney in nearby Clayton, Alabama, before the war. These

Alabamians were ordered to hold their ground and open fire. The 39th Georgia fell into position as support while Clayton tried to halt and assemble his division for a stand. He sent his staff officers flying to find his command and soon thereafter ordered McKenzie and the supporting Georgians to fall back.

The Louisianans of Brig. Gen. Randall L. Gibson's brigade in Clayton's Division also held together enough to make a stand along the pike about half a mile to the rear, based on Lee's exhortations. In the near darkness, Lee galloped up to these troops and tried to seize the colors of the 13th Louisiana so that he could lead the men, but the regimental flag bearer refused to surrender it, telling Lee, "No, general, you need not expose yourself in this way, just tell us where you want these colors and that is where we will take them." The other Louisianans yelled in support, and Lee knew he was licked. When Gibson joined Lee shortly afterward, Lee exclaimed to him, "Gibson, these are the best men I ever saw. You take them and check the enemy."[9]

Amid the chaos, with Gibson's men and other scattered units making a fighting withdrawal, Lee withdrew farther south on the pike into the Brentwood Hills about a mile to the rear, where Clayton had rallied Stovall's Brigade and formed across the road. Stovall having been separated from his troops in the mayhem, Clayton ordered Col. Abda Johnson of the 40th Georgia to take over. In "a few moments," Clayton claimed, his division and Pettus's Brigade of Stevenson's Division were in battle line. This position extended across the pike and east into woods near Travellers Rest, Hood's first headquarters. As Gibson's men fell into battle line with the others here, Lee had a drummer boy beat the long roll to rally and steady the troops.

Among the Union pursuers was Col. George F. Dick's 86th Indiana Infantry of Wood's corps, some of whom outdistanced their comrades and found themselves suddenly facing this unexpected Confederate line. The Union soldiers could hear the shouts and curses of the enemy officers and could tell they were having trouble keeping the line together. Occasionally, they saw Confederates turn and run for the rear. "One by one they went, until their officers saw it was the sheerest folly to try to hold them, when they all scampered," one Indianan noted.[10]

The 46th Alabama of Pettus's Brigade had earlier been swept up in the rout, but the regiment's commander, Capt. George E. Brewer, had noticed the disjointed nature of the Federal pursuit as he retreated on the pike with a few men "who were known to be cool and determined." Glancing back as they passed two abandoned Confederate guns, Brewer saw that the "enemy pursuing seemed but little better organized . . . but were simply straggling along, firing upon the Confederates." Brewer ordered the soldiers with him to "give the advance a few rounds," which they did, soon to be joined by a few others. "Something like a dozen stood together shooting as fast as they could load" and momentarily delaying the bluecoats. These Confederates then hastened down the pike and soon came upon Lee's crazy-quilt line, composed of 200 to 300 men crowned by some sixteen stands of colors, according to Brewer. More troops fell into the ranks here, and a few guns of Lee's artillery, which had managed to escape, also unlimbered and began banging away.

Among them were McKenzie's Alabamians, whom Clayton had earlier encountered. "Too much praise cannot be awarded the officers and men of this battery for the coolness and deliberation upon which they managed their guns under these trying circumstances," Clayton would later write of these artillerists. For now, however, in the blood, cold, mud, and rain along the pike, there was no time for reflection or compliments as the Confederates tried to plug the crumbled dam that had led to their undoing. Stevenson was trying to locate his other brigade—Cumming's—which, besides the 39th Georgia, had joined the masses on the pike. Stevenson later admitted that "amid the indescribable confusion of other troops" and the enemy's pressure, it had been impossible to hold his men together and they "became considerably broken and confused."[11]

The Confederates' primary tormentors on this pike were units of Wood's IV Corps. In the jubilation of cracking the

Union outer line at Nashville, December 1864.

Confederate line, many of these Union soldiers had bolted over the enemy gun pits after capturing prisoners, cannon, and flags and continued the pursuit. Brig. Gen. Nathan Kimball's 1st Division of the IV Corps, leaving behind about 900 prisoners taken when the division overran the Confederate defenses, resumed the chase on the pike. Maj. George Hicks's 96th Illinois of Brig. Gen. Walter C. Whitaker's 2nd Brigade spearheaded Kimball's advance, pressing the Southerners so closely that they captured a herd of cattle. The 3rd Division, commanded by Brig. Gen. Samuel Beatty, seized five field pieces in the bedlam of the Confederates' collapse—a grand way to celebrate Beatty's forty-fourth birthday. Wood's own guns, primarily Lt. Samuel Canby's Battery M of the 4th U.S. Artillery, were up by now, rumbling ahead with Kimball's advance and halting only to blast away at the Confederates, which "increased the confusion and hastened the flight of the enemy," according to Wood.[12]

The pursuit, however, did not resemble any Currier and Ives print depicting orderly ranks of Federals, bayonets perfectly aligned, trotting after a wildly panicked foe. Wood's men had been disorganized themselves in the day's jumbled attacks and the confusion of victory. With darkness gathering, most of them halted briefly to realign their units before resuming the chase at a cautious pace. Behind Wood, Steedman's troops occupied smoldering Peach Orchard Hill, for which so many of their comrades had paid in blood, and settled in and around the enemy works while awaiting orders. They also reorganized and hustled throngs of prisoners back toward Nashville.

Lee was in the process of trying to strengthen his Brentwood Hills line when he received word from Hood that the enemy was near Brentwood to his rear and threatening to cut the pike, Lee's only route to safety. Knowing that "it was necessary to get beyond that point at once, everything was hastened to the rear," Lee reported. At the village of Brentwood, on the pike about four miles from "the scene of disaster," as Hood described the battle, the main body of the army tried to right itself, like a proud warship shuddering from a lethal broadside.

Hood, "seconded by officers from various commands, endeavored to gather up the fragments of his broken forces," according to General Walthall. "The effort was attended with but partial success." Cheatham and Loring, another of Stewart's commanders, were among those who tried to form a line at Brentwood, but a Confederate soldier described this effort to stem the tide as "like trying to stop the current of the Duck river with a fish net."[13]

With the army in such massive disarray, Hood abandoned his emergency plan, ordering elements of Stewart's Corps and Cheatham's Corps, both of which retained some cohesion, to continue on toward Franklin. Hood later attributed this opportunity to attempt, at least, to regroup at Brentwood to the "promptness and gallantry" of Clayton's Division, "which speedily formed and confronted the enemy." This unit, Gibson's Brigade, and McKenzie's Alabama gunners were "acting as rear-guard of the rear-guard."[14]

Meanwhile, Stevenson had been able to reorganize his remaining troops—Cumming's Brigade, minus the 39th Georgia—"extricating them from the throng of panic-stricken stragglers from other commands who crowded the road." He was ordered to continue marching to Franklin and beyond, leaving Pettus's Brigade, which was still fighting with Clayton, at Hollow Tree Gap, about five miles north of that town, to assist in bringing up the rear. The Confederates benefitted from the fact that the triumphant Union troops were intermingled, exhausted, and confused as well, having not anticipated such a startling result to the day's battle. "It was a fortunate circumstance that the enemy was too much crippled to pursue us on the Franklin Pike," Lee noted. "The only pursuit made at that time was by a small force coming from the Granny White Pike." By the time Lee's Corps passed Brentwood, the Confederate cavalry was fighting only half a mile away from the Franklin Pike and hanging by a thread.[15]

On the Granny White Pike just south of the major fighting, a messenger galloped up to Rucker's cavalry brigade around 4:30 P.M. with a dispatch from Hood to Chalmers, ordering him to hold the road "at all hazards." Chalmers himself was away at the time, ironically having ridden minutes earlier to find Hood and receive instructions. In his absence, Rucker read the dispatch and posted some of his troopers to defend the road. These soldiers were unaware that the army was melting away a few miles to the north and northeast. They did know that a sizeable Union force was in front of them and had to be repelled. Rucker had no more than 1,200 troopers total and had been weakened hours earlier when his 7th Tennessee had been sent south to Franklin to help guard Confederate wagon trains. Rucker placed Col. David C. Kelley in temporary command of this first position and then rode with his escort and the rest of the brigade about half a mile to the rear. There they erected a barricade of fence rails and logs on the pike just north of its intersection with the Brentwood road and positioned two field pieces. If the Federals took the intersection, they could possibly cut the Franklin Pike at Brentwood, closing Hood's line of retreat.[16]

Known for his Sunday-morning sermons in camp, Kelley led Forrest's "old regiment." He had been described by a British observer earlier in the war "as brave a man as ever smelled gunpowder" and had done stellar work during the siege, using a few artillery pieces to bedevil the Union Navy on the Cumberland a few miles downriver from Nashville. Posting his guns on a bluff at Bell's Bend, he had managed to capture two transports and, along with a falling water level, effectively blockaded the river for several days prior to the battle. Earlier in the day, Rucker and Kelley had sparred with the enemy along the Hillsboro Pike before regrouping on the Granny White to help protect wagons and ambulances gathered at Brentwood. They and their troopers were about to face probably the sternest test of their lives.[17]

It had already been another banner day for the Union cavalry. Edward Hatch's troopers and Brig. Gen. Joseph F. Knipe's 7th Division captured fifteen more guns and several hundred prisoners. But fighting on foot and having covered significant ground, Hatch's and Knipe's bluecoats had to get their mounts before they could make an effective pursuit of the routed enemy, and "considerable time was unavoidably lost before the horses could be led to the men," Wilson stated. Hatch's 5th Division, followed by Knipe, was ordered to push down the Granny White Pike in an effort to reach the Franklin Pike and seal off Hood's line of retreat, but the delay meant they would move in the rainy darkness.

Furthermore, the horsemen would not have infantry support, and John Schofield would bear the blame for this, at least in Thomas's view. Schofield had been lethargic in the day's action, except for the attack of one brigade, Doolittle's, on Cheatham's position. After McArthur's successful action, Thomas ordered Schofield to pursue Hood, but Schofield remained tentative. Couch's division did not move until almost dark, and Jacob Cox's troops were halted before reaching the Granny White Pike because A. J. Smith's units—primarily McArthur's division—were on the road. McArthur's boys, however, had borne the combat burden for both days now and, exhausted, were recalled after advancing a short distance on the Granny White.

With Schofield not taking the initiative, the infantry pursuit stalled, which meant that Wilson's cavalry would have to block the enemy's escape alone, although it would still be "thousands against hundreds" in the Federals' favor. The Union troopers clattered south on the Granny White in such blackness that they "could hardly see their horses' ears" and in more numbers "than they could properly use in the dark on a single road," Wilson stated. The horsemen scattered little groups and individual Confederate soldiers on the pike as occasional lightning streaked the sky, illuminating other retreating Confederates in the nearby woods.[18]

The Union trap was not to be. A mile or so from the battlefield, Col. Datus E. Coon's 2nd Brigade of Hatch's division smacked into Kelley's Confederates, who had pieced together their own defenses with fence rails, logs, and anything else they could find. Coon's troopers, still running on adrenalin from their part in the capture of Redoubts No. 4 and No. 5 the previous day, closed in, and the firing crescendoed. "Pour it into them, boys! Pour it into them!" Kelley yelled as he rode behind his dismounted line, a slug tearing a patch out of the shoulder of his coat. "Kneeling or crouching down behind that rail fence, which constituted our only protection, we poured a constant stream of shot out into the night," Pvt. John Johnston of the 14th Tennessee Cavalry remembered. "We could see nothing, the mist and darkness had covered all in front, and we shot blindly out into the dark woods, our whole line from right to left being one continuous blaze of musketry." Not realizing that they were so outnumbered, Johnston and his Confederate comrades "were in fine spirits and sprang to our work with alacrity and enthusiasm." The Southerners fought scrappily, but the Federals quickly rolled over this position. A charge by Col. George Spalding's 12th (U.S.) Tennessee Cavalry, Coon's lead regiment, assisted by the dismounted 9th Illinois, sent the Confederates flying.[19]

According to Private Johnston, "The whole line seemed to give way at once," as the Confederates ran back to find their horses. "And we did not fall back any too soon, for the enemy had almost completely enveloped our left, and in a few minutes more would have been in possession of the pike in our rear." The Federals smashed Kelley's line, separating the 14th Tennessee, commanded by Lt. Col. Rolla R. White, on the left flank from the rest of the Confederates. Some of Kelley's men panicked, and cries of "ammunition is exhausted" hastened their scamper to get their mounts. Spalding, along with the 6th and 9th Illinois, pursued before running into Rucker's second barricade. By now, the fight was swelling out into the fields and woods on both sides of the pike.[20]

In the freezing rain and blackness, Hatch and Coon threw dismounted troopers around both enemy flanks as Spalding's men charged the defenses and punched through them as well.

"It was a scene of pandemonium, in which every challenge was answered by a saber stroke or pistol shot, and the flash of the carbine was the only light by which the combatants could recognize each other's position," Wilson noted.[21]

Rucker had been in the process of constructing his barricade and positioning some troopers when horsemen of his 12th Tennessee began streaming back from Kelley's line, warning of the Union threat. Rucker immediately ordered the Tennesseans to file in behind the makeshift defenses and try to strengthen them further while he rode to station the 7th Alabama on his left. By now, he had also been reinforced by the 7th Tennessee, which had returned from its escort assignment. After seeing to the Alabamians, Rucker rode back toward the pike. In the rainy darkness, he encountered mounted men whom he did not recognize and called for its commander. An officer rode up close to him, and both men quickly realized they were foes: Rucker was facing Spalding. In the ensuing confrontation, Rucker seized the bridle rein of Spalding's horse, shouting that the Federal officer was his prisoner, but Spalding yelled, "Not by a damned sight!"as he spurred his mount and wrenched away from Rucker's grasp.

Rucker quickly found himself tangled in a saber melee with Capt. Joseph C. Boyer, also of the 12th (U.S.) Tennessee. Boyer was gashed on the forehead, but Rucker was surrounded and at least one Union trooper yelled,"Shoot the man on the white horse!" The exhortation was punctuated by a scattering of shots, and a revolver round shattered Rucker's left arm above the elbow. The colonel's spooked mount then bolted, hurling him against some fence rails and to the ground, stunning him as Federals moved in to capture him. Amid the swirling firefight, Spalding's Tennesseans clashed with the Confederate 12th Tennessee, led by Col. U. M. Green. Two of these Southern troopers grabbed the reins of Spalding's horse on either side of him and demanded the colonel's surrender, but Spalding made another escape, his spurred horse bounding away. So intertwined were the rival forces that two Union battalions of the 12th Tennessee, led by Maj. John S. Kirwan and Maj. Jason A. Bradshaw, charged entirely through the Confederate lines. In the night, they returned by passing themselves off as the Confederate 12th Tennessee "in great anxiety to meet the Yankees," according to Coon.[22]

Edmund W. Rucker.

Union private Berry Watson of Company G., 12th Tennessee, snatched one of Rucker's flags, killing the Confederate standard bearer in the process. Moments later, a Southern officer, not realizing Watson was a Federal, rode up and said, "Stick to your colors, boys!" Watson cooly replied, "I'll do it," before galloping away with his trophy. Spalding promoted Watson to sergeant that night for his exploit.[23]

The cavalry fight here lasted long after dark before Rucker's troopers were finally overpowered. These Confederates were unaware of it at the time, but this stand cost the Federals any immediate chance of bagging Hood's army. Wilson later would describe the struggle as "one of the fiercest conflicts that ever took place in the Civil War." Rucker's 7th Alabama—including a company of young cadets from the University of Alabama—did stout work in holding the pike. This regiment, which, according to Chalmers, had "rested under some imputation of a lack of courage" when it joined the division, was aided greatly by the night and terrible weather, which likely prevented Wilson's horsemen from taking their objective. "In the main, the darkness which shrouded the field was decidedly propitious for the vanquished, for it concealed their fearful weakness, their shattered, disorganized condition," stated one Confederate account.[24]

Most of Chalmers' troopers re-formed overnight and were not pursued as they joined the rest of the Confederates streaming south. Kelley led what was left of his regiment to Brentwood while Lieutenant Colonel White of the 14th Tennessee, now the senior officer, collected as many of the rest of the men as possible. Leaving his Tennesseans as pickets, White spurred for the Franklin Pike with the remainder of the decimated brigade.[25]

The wounded Colonel Rucker was jostled by his Union captors before being lifted back on his horse and taken a short distance toward the rear, where Hatch questioned him around 6:30 P.M. "Forrest has just arrived with all his cavalry, and will give you hell tonight. Mark what I tell you," Rucker defiantly told Hatch, knowing full well that Forrest was really miles away.

During the interrogation, he again said that Forrest was on the field, a statement punctuated by a surprise volley from Confederate cavalry still in the vicinity. Based on Rucker's account, the Federals withdrew several hundred yards, and the colonel heard a command issued that "General Wilson has ordered everything in camp." Perhaps his ruse had worked. It is a better bet, however, that after two days of fighting, culminating in Rucker's stout resistance well into the cold, rainy night, that Wilson simply wanted to regroup and rest his men. Wilson later claimed the Federals were unsure of Forrest's whereabouts and whether they were facing him in this phase of the battle. He reflected that had Forrest indeed been present, "it may well be claimed that he could have made a better and more stubborn defense."[26]

While the cavalry battle flamed on the Granny White, Hood's jumbled troops jammed the Franklin Pike, tramping south as Stephen Lee tried to stabilize his rear guard and prevent any further damage in the event that Thomas launched a full-scale pursuit. "The whole army on this thoroughfare seemed to be one heterogeneous mass, and moving back without organization or government," General Bate reported. "Strenuous efforts were made by officers of all grades to rally and form line of battle, but in vain. The disorganized masses swept in confusion down the Franklin Pike, amid the approaching darkness and drenching rain."[27]

With night deepening, Lee posted Brig. Gen. James T. Holtzclaw's brigade to defend the Franklin Pike as the army's rear guard while he moved the rest of Clayton's Division, plus Pettus, farther south. Caught up in the earlier flight, Holtzclaw's men had been separated by the parallel stone walls along the road, but the majority had succeeded in regrouping about a mile to the rear. "When soldiers are in a stampede, they are without control, and this was our condition," one of his Alabamians recalled of the initial rout.

Holtzclaw, who would turn thirty-one the next day, was a Georgia native, but had grown up in Alabama. Declining an appointment to the U.S. Military Academy, he was a lawyer before the war. Shot through a lung at Shiloh, he survived the supposedly mortal wound and returned to duty about three months later, fighting at Chickamauga, Chattanooga, and Atlanta and earning his brigadier's rank in July 1864. When the army splintered that afternoon, he had watched incredulously as "almost instantaneously the line crumbled away till it reached me. I had no time to give any order or make any disposition to check the disaster." Now, reforming his soldiers across the Franklin Pike, Holtzclaw must have realized that the army faced worse catastrophe if the enemy pressed its advantage into the night.[28]

There would be no sweeping attack that night to finish Hood; the Federals were too disorganized, tired, and fought out to do anything else. Exhausted soldiers on both sides lay down for scant rest in the cold rain that night, with the Confederates spread out along the pike between Brentwood and Franklin. "All night long we fled," wrote one of Stewart's officers, who also recalled the woods filled with Confederates struggling toward the pike, many pleading for him to take them in the saddle behind him or give them a helping hand in the sucking mud. With Clayton's units and a portion of Stevenson's, Lee remained in his rear-guard role during the night. These troops, "our numbers constantly increasing" as they regrouped, halted some seven miles north of Franklin around 10 P.M. for a break. By this time, the downpour had intensified, and drowsy men found themselves in spreading puddles. Many stumbled to logs, tree branches, and even rocks to lessen their misery.

Some Union soldiers, at least in McArthur's ranks, were issued whiskey to celebrate their great effort and warm their bones. The 86th Indiana reassembled near where it had encountered Lee's rallied troops, the men talking excitedly about the day's events as they made their cooking fires, despite the conditions. "The boys almost hugged one another in the excess of their joyous good humor," a Hoosier wrote. Everyone agreed that it had been a great victory—and a backbreaking defeat for the Confederacy. The Southerners had fled their defenses "like the wild deer of the forest," they laughed. Others compared Hood's debacle with Braxton Bragg's defeat at Missionary Ridge.[29]

A few miles south, Hood himself set up headquarters that night at the Maney home near Franklin, his mood a universe away from the jubilant Indianans. Among the hundreds of soldiers resting or milling about nearby was Sam Watkins, with visions of the last few hours painfully and indelibly etched in his memory. The army "was in full retreat," he recalled years later of what he had endured.

> I saw many, yea, even thousands, broken down from sheer exhaustion, with despair and pity written on their features. Wagon trains, cannon, artillery, cavalry, and infantry were all blended in inextricable confusion. Broken down and jaded horses and mules refused to pull, and the badly-scared drivers looked like their eyes would pop out of their heads from fright. Wagon wheels, interlocking each other, soon clogged the road, and wagons, horses and provisions were left indiscriminately. The officers soon became effected with the demoralization of their troops, and rode on in dogged indifference.

The occasional roar of enemy artillery in the distance punctuated the scene. Watkins, his boot brimming blood and his uniform saturated with it, had commandeered a horse hitched to an abandoned wagon and made his way to Franklin, where a surgeon bandaged his wounds. Amazingly, he then went to find Hood to request a "wounded furlough" and located the general in his tent. "He was much agitated and affected, and crying like his heart would break," wrote Watkins, who received his furlough. "I pitied him, poor fellow. . . . I never saw him afterward. I always loved and honored him, and will ever revere and cherish his memory."[30]

Wood's corps bivouacked about a mile from Brentwood that night after a remarkable day. The IV Corps had captured fourteen artillery pieces, almost 1,000 Confederate prisoners, two flags, and hundreds of small arms at a cost of fewer than 1,000 casualties during the two days of combat. "It may be truthfully remarked that military history scarcely affords a parallel of a more complete victory," Wood noted of Nashville. Their haul likely would have been even larger had they not halted because of darkness and fatigue.[31]

Worn down, scattered, and hungry, the Union cavalry called off the pursuit in the wet blackness. Wilson ordered the halt around midnight with instructions for his commands to resume the attack in the morning. Hatch's and Knipe's divisions, along with John Croxton's brigade in the 1st Division, were on the Granny White Pike while Richard Johnson's 6th Division was situated on the Hillsboro Pike near the Big Harpeth River. Hatch's men camped near the barricades they had taken from Rucker.

As daylight waned, Thomas had ridden out over the smoky battleground and surveyed the panorama from Peach Orchard Hill, previously occupied by Lee's Confederates. He was jubilant—by his less-than-excitable standards, that is—and night was descending far too quickly for him to enjoy fully the fruits of this exceptional day. Seeing his men guarding long files of Confederate prisoners being marched back to Nashville, he raised his hat and shouted, "Oh, what a grand army I have! God bless each member of it!" Leaving the hill, Thomas rode west to check the progress of his cavalry. In the rainy darkness, he found Wilson on the Granny White Pike. "Dang it to hell, Wilson, didn't I tell you we could lick 'em?" the army commander exclaimed. "Didn't I tell you we could lick 'em, if they would only leave us alone?" Wilson knew Thomas was referring to the Washington authorities but was surprised by the profanity of his usually reserved commander.[32]

Before leaving the battlefield and despite the chaos, Hood had sent a staff officer to inform Forrest about the catastrophe and directed him to "rejoin the army with as little delay as possible," moving south via Shelbyville and Pulaski. Receiving the dispatch that night, Forrest immediately ordered Abraham Buford's division to fall back from the Cumberland River toward the Nashville-Murfreesboro Pike and guard Forrest's rear until he could move his artillery and wagons. Buford was to be prepared to unite with Chalmers's cavalry in order to protect the army's rear in the expected retreat. Pelted by icy rain, Forrest's somber troops struck out overnight to try to find Hood's army—or what was left of it. "Then began a march that had few parallels in the war for downright hardship and suffering," noted Colonel Olmstead, "every circumstance conspired to make it such."[33]

Union horsemen escorted the bleeding Colonel Rucker to the Tucker family house, which was serving not only as a field hospital for the cavalry, but also as temporary headquarters for Wilson and Hatch. Federal surgeons treated his arm as best they could there, but it was a serious injury, and the arm was amputated. Saying that he wanted to make Rucker more comfortable, Hatch offered the colonel his bed, which was accepted. There was another bed in the room and sometime during the night, Wilson entered and sat down on it. "He [Wilson] did not retire, however, but sat up in that bed, cross-legged like a tailor, all night, writing orders and receiving despatches [sic]," Rucker remembered. "I do not think that either General Wilson or I slept a wink. I certainly didn't. General Hatch laid down on the floor by my side, and (God bless him) got up frequently during the night and gave me water, and the next morning . . . he provided me with a small flask of good whiskey."[34]

A few miles away, John Johnston of the Confederate 14th Tennessee and another soldier were among Rucker's men making their way to the Franklin Pike after the clash at the barricades. Reaching the pike from a side road, Johnston was shocked by the sight of the beaten army before him, streaming south, since he and his comrades were unaware that Hood had been defeated. "Just as we reached the pike, the clouds parted and the moon came out and flooded the scene with a brilliant light," he recalled. "My heart sank within me when I came thus upon our routed army, for, strange to say . . . we had heard no sound of battle but our own, and had very little information as to what was going on over on our right. But now I realized that the battle was lost." The despondent Johnston and his friend headed back a short distance on the side road, found some forage for their horses, and settled into a fence corner for whatever rest they could get.[35]

That night, Thomas issued general orders thanking his troops for their "unsurpassed gallantry and good conduct displayed" in the two-day battle. "A few more examples of devotion and courage . . . and the rebel army of the West, which you have been fighting for three years, will be no more, and you may reasonably expect an early and honorable peace." Also contained in the orders were congratulations sent from President Lincoln, Secretary of War Stanton, and General Grant after the Union success on December 15, though the messages had not been received by Thomas until the morning of the sixteenth. "Please accept for yourself, officers and men the Nation's thanks for your good work of yesterday," Lincoln had wired. "You made a magnificent beginning. A grand consummation is within your easy reach; do not let it slip."[36]

Thomas was still about eight miles from Nashville around 6 P.M. when he sent a blanket reply to Lincoln, Stanton, Grant, and Andrew Johnson for their congratulatory messages regarding the December 15 battle. He also updated them on the second day's grand results and the chase that was unfolding even as the dispatch was being transmitted. "I have ordered the pursuit to be continued in the morning at daylight, although the troops are very much fatigued," he wrote.[37]

With the combat shifting south, the battleground was left behind, a grim collage of dead men and horses, wrecked caissons and wagons, and a now-haunted woodland, all lit by fingers of jagged lightning and soaked by the ongoing rain and sleet. Civilian members of the Christian Commission joined Union corpsmen in scouring the torn terrain with lanterns and torches to find the wounded; their compassion initially extended only to Union soldiers while injured Confederates were left to endure the awful conditions. The city's hospitals were quickly filled, and churches, private homes, and the courthouse also were used to treat the casualties. In the coming days, families with southern sympathies took in wounded Confederates. Of the two-day battle, Thomas reported taking 4,462 prisoners, including 287 officers of all grades (3 generals among them), 53 artillery pieces, and thousands of small arms in addition to the undetermined dead and wounded that the Confederates left behind. Of the 3,000 or so Union casualties, fewer than 400 were killed. The battlefield cleanup would take about four days, and with Christmas nearing, the Federals allowed residents to take food and gifts to the Confederate prisoners.[38]

The biggest fish netted by Thomas that day was Old Allegheny Johnson, who had been captured with much of his division—not the first time Johnson had been subjected to such an embarrassment in this war. "The Army of Tennessee has sustained no greater loss than that of this gallant and accomplished soldier," Stephen Lee later noted of the forty-eight-year-old Virginian who had established much of his combat resume in the eastern campaigns. Severely wounded in the lower leg in May 1862, he was hit again on the third day of Gettysburg and subsequently hobbled about with a stick. Defending the Bloody Angle at Spotsylvania on May 12, 1864, he had been captured along with the rest of his men. After his exchange a few weeks later, he reported to Hood in Atlanta in late August. On foot when the army unraveled at Nashville, he had been unable to escape because of his immobility.[39]

The two other captured Confederate generals were Brig. Gen. Henry R. Jackson and Brig. Gen. Thomas Benton Smith, both commanders in Bate's Division. Jackson also was dismounted when the dam ruptured and vainly tried to make his escape. His boots weighted with mud, he was soon overtaken by Federal infantrymen. Smith was seized in more dramatic fashion as he and the bulk of his brigade were overpowered in the assault on the Confederate left. Johnson and Jackson were taken to Thomas's field headquarters at the Hale home that night, where they were treated to officers' mess, cigars, and a flask by members of Thomas's staff. Smith, however, was not so lucky. As he and other Confederate prisoners tramped toward the Union rear, he was involved in an altercation with a Federal officer, who slashed him several times about the head with his sword. Now Smith clung to life in a Union field hospital, his brain exposed by the deep wounds.[40]

Amid the Federals' tired euphoria during the night, a mental error that would be overlooked in the Union command chain resulted in an order that would greatly influence the outcome of the campaign. At the Hale house, Thomas napped and awoke from a "deep sleep" to issue orders for the army's pontoon train, commanded by Maj. James R. Willett, to leave Nashville as early as possible on the seventeenth and join the army in the field. Willett was to move "on the Murfreesborough [sic] Pike, being prepared to report with it [the train] to the commanding general at any point between Brentwood and Columbia." Thomas obviously was planning a vigorous pursuit to destroy Hood. Capt. Robert H. Ramsey, the assistant adjutant who wrote the order, did not notice—or did not question—the fact that the Murfreesboro Pike would lead Willett *away* from Brentwood and Columbia and that Thomas must have meant the Franklin Pike. The immense consequences of this mistake would be felt three days later.[41]

In the slush and cold on the Franklin Pike, Hood's masses hurried south, and the soldiers watched their backs as the warm glow of Nashville's once-promising lights disappeared behind them. Beyond any battle statistics, some Confederates would later marvel how any of them had escaped Nashville. "The rout and retreat were inevitable. . . . The only wonder is that he [Thomas] did not capture us all," stated W. O. Dodd, one of Chalmers's men. Maj. James D. Porter, Cheatham's assistant adjutant general and a future Tennessee governor, echoed Dodd's sentiment: "There was no serious resistance to the Federal advance; it was a battle without an engagement or a contest; and the wonder is that Thomas, with a large and well-appointed army, more than treble the strength of Hood, did not press his right, seize the Franklin turnpike and capture the entire army." Porter also contended that "if Grant had been in command of the Federals, our little army would have been captured."[42]

Still, not even the most ardent Confederate would have denied the magnitude of the whipping they suffered at Nashville. As one Northern newspaper described it, "Gen. Thomas got Hood right where he wanted him and then put his hands upon him."[43]

CHAPTER 6

"Saber and Pistol against Stout Hearts"

SATURDAY, DECEMBER 17

The chilling rain continued to buffet the soldiers overnight, and morning broke dark and cloudy. Both armies were on the move early, sharing the misfortunes of intense fatigue, cold and aching limbs, drenched and muddy uniforms, and few rations. The nightmare was only beginning.

Basically all the troops Thomas had used in the Nashville fighting broke camp to seek and destroy Hood. Wilson's troopers rumbled south around 5 A.M., leaving behind the ruined barricade where Rucker had held them up. Knipe, Hatch, and Croxton took the Brentwood Road east along Richland Creek to reach the Franklin Pike at Brentwood. From there, Croxton moved out on the Wilson Pike while the others, with Knipe's division leading, wheeled south on the Franklin Pike. "It was killing work for both sides," Wilson related. "The rain was still pouring and the fields on both sides of the road were soaking wet." Soldiers would recall how the rain froze onto their weapons and how their numb fingers forced them to use both hands to cock muskets and pistols.[1]

On the Franklin Pike, upon which Wood's IV Corps was to continue its advance this morning, the cavalry had priority at Brentwood since they would be able to make up ground on the enemy more rapidly. Wilson had been gracious to the wounded Rucker, but papers taken from the officer helped him formulate his plan of attack on the first full day of the pursuit. Overnight on December 16–17, he sent at least two messages to

Gen. Richard Johnson, ordering him to move on Saturday down the Hillsboro Pike to reach the Big Harpeth River and possibly flank the retreating Confederates at Franklin.

From Rucker's documents, Wilson knew that the Confederates' main wagon trains had been sent south to Franklin even before the battle was decided and that Chalmers's cavalry remained his main obstacle in this sector. "Go for him [Chalmers] with all possible celerity, as Hood says the safety of their army depends upon Chalmers," Wilson told Johnson in one dispatch. He added that he and the rest of the pursuing cavalry were headed toward Franklin and hoped to meet Johnson there. In a later message, Wilson ordered Johnson to "shove him [Chalmers] as closely as possible; give him no peace . . . time is all he wants. Don't give him any. I will meet you somewhere on the [Big] Harpeth River tomorrow with the whole force. This has been a splendid day."[2]

Schofield's and Smith's infantry marched on the Granny White Pike while Steedman was behind Wood on the Franklin Pike. Knipe's 7th Division would be the spearpoint on the Franklin Pike, followed by Hatch, with whom Wilson rode with his headquarters staff. Knipe was a tough veteran, a forty-one-year-old Pennsylvanian who had tasted combat from the Shenandoah Valley in 1861 to Antietam, where he briefly led an infantry brigade, Gettysburg and Atlanta. Despite four battle wounds, he remained a hard charger.[3]

Meanwhile, the Confederates were still trying to restore some semblance of order as soldiers attempted to find and rejoin their fractured units during the night. The main army plodded south on the pike toward Franklin. Stewart was first in line, followed by Cheatham and Lee, the latter supported by Chalmers's cavalry, but much of the army remained a jumbled mob. The remnants of Chalmers's Division—still just Rucker's Brigade—had camped near the army's rear guard for a few hours overnight, and by early morning, they were joined by Col. Jacob Biffle's brigade, composed of only two Tennessee regiments, which had come in from Hood's right after the army collapsed.

Chalmers rejoined his horsemen after missing the fight at the barricades. The cavalry also was bolstered by the overnight arrival of Abraham Buford's command, with a couple of pieces of Forrest's artillery, after a forced march during the night. Buford's men had been posted on the Lebanon Pike about fourteen miles from Nashville on the sixteenth and had heard the boom of cannon throughout the day. When an officer arrived at their camp after midnight with the ominous news of Hood's debacle, there had been a "stupefying silence" before the command prepared to ride, a Kentucky trooper recalled.[4]

With Holtzclaw serving as rear guard, the rest of Clayton's Division and Pettus's Brigade had marched south until 2 A.M. on Saturday, when they halted to rest about seven miles from Franklin. They resumed their march around 5 A.M. and covering some two miles before reaching Hollow Tree Gap and taking defensive positions. Stovall's Brigade, supported by a section of Bledsoe's Missouri battery, was posted to the right of the road while Pettus's men were on the left. Clayton's other two brigades—Holtzclaw's and Gibson's—were in support. "A good many soldiers had come in through the night and early hours . . . so that it looked more like an army again," related one of Pettus's officers. Still, the fact that Bledsoe's gunners were assigned to Cheatham's Corps but now were fighting in the rear guard with Lee's command is mute evidence of the army's disarray, especially in the artillery. Holtzclaw had stood his ground until well after darkness halted the combat the night before and then had pulled back slowly, rounding up stragglers as he went. He rested his troops around 11 P.M., some four miles from Hollow Tree Gap, and then moved around 3 A.M., reaching the gap and filtering in behind Pettus. The exhausted Confederate rear guard would not have to wait very long for action.[5]

Elements of Stewart's Corps reached Franklin by about 3 A.M. and were hustled over the Harpeth before they were allowed to rest for a few hours. The Confederates had been able to lay a pontoon bridge at the pike crossing and also had access to the railroad trestle span near Fort Granger, the old

Union stronghold overlooking the town from the north bank. Chalmers's and Buford's horsemen also arrived at Franklin in the early morning. Hood ordered Chalmers to assume overall cavalry command until Forrest came up and to report to Lee to assist the rear guard.

Franklin itself remained packed with hundreds of soldiers from both sides who had been wounded in the November 30 battle and were still recuperating. Some of the Confederates, well enough to attempt travel, joined Hood's exodus, but most would be left behind. The town also contained a vast store of arms and ammunition, most of it captured from or abandoned by the Federals. A number of Confederates who had lost their weapons in flight were rearmed at Franklin. There also may have been some looting of stores and homes, based on Union newspaper accounts.[6]

The town still reeked of death, and scenes of the human slaughter that had occurred there lingered. The stench of dead men and horses permeated everything, and the rains had washed away shallow graves, leaving some heads and limbs of soldiers protruding from the ground as if struggling to rejoin the living. A few Confederates found time to perform a solemn task before leaving the town. Among the thousands of Southern dead buried at Franklin was Brig. Gen. States Rights Gist, a South Carolinian who led a brigade in Cheatham's Corps. As the Confederates retreated from Franklin, Gist's body was exhumed by his personal servant, Wiley Howard, or by soldiers of his brigade, possibly both. The remains eventually were returned to Columbia, South Carolina, where Gist rests today.[7]

Some Mississippians of Brig. Gen. William F. Brantley's brigade had escaped being swallowed up with the rest of Johnson's Division and rejoined the army near Franklin after being separated amid the rout. These troops had fled east from the battlefield and then south, paralleling the Franklin Pike. Guided by a local resident, the brigade reached the pike behind Lee's battle line. "Up to this time we had no straggling . . . as all feared capture," recalled Sgt. Robert A. Jarman of Company K, 27th Mississippi, "but when the men found out that a line of battle was between them and the enemy, they began to straggle." By the time the soldiers halted after midnight south of Franklin, "there were only four men in the consolidated company to stack arms." The Mississippians regrouped somewhat overnight, Jarman and his companions able to draw full rations and noting that "we had for our mess as much as we cared to pack with us next day." He added that many stragglers came in early "before we got up, for they were hungry."[8]

A few miles to the north, John Johnston, the Tennessee trooper from Rucker's Brigade, awoke in the fence corner early that morning to a strange silence. "There was not a sound or sign of impending battle, all was as peaceful and quiet as if no war had been," he noted. Johnston and his companion mounted and rode south on the Franklin Pike, which only hours before had been packed with Hood's infantry. Now they passed only an occasional straggler camped by the roadside. Reaching Hollow Tree Gap before 7 A.M., Johnston claimed that he saw Hood there with Lee's rear guard. Accompanied by his staff, Hood "was sitting on his horse very quietly, and was looking up the road as if expecting the appearance of the enemy. . . . He had a worn and dejected look."[9]

Union troopers of Bvt. Brig. Gen. John H. Hammond's 1st Brigade of Knipe's command soon smacked into enemy cavalry south of Brentwood on the Franklin Pike and drove them back toward Hollow Tree Gap, where Lee's rear guard awaited. All along the road, the Federals continued to see the stark evidence of a mortally wounded army. Wrecked and abandoned wagons had been pushed to the roadside. Shattered muskets that Confederates had smashed were in the ditches. Ammunition of every caliber had been dumped out along the route, and boxes were cracked open, their assorted contents soaked by the rain.[10]

Around 8 A.M., Knipe's division appeared before the gap, and Hammond immediately deployed and charged, shoving back the few Confederate horsemen who tried to confront them "in a most shameful manner," according to Clayton.

Joseph F. Knipe.

Earlier in the morning, some of Chalmers's men had needled Lee's infantrymen about running away as the cavalry rode north on the pike to meet the expected enemy pursuit. "They were going back to show us how to whip Yankees, so we need not be afraid any more," recalled one of Lee's officers.

Now the infantry guarding the gap heard sporadic gunfire and the dull throb of horses' hooves on the pike. Minutes later, the road was filled with horsemen in blue coats. Lee's soldiers quickly saw that many of the cavalry were Chalmers's troopers wearing captured Union overcoats—the same ones "who were going to show us how to fight Yankees," a captain observed. Mixed among the Confederates were some of Knipe's men, primarily the 19th Pennsylvania. The Federals pursued the Confederate riders through the ranks of the butternut infantry, sabering soldiers left and right before they were repulsed with the loss of a stand of colors and a few prisoners.[11]

Knipe made another mounted frontal assault within the hour, but stout musketry from Stovall's and Pettus's men, along with Bledsoe's artillery blasts, temporarily stymied the Union onslaught. The cavalry fell back and left dead, wounded, and several guidons scattered in the sullen woods and fields. The enemy "commenced a most vigorous pursuit, his cavalry charging at every opportunity and in the most daring manner," Lee recalled of this phase of the campaign. "It was apparent that they were determined to make the retreat a rout if possible."[12]

The Federals were too many and soon lapped around both of Lee's flanks, threatening to knife across the turnpike well to his rear and surround him. Gibson's men and a regiment of Buford's troopers, the 8th Kentucky Mounted Infantry under Lt. Col. Absalom R. Shacklett, fought off at least one attempt to seize the road as Lee ordered a hasty withdrawal from the gap to the Harpeth around 10 A.M. By now, most of the rest of the army was well south of the river, including the rest of Stevenson's Division, minus Pettus's Brigade. Knipe's men bagged about 100 prisoners, mostly Gibson's Louisianans, while suffering losses of 22 killed and wounded and 63 captured, all from the 10th Indiana and 19th Pennsylvania. Marched to the Union rear under guard were Col. Samuel E. Hunter of the 4th Louisiana, a number of his men, and a large portion of the 30th Louisiana. Among the war trophies taken, Knipe's troopers seized flags from the 4th and 30th and two sets of regimental band instruments, one silver, the other brass.[13]

Hustling south, Lee's men found scant respite as they approached the river: their fight at the gap had apparently forced the Federals to regroup quickly. Reaching the Harpeth by late morning, Lee and Clayton aligned Gibson's and Pettus's units on a bluff less than a mile from the river and the pontoon bridge in a horseshoe-shaped position. Gibson's Louisianans, now less than 500 strong, were posted in an earthwork, and the Confederates also deployed two guns and some of Buford's cavalry. The rest of Clayton's Division teetered over the pontoons and formed in support on the south side, in the town. By now, the rest of the army, including the remaining wagons and guns, were over the river, and engineers had begun disassembling the bridge.

The brief lull in fighting ended before noon. "The enemy having retreated we followed rapidly," according to Hammond, whose 9th Indiana took the lead toward the Harpeth. Lee noted that "the enemy appeared in considerable force and exhibited great boldness." The Federals soon attacked in force, with three cavalry columns rumbling down on the overmatched Confederates. The 9th Indiana, supported by the 10th Indiana and the 4th Tennessee of Hammond's brigade, were the attackers here. Buford's horsemen were brushed aside in quick order. In Franklin, Holtzclaw wrote that the Confederate troopers were shoved "in confusion into the river."

Watching the men in blue thunder toward them, the Confederate infantry held fire until the bluecoats were in close range. "What a moment of suspense and expectation," recalled one Southerner. "How the brain works in moments like these! But at last the general [Lee], rising in his stirrups as he sat on his gray horse, gave the command in stentorian voice 'Fire!'" The air crackled with musketry, but the two howitzers were silent as the cannoneers frantically realized that the friction primers were wet.[14]

The artillerists desperately worked on the guns and managed to fire about ten rounds, but the Federals were now too close and too many for them to have much effect. Outflanked and outnumbered, Gibson ordered the gun crews to limber up and fall back over the Harpeth. "The cavalry of the enemy charged all around us," Gibson wrote, adding that Federal troopers rode within less than 100 yards of the cannoneers as they retreated, firing their revolvers at them. Gibson's men fought their way to the river "entirely surrounded," suffering forty casualties, including ten killed. Added to the Confederate losses were about seventy-five men from Holtzclaw's Brigade, who had been separated from their command in the fighting at Hollow Tree Gap but found their way back to the pike to join Gibson, Holtzclaw, and the rest of his troops already posted on the south bank. Gibson ordered these men to cover the retreat of his brigade and the guns, which they did before they were cut off, most of them being captured. Pettus's Brigade had held firm but also had retreated by now, the rear guard tumbling toward the bridge and hard pressed by the bluecoats. It was a chaos of horses' shrieks, carbines and Colts, and yelling men as the Confederates jammed the span. One soldier stumbled and fell, begging for help as he struggled against the mass to regain his footing, but no one stopped. "The last I saw of him, he was still wallowing in the mud and the men were running over him," recalled George Brewer of the 46th Alabama.[15] Maj. Eugene F. Falconnet of the 7th Alabama Cavalry, upon seeing Gibson's units being assailed as they were about to cross, drew his revolver and, "gathering less than 100 brave followers, dashed upon the enemy, more than twenty times his number," Clayton stated.[16]

Clayton's other troops, taking in the spectacle from Franklin, were basically powerless to help their comrades since the Union forces were out of musket range, but Bledsoe's two guns, unlimbered on Front Street amid Holtzclaw's infantry, began lobbing shells that burst above the heads of Knipe's men, causing them to retreat briefly. Forrest's guns, which had arrived with Buford's cavalry, also played on the Federals, according to at least one account. This shelling allowed the Confederates to complete their crossing and sink the pontoon bridge. Despite a stinging fire from Union sharpshooters, a party of pioneers led by an engineer captain on Lee's staff sent the railroad trestle span crashing into the river as well.

Other than Falconnet's "one bright exception," Clayton later noted his disgust for the performance of the Confederate cavalry at the Harpeth, claiming that it was responsible for the capture of Holtzclaw's isolated soldiers. "For this occurrence, I think no one [is] to blame but our cavalry, who, all day long, behaved in a most cowardly manner," he reported. Gibson and Holtzclaw also noted the "stampeded" cavalry which contributed to their losses.[17]

As the rear guard hurried through the town, there were unexpected explosions of cannon fire from another direction as a second Union force, which had been able to ford the Harpeth downstream, was even then preparing to attack. Richard Johnson's cavalry division of about 2,000 men had been in the saddle since 4 A.M. and had reached the Harpeth a few miles west of Franklin about the time Lee was retreating from Hollow Tree Gap. Despite the fact that his scouts told him the road was open, Johnson had made a cautious advance on the Hillsboro Pike that morning, taking some six hours to cover the nine miles to the Harpeth by horseback. Now, however, he was in a prime position to surprise Lee's troops as they prepared to leave Franklin. With the river rising rapidly because of the rain, Johnson hurried his troopers over, especially the guns of Battery I of the 4th U.S. Artillery, commanded by Lt. Frank G. Smith. After fording, Johnson's cavalry pressed down the south bank, and Smith's gunners unlimbered on a bluff overlooking the town around 10:30 A.M. The cannoneers opened fire, hastening the enemy evacuation.[18]

Stephen Lee later claimed that the presence of the hundreds of wounded caused him to leave Franklin to the Federals shortly after noon without much of a fight. He wrote that "not wishing to subject them and the town to the fire of the enemy's artillery, the place was yielded with but little resistance." Johnson, however, saw matters somewhat differently, writing that the Confederates likely believed they had been outflanked by an overpowering force when his division surprised them: "I have often supposed the rebels imagined that the greater part of our army was on the south side of the Harpeth . . . and had it been known that we were completely cut off from our army by high water, they might have turned against us and made it very uncomfortable, even if they had failed to kill or capture the last one of the command."[19]

Johnson did not mention that he missed an opportunity to trap much of Lee's Corps and, more importantly, prevent the destruction of the Harpeth bridges. Johnson's failure—or Knipe's, for that matter—to secure at least one of the spans meant little for the recapture of the town. Its import came days later when Union supplies crucial to sustaining the chase were held up at the Harpeth while bridges were reconstructed. As it was, the river was not yet high enough on this day to keep Knipe's troopers from fording near the remains of the railroad span and joining Johnson's horsemen in a wild ride through Franklin's streets. Johnson's bluecoats, primarily Col. Israel Garrard's 7th Ohio of Col. Thomas J. Harrison's 1st Brigade and Hammond's 4th Tennessee, charged through the town on the heels of the Confederates, snatching some prisoners. Before leaving, some of Lee's soldiers set fire to a freight house containing seven wagons loaded with ammunition. With a massive explosion looming, a civilian with a ladder ran to the building and threw buckets of water on the burning roof. Some cinders and smoldering shingles dropped onto the wagons, but the man extinguished the blaze, averting disaster. Garrard's boys would have pressed on, but Johnson recalled them to reorganize, not knowing what they faced south of town.[20]

Before evacuating Franklin, Lee replaced Clayton with Stevenson's Division as the rear guard, along with Chalmers's cavalry. Stevenson re-formed his command with the return of

Pettus's battered brigade. Like the rest of Clayton's command, Stovall's Brigade had been in the teeth of the combat all day to this point and had helped repulse the repeated Union attacks, including one charge that resulted in the capture of 75 to 100 men, an enemy flag, many horses, bridles, and saddles, and "such other things as constituted the outfit of a Federal cavalryman." Stovall himself had not yet been able to rejoin his troops, and the brigade was temporarily commanded by Col. R. J. Henderson of the 42nd Georgia. Henderson had replaced Maj. Abda Johnson, who led the brigade just after the December 16 rout.

Pettus's men halted for a few golden minutes of rest after crossing the river, but not long enough to refresh them from the almost non-stop entrenching, fighting, and marching of the past two days. "The night of the 16th had been spent in moving to the new line and intrenching, the day following in fighting, most of the night in marching and reorganizing, and on the 17th we had been fighting and marching, so we were much worn with loss of sleep and active work," related the Alabamian George Brewer. "If it could be called rest, it was brief."[21]

In retaking Franklin, the Federals found themselves in possession of 1,500 wounded Confederates and about 200 of their own injured comrades from the great battle. The Union wounded "were greatly delighted at getting once more under the shadow of the stars and stripes," Johnson related. Many of the men limped or crawled to windows and whooped for joy. About 17,000 rations also were seized. Among the Confederate wounded who had been able to escape was Tennessee captain John W. Carroll of Forrest's cavalry, who had been shot in the left foot at Murfreesboro and who had been recovering in Franklin. With Hood retreating, Carroll and James Record, a soldier in his company, started south in a one-horse wagon drawn by a mule, just ahead of the fleeing army. Carroll had his right shoe off so that he could use that foot to support the injured one from the wagon's jolts and bumps. In the severe cold, Carroll's good foot soon became frost-bitten, "so much so that the skin and toe-nails all came off together." His troubles were only beginning.[22]

As the fighting crackled at Hollow Tree Gap that morning, the Union IV Corps began to slog south on the Franklin Pike after a 4 A.M. reveille. Wood had received orders from Thomas around 12:30 A.M. that he should continue the pursuit "as early as practicable." Wood instructed his division commanders at 6 A.M. to move out as soon as they could and, "if the enemy should be overtaken, to press him vigorously." Wood's three divisions would move in a line extending over the pike, each with a brigade deployed and the rest of the troops marching in column behind them. Kimball was on the right, Elliott's 2nd Division in the center and Samuel Beatty's 3rd Division on the left. The corps did not fully get underway until almost 8 A.M., but then made good progress despite the rain and worsening roads. The columns were held up a short time around 10 A.M. to allow some of Wilson's cavalry to pass ahead of them. "The morning . . . demonstrated plainly that the enemy had fled from our front, and the ground strewn with arms, accouterments, and munitions of war showed that his retreat had been both hasty and irregular," Beatty wrote.[23]

Wood's soldiers were tired but buoyed by the excitement of the Nashville triumph and eager to take advantage of the opportunity before them as they trudged through the muck, picking up Confederate stragglers and deserters. Smith's XVI Corps, Schofield's XXIII Corps, and Steedman's division also were afoot on Saturday, but the IV Corps would be Thomas's spearhead in the infantry operation. "Among the men the feeling was quite general that the victory of yesterday, if properly followed up, would result not only in the capture of Hood's entire army, but in the speedy termination of the war," recalled a soldier in the 36th Illinois of Elliott's division. "On every side were heard expressions of hope, mingled with shouts of exultation."[24]

Others still had respect for their enemy, whom they had faced on many fields, and were greatly surprised at the level of the Confederates' disintegration. "We had on other occasions followed the retreat of this same great army," said the Ohioan L. W. Day of Kimball's division. "We had passed through their camps soon after they had left them, but never had we witnessed such a scene as was here presented." For some distance, the pike's shoulders were littered with guns, bayonets, belts, cartridge boxes, knapsacks, canteens, camp kettles, and various clothing. The men marched past abandoned caissons and overturned wagons. "Everything that could hinder their flight seemed to have been flung away," Wood said. "The whole line of march of the day bore unmistakable evidence of the signalness [*sic*] of the victory our arms had achieved and the completeness of the rout. The road was strewn with small-arms, accouterments, and blankets."[25]

Hood established his headquarters at Spring Hill by early afternoon. Here, he sent a telegram to Secretary of War Seddon, with a duplicate to Beauregard, informing them of the previous days' battles and of the army's retreat. This was his first official report about the catastrophe. Of the back-breaking attack the day before, Hood stated that, "all their [the enemy's] assaults were handsomely repulsed with heavy loss till 3:30 P.M. when a portion of our line . . . suddenly gave way, causing in a few moments our line to give way at all points, our troops retreating rapidly down the Franklin Pike. . . . I still have artillery enough with the army, and am moving to the south of Duck River." Hood also was already preparing for the possibility that his army would have to retreat beyond the Tennessee, although his plans remained fluid at this point. He wrote to the commander at Corinth to direct the engineering officer there to gather "all the pontoon boats (with ropes and flooring) that he has on hand" and send them to Barton Station, a stop on the railroad between Tuscumbia and Cherokee Station. The officer was also ordered to collect "sufficient transportation to forward the boats, &c., to any point on the river that may be designated."[26]

Wilson reassembled the cavalry he had on hand at Franklin early in the afternoon and quickly sent them tearing after the Confederates, with Knipe taking the Columbia Pike while Johnson marched southwest on the Carter's Creek Pike, trying to hit the Confederates at or near Spring Hill. Hatch's 5th Division troopers were on the scene by now to reinforce Knipe after being held up much of the day on the increasingly bad roads. Meanwhile, Croxton was somewhere to the left, looping southeast toward Lewisburg. Wilson hoped this three-pronged movement of about 10,000 troopers would allow him to envelop and cut off a sizeable portion of the Confederate army. The morning's work had netted 413 prisoners, excluding the wounded in Franklin, as well as three flags. There was little letup in the fighting after Franklin changed hands, and the combat south of town became a moving series of sharp but sporadic firefights as Wilson's horsemen engaged Confederate cavalry and Lee's infantry. "During the day we were almost constantly engaged with the enemy, who followed us vigorously with a strong force, often in close encounters," General Chalmers wrote.[27]

"The rebels are on a great skedaddle," Wilson wrote to Thomas from Franklin around 1 P.M., also informing him of his cavalry's dispositions. "The prisoners report the rebel army in a complete rout, and all the Tennesseans are deserting." Events were unfolding so rapidly that Wilson had to update his dispatch twice before sending it: the Confederate rear guard was supposedly in position in the hills just south of town. "The Harpeth is rising rapidly; all bridges down. Shove up the infantry and get up the pontoons." Knipe had snared five battle flags and 300 prisoners.[28]

Even as Wilson composed his message, his horsemen were engaging in the afternoon's first serious encounter some two miles to the south, near where the Confederates had formed for their assault on November 30. Lee's orders to flip-flop his divisions had not yet been implemented since Holtzclaw's weary men were trudging over the grim landscape when they were hurried into line around 1 P.M. just outside some of the trenches to fend off the bluecoats. The Union troopers "dashed up to within 300 yards of my line, firing carbines and pistols," Holtzclaw reported, but were driven back by three or four volleys of musketry. His brigade then withdrew in line, halting every few hundred yards to keep the enemy at bay before reaching the relative safety of a gap to the south. Lee estimated that this action, along with the destruction of the two Harpeth bridges, gained four to five hours for the retreating army.[29]

In another blow to Hood's senior leadership, Lee was seriously wounded in the foot by a shell fragment in this scrap. The shrapnel took off a spur and cut through his heel. The general was mounted on the pike and accompanied by General Gibson, a physician named Stewart, and Col. Robert Lindsay of the 16th Louisiana of Gibson's Brigade when he was hit. Lee refused to relinquish command, however, and directed his corps from an ambulance. The stop-and-go fighting between the Union cavalry and Hood's rear guard sizzled through the rest of the afternoon, with the major drama yet to come.[30]

The Union IV Corps began arriving on the north bank of the Harpeth at Franklin around 1:20 P.M., but the swelling river and lack of bridges prevented Wood's infantry from following the cavalry, leaving Wilson on his own. Wood made a game effort to follow. The 9th Indiana of Col. Isaac Suman received orders around 2 P.M. to construct a makeshift span using whatever timber the men could find. "It is doubtful whether he [Suman] will succeed in putting one up, as the river is rising rapidly," Col. Joseph S. Fullerton, Wood's chief of staff, wrote at the time. In Franklin around 1:30, Wilson fired off another update to Thomas: the Confederates had started passing through town early on the sixteenth. "One of our surgeons here says he never saw a worse rabble; they are completely demoralized." Wilson also noted that he knew nothing of Forrest's whereabouts although he had reportedly withdrawn from Murfreesboro the previous day, which was accurate.[31]

Thomas, however, had received some heartening news about Forrest from Schofield this day: "the universal testimony of rebels, officers, and men is that Forrest was killed certainly at Murfreesborough [sic], where they admit their cavalry was badly whipped." From Murfreesboro, on the same date, General Rousseau also reported Forrest's death. Word spread to

Northern newspaper correspondents with the army, but Wilson, on the eighteenth, informed Thomas that a prisoner "just taken states that Forrest, with Jackson's division of cavalry and two brigades of infantry, left Murfreesborough day before yesterday for Columbia, where he may be today." This was the most accurate information the Federals had about Forrest, who even then was riding hard for Columbia.[32]

This amazing day ended with a collision at nightfall about six miles south of Franklin as the Federal cavalry seriously pressed the gray rear guard. "A more persistent effort was never made to rout the rear guard of a retiring column," Stephen Lee wrote of the almost continuous harassment throughout the afternoon. In a foggy rain, the Confederates deployed for battle in open fields on both sides of the pike, with a battery on a slight rise. It was about 4 P.M., and Stevenson had decided to make a stand with the West Harpeth River about a mile to his rear. Wilson later claimed that the enemy likely made their fight because they were "apparently exhausted with rapid marching." He also said that in the mist and failing light, Hatch's troopers, "who had become somewhat intermingled with the sullen and taciturn Confederate stragglers, began to doubt that the ranks . . . looming up in their front were really those of the enemy's rear-guard." There was a "momentary hesitation" by the Federals, which allowed the Confederates to pull their guns into position and post their infantry.[33]

The Confederates consisted of Pettus's Alabamians, Cumming's Brigade of Georgians led by Col. Elihu P. Watkins, Chalmers's and Buford's cavalry, and three 12-pounder guns of Douglas's Texas battery commanded by Lt. Ben Hardin. Eyeing this position, Wilson deployed Hatch on the left of the pike and Knipe on the right—both with their artillery—and posted his own bodyguard, 180 men of the 4th U.S. Cavalry led by Lt. Joseph Hedges, on the road in his center. Hedges's men were far from a pretty-boy escort; the 4th's combat resume stretched from Missouri-Kansas border clashes to Atlanta. Hatch's men, who had been in so much of the toughest combat the previous day, had not been engaged today until this encounter.

The Union gunners, primarily Hatch's Chicago Board of Trade battery, opened with blasts of grape and canister, and Hedges ordered the charge. In columns of four, the yelling troopers rumbled, sabers drawn, down the road toward the enemy line about 300 yards away. Stevenson claimed that he "found it impossible to control the [Confederate] cavalry" and that the gray troopers retreated in disorder when the Federals came on in force, "leaving my small command to their fate." Knipe's horsemen, mainly Hammond's troopers, clattered around the Confederate right flank, getting into the rear, their Spencers snapping, while Coon's brigade of Hatch's command spilled around Stevenson's left.

In the gathering darkness, the Confederates at first were unsure if the approaching horsemen were friend or foe since so many Southern cavalrymen, like the rest of Hood's army, wore capture Union clothing. "This was a critical moment, and I felt great anxiety as to its effect upon the men, who, few in numbers, had just had the shameful example of the cavalry added to the terrible trial of the day before," Stevenson noted.[34]

In seconds, there was no doubt about the identity of the oncoming riders along the pike as Hedges's troopers barreled into Stevenson's line. Confederates dove out of the way of the galloping horses. The white spit of small-arms fire and the wicked glint of swinging blades punctuated the gloom. "They swooped down on us with pistols, carbines, and sabers, hewing, whacking, and shooting," recalled George Brewer of the 46th Alabama of Pettus's Brigade. There was a tornado of hand-to-hand fighting, bayonets against swords, but the Confederates held, and the Federals spurred to safety. Hedges, however, found himself trapped within the enemy position, but his quick thinking likely saved him from death or capture. Realizing his predicament, he threw away his hat and shouted, "The Yankees are coming, run for your lives!" The Confederates' ensuing confusion allowed him to escape. Before this day's last fight was over, Hedges apparently repeated this ploy twice more to elude capture.[35]

By now, the Union men were assailing Stevenson from front, flank, and rear. Coon dismounted his 9th Illinois, and the troopers poured carbine volleys into the enemy position. The overall pressure caused the Confederates to falter. "It was the most trying experience I had during the war," Brewer said. "I knew there was no chance of escape, but by fighting, so I ran along my line, entreating the men to stand as our only chance, for we would never get away in the large, open grounds around us, for there were enough of them to give three or four mounted men to chase down each fellow afoot. I suppose the commanders of the other regiments did likewise, for in a little while the lines were steady, with a grim determination on every face, using shot or bayonet as needed."[36]

With the troops seemingly stabilized, Stevenson ordered Pettus and Watkins to form three sides of a hollow square and make a fighting withdrawal across the West Harpeth, which they were able to do. Hardin's gunners, meanwhile, had blasted at the enemy with at least one volley of canister before limbering up to escape. "Seeing what was about to burst upon him, the battery commander opened with canister at short range, but had hardly emptied his guns before the storm broke upon him as well as upon the entire rebel line," Wilson recalled. Hardin's cannoneers had struggled about half a mile down the turnpike before the wheels on the lead gun broke down—or were incapacitated by Union horsemen, based on conflicting accounts—trapping the Texans and their battery on the muddy road. Whatever the case, the bluecoats quickly overrode them, sabering and scattering the artillerymen, slashing harnesses, and freeing the battery teams so that these pieces would remain where they were. These guns were captured by Hatch's men, and the general himself was riding with the troopers who seized them despite the fact that he had lost his revolver and was armed with a riding crop. The Confederates retook them briefly but, with no way to move them, had to abandon them.[37]

Just south of the river, Stevenson halted briefly to reorganize his units before continuing in the darkness. As he prepared to resume his retreat, Hatch hit him again, the Union men riding almost into the Confederate ranks before both sides recognized the enemy. "The scene, like that of the night before, was one of great confusion, but every musket-flash and every defiant shout was a guide to the gallant and unrelenting pursuers," Wilson noted. The bark of Union Spencers and Confederate muskets ripped the night in combat that "for fierceness exceeded any the regiment ever engaged in," according to a sergeant in the 2nd Iowa Cavalry of Coon's brigade. There was desperate fighting along a roadside fence where a number of Southerners were hunkered.

With the Confederates often in Union overcoats, a soldier had to think twice before pulling the trigger or slashing at the man next to him—a dilemma for both adversaries. A Federal private named Backus aimed his carbine at a Confederate, ordering him to surrender, but the man responded with a gunshot, which missed. As Backus prepared to shoot him, the Confederate called for mercy, and the private responded with a shot that also missed. Now the Confederate lunged toward Backus, drawing a revolver from his belt and shouting, "Damn you, I'll teach you to shoot at me after I have surrendered." Backus dropped his attacker with the butt of the carbine, jacked another round into the chamber, and killed him. Moments later, a Confederate fired at Backus at close range, tearing off two of his fingers. Another Federal lost an eye before he escaped a hand-to-hand struggle with a Confederate officer.

Pressed in front by Hatch, Stevenson soon realized that other Union troops were boiling up toward the pike behind him. These were some of Knipe's men, primarily Hammond's brigade, who had crossed the West Harpeth and were threatening to cut off the Confederates' retreat. Stevenson's units withdrew, running south on the road in the mud and blackness.[38]

Meanwhile, Clayton's spent division had been halted on the turnpike a short distance to the south when it received word that Stevenson was under duress and the enemy was threatening to engulf him. Clayton immediately ordered his men into a battle line along the road, facing north. Stovall's Brigade, commanded by Col. R. J. Henderson, was on the right, Gibson in the center, and Holtzclaw on the left. Holtzclaw had posted his brigade when "another of the many cavalry stampedes from Chalmers's division occurred," he reported. The retreating cavalry threatened to disorganize his infantry. As he tried to keep his men aligned, get the cavalry out of the way into positions to his left, Holtzclaw suffered a "severe contusion" to his ankle. The injury was so painful that he was incapacitated for several hours. With the Federal cavalry bearing down, Col. Bushrod Jones of Alabama was suddenly thrust into brigade command.[39]

Hearing the escalating gunfire to the rear, Clayton ordered Jones to move forward in a battle line. Leaving Gibson in temporary command of the other two brigades, Clayton and his staff also rode north on the pike to find Stevenson. Jones had advanced to the proximity of Stevenson's retreating troops but was threatened by elements of Hammond's brigade to the west. Clayton then rode to Pettus, who was nearby, informed him of his support, and then started back to his own command. By now, it was dark, and as Clayton neared Gibson's position, he saw a cavalry column enter the road a few paces ahead of him. A Confederate infantryman ran up to the general and whispered, "They are Yankees." Clayton wheeled his horse away from them and, dodging several bullets fired by his own men in the confusion of the night, found Gibson and informed him of this threat. A volley from Gibson's men dropped some of these Federals and drove off the others.

Clayton and Gibson then moved the two brigades behind a fence for better defense. Shortly thereafter, the Confederates saw troops coming toward them on the pike. Clayton yelled for them to identify themselves and received the reply, "Federal troops." The Confederates answered with lead, emptying more saddles and capturing a stand of colors. Hammond's 10th Indiana, supported by the 9th Indiana, bore the brunt of this action. The 10th, commanded by Lt. Col. Benjamin Gresham, fought with "saber and pistol against stout hearts and clubbed muskets, with the pall of darkness still over all," Wilson stated.

"Both [Indiana regiments] suffered, but are repaid in the knowledge that this attack caused the abandonment of . . . cannon by the enemy," Hammond reported. Gresham himself was nursing five broken ribs after being knocked from his horse by a sturdy Confederate swinging a rifle in the previous night's fighting on the Granny White Pike.[40]

Despite the criticism from Stevenson, Holtzclaw, and others, the gray cavalry was immersed in some of the toughest combat in this phase of the retreat, with their generals just as—or more—involved in actual fighting than their infantry counterparts. Abraham Buford was assailed by a Union trooper who twice slashed at him over the shoulder with a saber. General Chalmers quickly came to Buford's aid, killing the Federal with two revolver shots. Chalmers also captured another Union soldier amid the engagement. Apparently in the same encounter, another bluecoat swung his saber at Buford, but the blade was diverted by a Confederate trooper using the barrel of his empty carbine. Buford, a big man weighing about 300 pounds, then grabbed his assailant and yanked him from his horse. Squeezing him so tightly that the Federal later said it was like being "hugged by a bear," Buford spurred to safety with his prisoner.[41]

The darkness added another dynamic to the fighting. At one point, a Union lieutenant rode up to some unidentified troops, tapped one of them on the shoulder, and asked to what command they belonged. "19th Tennessee, Bell's Brigade, rear guard," the Confederate replied. The lieutenant scampered back toward Hatch's line, and these Southerners soon came under Federal artillery fire. One of Hatch's privates was engaged in a one-on-one fight with a Confederate when the Union soldier snatched a revolver from the Confederate's belt and killed him with it.[42]

Troopers of the 2nd Iowa found themselves in a vicious struggle for possession of a Confederate banner. Pvt. Dominic Black was about to saber the flag bearer when a member of the color guard shot him through the heart. First Sgt. John Coulter of Company K, wrenched away the standard, and a bullet almost immediately ripped into his shoulder. Coulter swayed to the rear with the flag; five dead Confederates and two or three Iowans were sprawled within a few feet of the spot were it was captured. The color sergeant of the 2nd's Company F was killed nearby, minutes after he himself had slain a Confederate who demanded his flag.[43]

Reinforced by Jones, Stevenson held his ground in a large beech grove along the pike despite several Federal assaults, including artillery fire. Jones and his men found themselves facing a blistering sleet of carbine fire from the 9th Illinois Cavalry of Hatch's division and were forced back. "I never heard better volleys fired over a grave than these Illinois boys fired that night," an admiring Iowa trooper wrote after the war. By now, units on both sides were badly disorganized, positions were confused, and in the rainy cold, Union momentum had been blunted again, as on the previous night.

In battle line, Stevenson cautiously retreated about a mile before realizing the enemy seemed to have called off the onslaught. He then put his troops back on the pike and continued his march "in the ordinary manner." Clayton also had moved out after the firing died down, and the two divisions marched a few miles south to Thompson's Station, where they encamped and the exhausted men collapsed in the mud to sleep. Like the rest of the troops, Pettus's Alabamians "laid our weary bodies down for much needed rest," Captain Brewer wrote. The Confederate cavalry, now reassembled, passed a short distance to the south and bivouacked at Spring Hill, near the army's main body. "It was a dreadful night, the mud about a foot deep was frozen, but not sufficiently to bear the weight of our horses and the artillery, recalled James Dinkins, one of Chalmers' horsemen.[44]

Spread about Spring Hill, the Army of Tennessee had already bivouacked in order of march and was unmolested overnight because of the tenacious fight put up by Lee's infantry and the cavalry. The bulk of the army was now some twenty-one miles south of Brentwood, where much of the day's nightmare had started before sunrise. Most of the weary troops had halted after dark while the rear guard remained under duress. "The weather, still wet, was very cold, the roads desperately muddy, horses and men so hungry and jaded that despondency was now stamped upon the sombre [*sic*] features of the hardiest," read one Confederate account of this stage of the march.[45]

Although he had not played an active role in the rear guard's actions after his wounding, Lee managed to remain in command until that night, when he relinquished his corps to Stevenson. The South Carolinian had "displayed his usual energy and skill in handling his troops" before he had to retire, Hood wrote. Lee gave more credit to Stevenson, "to whom the army is much indebted for his skill and gallantry during the day." Forty-seven years old, Stevenson was a Virginian and 1838 West Point graduate who had served on the frontier and in the Mexican War. A veteran of the western campaigns, he had seen action at Vicksburg, where he was captured; Chattanooga; and Atlanta.[46]

With scarce rations and forage, the Union cavalry was recalled and went into camp at the river, where some troopers stirred campfires left by the Confederates. Bugle calls echoed in the night, summoning other bluecoats back from the wild country to the relative safety of their units. "Men and horses were ravenously hungry and almost worn out with three days of continuous marching and fighting, and there was nothing left but to bivouac on the field," Wilson later recalled, adding that the chase was kept up "till both men and horses were so blown that they could go no farther into the darkness." Among the returning horsemen was the jubilant Lieutenant Hedges, who would be awarded the Medal of Honor in 1898 for his actions in this clash.[47]

At 6 P.M., Wilson sent a dispatch to Thomas stating that he had "bust up" Stevenson's infantry and an enemy cavalry brigade, capturing three guns amid "several beautiful charges." Wilson also noted that there had been a great deal of night fighting and that his men were scattered, but that he was regrouping at the river. "Hatch is a brick!" he ended, complimenting his division commander. About an hour later, he sent another message to Thomas, lauding Knipe for his involvement in the action and giving more details about the engagement: "If it had only been light, we would certainly have destroyed their entire rear guard; as it was, they were severely punished." Wilson added that he badly needed forage and would assemble his troopers, except Croxton's brigade, at the river that night. Johnson had to be near the right flank, he told Thomas. "As soon as it is light in the morning, and everything fed, I will push forward." Wilson also issued orders that his officers should be "very active" in finding forage and ensuring that all mounts were well fed—before morning, if possible.[48]

The Federals still were unsure whether they were facing Forrest, although Wilson seems to have convinced himself by now that he was. "The rebel force was found to be Stevenson's division . . . under command of General Forrest, who had just returned" from Murfreesboro, he wrote in a report on February 1, 1865. Years later, Wilson claimed that the Confederates' stout fight at the West Harpeth "showed that a mastermind had taken charge"—that genius thought to be Forrest, which was not the case.[49]

A few miles to the east, Croxton's troopers bedded down after a long day of their own. They had plodded through the countryside, gathering isolated Confederates as they went, before swimming the Big Harpeth at McGavock's Ford and heading down the Lewisburg Pike. With 130 prisoners, Croxton bivouacked that night near Douglass Church, about four miles south of Franklin. The route was familiar to Croxton, since he was basically retracing the movements he had made on the day of the Franklin battle—only this time he was out of rations.[50]

To the west, Richard Johnson's division had moved south on the Carter's Creek Pike from Franklin and, by sundown, was well within striking distance of the enemy's Spring Hill encampments. He would attack the next morning. The Union infantry, meanwhile, remained stranded miles to the rear on the north bank of the rapidly rising Big Harpeth at Franklin.

Wood's bridge builders had struggled through the afternoon. They had made little progress and were frustrated since they could hear the clatter of firing to the south as Wilson's men engaged the Confederates.

By 5 P.M., Wood had received a note from Thomas, stating that he should cross as soon as a pontoon bridge reached him or Suman's work was done. The sun descended and the infantry waited as the Hoosiers labored and no pontoon train appeared. Wood sent orders to his division commanders that the span likely would not be completed until well after midnight and that they should let the troops "rest as they can."

Shortly afterward, at 7 P.M., Suman informed Wood that the river still was steadily on the rise and that he was skeptical a bridge could be built at all, although he would continue working. Wood sent word to Thomas an hour later that the river's strong current, flooding, and driftwood plunging downstream made the bridge construction impossible. "I see no other way than to wait for the pontoon train," he stated. "This should be hurried forward, for I am confident we cannot cross until it comes up. If you will hurry that forward, we will put it down and cross immediately." At 9 P.M., Wood sent a dispatch to Wilson apprising him of the infantry's situation. "If the pontoons get up tonight, I hope to get off early in the morning, and will use all possible dispatch in getting up to you," he told the cavalryman. "I congratulate you and your command on your distinguished success today."[51]

While Wilson and Wood led Thomas's advance, a good portion of the rest of his army also had slogged south that day. By an alternate road to the southwest, Steedman's division had also reached the Big Harpeth near Franklin, encamping on the north bank that night. The XVI Corps had moved south on the Granny White Pike that morning and then filtered into position to march in the rear of Wood's corps. Schofield's corps, which had done so much damage to Hood at Franklin, would bring up the rear of Thomas's pursuit, including the main wagon train. Schofield had been relegated to this position because Thomas remained upset about Schofield's lack of initiative in attacking when Hood's army was broken on the sixteenth.[52]

At his field headquarters a few miles north of Franklin around 8 P.M., Thomas wired Grant and Halleck identical messages about the day's progress as he knew it at the time. The Confederates had been pushed out of the town, which yielded about 1,500 Confederate and 150 Union wounded in the various makeshift hospitals (the figure was closer to 2,000 total). Knipe's thrust through Franklin resulted in the capture of approximately 250 prisoners and five battle flags with minor loss to the Federals. Johnson's cavalry also had taken an unknown number of Confederates. "Citizens . . . represent Hood's army as completely demoralized," Thomas told them. "The enemy has been pressed today both in front and on both flanks" with more prisoners taken but not yet reported, he said. "My cavalry is pressing him closely tonight, and I am very much in hopes of getting many more prisoners tomorrow."[53]

Shortly afterward, Thomas received word from Wilson about his collision with Stevenson's infantry and passed this intelligence on to Halleck. Since his headquarters had basically been in the saddle since the rout, Thomas still was gathering details about the immensity of his Nashville victory. That night, he learned that A. J. Smith's veterans had captured Confederate general Johnson and most of his division in the climatic assault on the sixteenth. Just before 11 P.M., he responded to Wilson's two earlier dispatches about the West Harpeth fight, stating that he agreed with Wilson's suggestion to feed the men and horses and push on early in the morning.[54]

Amid the Confederate camps south of Spring Hill, A. P. Stewart issued orders for his corps' movements at daybreak on the eighteenth, with Walthall to lead, followed by Loring. Additionally, all wagons and ambulances were to be started at once toward Columbia. The ambulances, brigade ordnance trains, and tool wagons were to be stopped north of the Duck River while the corps' other wagons were to cross to the Columbia side and be parked, awaiting the arrival of the other vehicles; Loring's quartermaster would be in charge of the column.

Stewart also received orders from Hood that night not to "burn the railroad" in the Spring Hill vicinity since there was a train still to head south from there. Stewart also ordered a battery from Storr's Battalion of artillery back to the village early the next morning to support Cheatham.[55]

Meanwhile, Thomas had an ace yet to play, and if there was a "fair prospect" of the Tennessee River rising as expected, there also was a good chance that Hood's army could be captured en masse or obliterated. In his message to Grant and Halleck that night, Thomas informed them that he had requested Acting Rear Adm. Samuel P. Lee, commander of the U.S. Mississippi Squadron, to send gunboats up the Tennessee "to destroy Hood's pontoon bridge, if possible, and cut off his retreat." The vessels also could be used to ferry Union reinforcements from western Tennessee if they were needed. If the navy could dam the Tennessee with gunboats, Hood would be cut off, and the remnants of one of the Confederacy's two principal armies would be trapped against the river. From his headquarters at Clarksville, Tennessee, on the Cumberland River that day, Admiral Lee complimented Thomas's triumph, but there was no word yet about how the navy would react to the army's request for assistance.[56]

The fifty-two-year-old admiral had an impressive service record and was another of the Virginia Lees. His grandfather, Richard Henry Lee, had been a statesman during the American Revolution. Lee had entered the navy when he was thirteen and, in almost forty years, had seen action from the East Indies to the Mediterranean and through the Mexican War. In the present conflict, he had served in the campaign to capture New Orleans and in blockade duty off Charleston, South Carolina, before being assigned command of the North Atlantic Blockading Squadron, which had been increasingly efficient in stifling Confederate sea commerce. Lee had been transferred to head the Mississippi Squadron in October, and this would be his first—and ultimate—test in that capacity.

CHAPTER 7

"The Print of Bloody Feet in the Snow"

SUNDAY, DECEMBER 18

In the miles of grim trenches and forts scarring the Virginia countryside around Richmond and Petersburg, soldiers on both sides heard the roar of 200 Union guns fired in honor of Thomas's Nashville victory on the morning of December 18. Some 650 miles away, amid the mixed stench of human filth, mule dung, and soaked wool uniforms, there was no martial glory for the victors or their foe as the Tennessee drama reopened in and around the hamlet of Spring Hill. Hood's columns were on the march early, with Stewart's Corps taking the advance toward Columbia, followed by Cheatham's and Lee's Corps, which was now led by Stevenson. Some Confederates remained in the village when Federal cavalry hit them before noon. Richard Johnson had his bluecoats plunging south on the Carter's Creek Pike by 5 A.M. before taking a dirt road that brought them into Spring Hill from the west, where they flushed out these Confederate stragglers by about 11 A.M.

Wilson's other horsemen were in the saddle by then as well, "pressing forward to his [Johnson's] assistance," Wilson stated in a report to Thomas. "I will push them as rapidly as I can toward Columbia tonight." He had earlier told Thomas that he had seventy or eighty wounded men scattered in houses along the road and requested ambulances for them. Croxton, on Wilson's left flank, had been ordered on the seventeenth to try to attack from the Lewisburg Pike, but for reasons that are unclear, he was not a factor in catching Hood at

Spring Hill, although the 2nd Michigan Cavalry, at least, may have seen some action there. Croxton would not be a major player in the campaign again until December 24.[1]

The countryside had been basically picked clean of provisions when the armies fought and marched through the same region weeks earlier. Now, even two days into the chase, Wilson recognized that his troopers would suffer because of this, but not as much as the Confederates. "There was, indeed, no choice for them but to imitate the French in the retreat from Moscow," he reflected after the war, "to take a drink, tighten their belts and hit the road to the rear at the best gait they could make. It was but little better with the victors."[2]

Indeed, the Confederates would have scant rations. Most subsisted on parched corn or corn pone and, occasionally, bacon fat. The infrequent capture of a pig or chicken offered a rare feast. In the merciless weather, however, their lack of shoes, clothing, and blankets was the cruelest deficiency, compared to the well-uniformed and well-equipped Union forces chasing them. Major Porter of Cheatham's staff watched barefooted soldiers butcher a cow or steer, divide the skin, and bind their feet in the rawhide.[3]

Stewart's troops crossed Rutherford Creek, some four miles north of Columbia, and were at the Duck River by early afternoon. Stewart camped in a battle line on the narrow river's north bank to cover the army's passage into Columbia, with Walthall's Division digging in on the left and Loring's men on the right.[4]

During the day, Cheatham's troops replaced Lee's Corps as the rear guard and dug in about two miles south of Spring Hill so that some of the army's wagon trains could get over Rutherford Creek. Cheatham held off Wilson's thrusts until the afternoon when his corps pulled back across the creek, burning the bridge behind them. Chalmers's cavalry covered his flanks and rear. Before leaving Spring Hill, Chalmers was reinforced by another of Forrest's brigades—Brig. Gen. Frank C. Armstrong's—which Forrest had ordered ahead of his main column, which was struggling to reach Hood. Cheatham

Frank C. Armstrong.

entrenched on steep, high ground just south of the creek that night, with Chalmers also posted to guard the creek crossings. The fact that Cheatham's Corps, which had been mauled and badly disorganized in the Franklin and Nashville fighting, was able to assume rear-guard duties somewhat contradicts Union accounts that Hood's army was a fleeing mob during the retreat. But the fact that Cheatham had fewer than 1,500 men at the creek attests to the immensity of the Confederate calamity.

At the Duck, the Confederates were already crossing some wagons, artillery, and troops on a pontoon bridge located near an old mill about a half mile above Columbia. Realizing the extreme need for draft animals, Hood issued an order that day stating that all horses and mules "taken from artillery and wagons lost in the recent engagements or on the retreat will be at once turned over" to Maj. A. L. Landis, the army's inspector of field transportation.[5]

While the Union cavalry burned Hood's remaining heel, Wood's infantry remained at a standstill north of the Big Harpeth until well after sunrise on Sunday. Suman's Hoosiers had labored through the night to build their bridge, struggling against the current. By about 7:30 A.M., a reinforced span was ready, and orders were sent to division commanders to cross immediately. Since Wood's men had arrived at the Harpeth, eighteen precious hours had been lost while the infantry stewed and waited. In a pounding, continuous rain, Kimball went over Suman's bridge first, followed by Elliott and Beatty; each division was accompanied by an artillery battery. The rest of Wood's guns, as well as trains of ammunition, hospital, headquarters, and regimental baggage wagons, followed.

Of the Confederate wounded in Franklin, an Illinois soldier in Elliott's division noted that they were "left to the mercy and care of their victorious enemies—a change most gratifying to the majority, for the poverty of the South in medicines and the wretched management of their Sanitary Department was not conducive to the alleviation of suffering and the healing of wounds." The soaked infantry did not linger in the town, and by 8 A.M., the head of Kimball's column was south of it on the turnpike.[6]

The wounded Stephen D. Lee remained with the army on Sunday and issued General Order No. 67, commending his soldiers for their conduct in the battle: "I desire to express to the officers and men of my command my high appreciation of the good conduct and gallantry displayed by them at Nashville . . . and to assure them that they can be held in no manner responsible for the disaster of that day."[7] Also taking time to write that day was Col. Andrew J. Kellar, commanding Strahl's Brigade of Cheatham's Corps, but he expressed more frustration and defiance than Lee. Writing to Maj. A. P. Mason, Hood's assistant adjutant general, Kellar wanted to clarify, in his view, what had happened to the army on the afternoon of December 16. He blamed Tyler's Brigade of Bate's Division in Cheatham's Corps for the rout. Commanded by Brig. Gen. Thomas B. Smith, who was captured, this brigade had occupied a hill west of the Granny White Pike, but this position had been "given up to the enemy without a struggle," Kellar claimed.[8]

By about 1 P.M., Wilson had pushed some two miles south of Spring Hill—within eight or so miles of Columbia—and had halted to issue rations and ammunition and groom the horses. "All our efforts to bring the rebels to a stand this morning have failed, though their alluring positions have carried us to this place," Wilson dispatched Thomas. "All indications are that the rebels have no intention of halting this side of Columbia."[9] Wilson's men had had nothing to eat since the previous day, no forage was available, and everyone was exhausted after slogging through the rain and muck along the turnpike while still failing to bring the enemy to bay. Wilson decided to camp there.

As his troopers settled into their soggy bivouac, Wilson studied his maps, trying to guess the route the retreating Confederates would take if they retreated to the Tennessee and the expected crossing point at Florence. The Federals thought Hood still had his pontoon bridge in place there, which was not the case. Wilson believed that Hood, upon reaching Columbia, would take a shorter route via Mount Pleasant and

Lawrenceburg to Florence—about fifty-three miles—rather than going through Pulaski, a distance of more than sixty miles to the river. Wilson told Thomas all of this, advising that the army march toward Eastport, Mississippi, located on the Tennessee well west of Florence, and crowd the Confederates from that flank. Even now, Wilson was thinking of how the chase could be continued south of the river. "If it is intended to carry the pursuit beyond the Tennessee . . . and gunboats can control it as far as Eastport, we could lay a bridge and cross the whole army there." Hood had made no decision to retreat to the Tennessee at this point.[10]

Lead elements of Wood's IV Corps trudged into Spring Hill around 3 P.M. as the incessant rain finally eased. In the distance, the men heard the erratic popping of carbines as Wilson's boys skirmished with the enemy. About this time, Wood received a message from Wilson regarding the cavalry's halt. Wilson told Wood that he had learned that the Confederates had two pontoon bridges over the Duck River at Columbia and that, according to "a little girl who has just arrived from Tuscumbia," there were no troops at Tuscumbia. "Persons say that Hood cannot get across the Tennessee River, as our forces at Memphis had repaired the [Memphis & Charleston] railroad as far as LaGrange [Tennessee], and were marching out to attack him in flank." In truth, there was no Union force en route from Memphis to intercept Hood, but there would be some action toward this end in a few days.[11]

Wood wasted little time before plowing ahead from Spring Hill. His first units reached Wilson's position within an hour. From this point, after a brief rest, the infantry marched about another mile before bivouacking around 4:45 P.M. Since leaving Franklin that morning, the IV Corps had covered ground they had been forced to relinquish to the enemy less than three weeks earlier. Now they returned as conquerors, much to the chagrin of pro-Confederate civilians along the way. "The 'natives,' then so jubilant over the idea of the 'Yanks' being driven from the country and hurled back upon Nashville . . . now experienced an entire revulsion of feeling," a soldier in the 36th Illinois wrote. "The tables were turned, and a more forlorn and disconsolate set of bipeds were seldom seen." Still, it was a grinding march. The soaked infantry picked their way along the pike in ankle-deep mud, their shoes filled with watery sand and grit.[12]

Now leading Thomas's pursuit, Wood's men were about three and a half miles from Rutherford Creek when they went into camp in battle line, the 1st Division on the right of the road, the 2nd Division on the left, and the 3rd posted in the rear of the 2nd, all facing south. "The enemy's rear guard but a short distance ahead," Colonel Fullerton of Wood's staff wrote of the day's activity in his journal. "It ran rapidly whenever it was approached by the cavalry," but the infantry did not make solid contact before halting for the night.[13]

Hood himself reached Columbia that Sunday and established headquarters at the home of the Vaught family, where he would spend two nights. Chaplain Charles Quintard visited him during the day, and Hood showed him the letter from Kellar faulting Bate's soldiers for the break that initiated the disaster. Others were blaming Bate's troops as well, including the chaplain, who wrote that when that division broke, "the whole army seems to have fled like a pack of whipped hounds." Bate's Division also had performed poorly at Murfreesboro, drawing criticism from Forrest. Quintard considered Bate "a most gallant man," but described the actions of his troops as "shameful." Based on the chaplain's account, Hood believed that he had gotten the best of the Federals all day on the sixteenth but that the last enemy thrust had sealed the Union victory.[14]

Milling in and about the town and looking for friends, lost units, or something to eat, the Confederates were painfully aware that the enemy smelled blood and was coming after them. General Walthall related that the men knew "their situation was one of extreme peril, and the serious and discouraging disasters which had but recently befallen us were well calculated to bring all commands into a state of disorganization." Randall Gibson and his men enjoyed a reunion with survivors of the 4th Louisiana Battalion, also of their brigade. The

Chaplain Charles T. Quintard.

4th had been shot to pieces in the Atlanta fighting and had not participated in the Franklin and Nashville battles, being left in the Columbia area to guard Hood's rear.[15]

Hood by now hoped to re-form his troops and remain in Tennessee by establishing a defensive line on the Duck. At the Vaught house that night, Quintard led prayers and then was among a group of officers who conferred with Hood about this possibility. Two of those present felt that a further retreat would aggravate demoralization and spur desertions, especially in the Tennessee regiments. Others reasoned that if the army held firm at the river, the Confederates could reestablish their own state government and claim a successful campaign despite the Nashville debacle. One officer told Hood that God favored the Confederacy but that "it was still very apparent that our people had not yet passed through all their sufferings"—an opinion the general shared. Forrest and his cavalry were returning, which would bolster the army, but when the discussion broke up, Hood remained undecided.[16]

Forrest and the rest of his force reached Columbia later that night after a grueling march of about sixty miles, and the cavalry chief met with Hood at the Vaught house. From the Murfreesboro area two nights before—disobeying Hood's order to march via Shelbyville—Forrest had moved to Triune, where his wagon train, as well as his sick and wounded, were located. After sending Armstrong's Brigade ahead to link with Chalmers, Forrest pushed his main column of cavalry, infantry, and wagons toward the Duck ford at Lillard's Mills, hoping for a speedy junction with Hood, but his efforts were hampered by a variety of problems, such as a lack of shoes in the infantry, issues posed by livestock and 400 Federal prisoners, poor roads, and cold weather. According to Col. Charles Olmstead, "Everything combined to weigh down heart and soul with a deep sense of depression."

At Lillard's Mills, Forrest saw that the Duck was rising rapidly and "ordered everything to be hurried across." Some of his wagons made it over, but the river soon became impassable, and Forrest had to take another route to Columbia. By the time they reached the town, Olmstead's command alone had lost 300 to 400 men who had dropped by the wayside, unable to keep up the pace. Many of the infantrymen rode double with the cavalrymen, while others were mounted on mules and oxen, read an account in the *Richmond Daily Dispatch.* "It was said to have been a most ludicrous cavalcade as it marched through Columbia. Nobody else save Forrest could have saved the men in that expeditious style."[17]

The forty-three-year-old Forrest was horseshoe hard, one of the toughest and most innovative commanders in either army. Forrest was the Grim Reaper in the saddle, and if the Confederates had found a few others like him, the war might have unfolded much differently. While J. E. B. Stuart was the parlor darling of the South, the starry cavalier who galloped into legend on the main stage of the eastern front, Forrest was an unassuming brawler who cared more about bludgeoning the enemy by all means possible than he did about garnering headlines and society invitations. "Over six feet in stature, of powerful frame, and of great activity and daring, with a personal prowess proved in many fierce encounters, he was a king among the bravest men of his time and country," related Confederate major general Dabney Maury, who served with Forrest in the western theater.[18]

Born near the village of Chapel Hill, a few miles east of Columbia, in what was then Bedford County, Tennessee, Forrest had little formal schooling, but had risen to become a prosperous planter and slave trader when the war began. Enlisting as a private in the 7th Tennessee Cavalry, he raised and equipped a mounted battalion at his own expense and was elected its lieutenant colonel in October 1861. He participated in the defense of Fort Donelson and was elected colonel of the 3rd Tennessee Cavalry in spring 1862. After the Confederate defeat at Shiloh, Forrest was severely wounded in the hip and back while covering the army's retreat on April 8, 1862.

Within a few weeks, however, he had made a surprising recovery and, in June, was assigned command of a cavalry brigade in the Army of Tennessee. He captured a Federal garrison and its stores at Murfreesboro weeks later and was promoted to brigadier general in July. Preying on enemy communications in western Tennessee and operating in northern Georgia, Forrest fought at Chickamauga, despite being wounded in the preliminary fighting. But a feud with Braxton Bragg, then commander of the army, resulted in Forrest requesting and receiving an essentially independent command.

His fame spreading, Forrest rose to major general in December 1863, but the darkest blotch on his war career was looming.[19] Forrest's cavalry captured Fort Pillow, Tennessee, an outpost on the Mississippi River, on April 12, 1864. After his men overran the Union garrison, about half of which was composed of U.S. Colored Troops, the Confederates butchered a large number of the defenders, especially the black soldiers, after they surrendered. (The Confederates contended that the Federal casualties were inflicted during the fighting.)

Outnumbered three to one, Forrest routed a Union force at Brices Cross Roads in June, demonstrating the advantages of using cavalry as mounted infantry. Forrest had such an effect on the Federals' western war effort that Union commander William T. Sherman seemed unable to mention him in correspondence without describing him as a "devil." "Forrest is the very devil," he wrote to Secretary of War Edwin Stanton shortly after the battle, adding that he was gathering a force to eliminate Forrest. "There never will be peace in Tennessee till Forrest is dead."

In fighting at Tupelo on July 15, Forrest suffered his third combat wound of the war when he was shot in the right foot. Undeterred, he directed his troops from a buggy, dispelling the rumor that he had been killed. Forrest continued to operate in western Tennessee and northern Mississippi, striking enemy supply and communications lines, until he was ordered to coordinate with Hood. In October, he requested leave due to failing strength, but was turned down.[20]

At the Vaught house, Hood and Forrest talked about the army digging in on the Duck, but several accounts state that Forrest advised against it, telling Hood that the army was not

Nathan Bedford Forrest.

strong enough to stay put and that it should retreat beyond the Tennessee River and out of immediate danger. Another version claims that Hood told Forrest that he felt the weather, bad roads, and broken-down condition of his draft animals would prevent his escape. Forrest answered that to remain at Columbia meant the army's certain destruction, but if he was given 4,000 infantry to augment his cavalry, he could hold off the Federals until the army was over the Tennessee. At least one other account of this meeting concludes that the two generals concurred that the Confederates should withdraw as quickly as possible. Whatever the case, Hood wrote that "I became convinced that the condition of the army made it necessary to re-cross the Tennessee River without delay." Hood's decision also was based on discussions with Isham G. Harris, the Confederate governor of Tennessee, who agreed that "it is the best we can do."[21]

The Federals continued to scoop up prisoners on Sunday, the most notable being Brig. Gen. William A. Quarles, who had been severely wounded in the left arm by a cannonball at Franklin on November 30 and was recuperating at Carnton, the John McGavock family mansion south of town. Quarles, a thirty-nine-year-old Virginian, had been told of the army's Franklin evacuation the previous day but could not be moved. With Union troopers nearing, he ordered several of his attendants to leave him. These men piled into an ambulance, raised a yellow hospital flag, and made their escape, passing Federal horsemen who did not stop them. Nevertheless, Quarles was eventually captured and taken to a Nashville hospital; he would remain a prisoner until after the war.

At Wilson's headquarters that night, captured stragglers and deserters still described the enemy as demoralized, but there was also more ominous news. A prisoner said that Forrest, with Jackson's Division, was en route to Columbia to join Hood, meaning that Wilson likely would soon be facing the vaunted Confederate cavalryman. Wood also was aware of Forrest's presence, and Fullerton noted that despite the reports and rumors of his death, Forrest supposedly had already rejoined Hood, bringing with him cavalry and infantry from Murfreesboro. Indeed, Wilson claimed he had been opposed by Forrest since the December 17 clash at the West Harpeth.[22] Night brought more torrential rains and cold temperatures, but most importantly for the Union cavalry, it also saw the arrival of a few wagonloads of supplies, based on one of Wilson's reports.[23]

Thomas rode into Franklin late in the day and decided to employ more of his chess pieces against Hood. He ordered Steedman and his provisional division to move from there to Murfreesboro and then embark south on the Nashville & Chattanooga Railroad to Decatur, Alabama. Steedman was also to reoccupy strategic points that had been abandoned when Hood advanced. From Decatur, Steedman was to take command of a force consisting of his soldiers and Union garrison troops and strike west to destroy the Confederate bridges that were believed to be in place across the Tennessee at Tuscumbia.[24]

Overnight, Wood received orders from Thomas that the cavalry, which was encamped behind his infantry, would move out at 6 A.M. and that his corps should be prepared to march by 8. Thomas also had sent orders to Wilson to "press directly after the enemy to-morrow, and await the developments . . . before deciding upon your future route."[25]

CHAPTER 8

"The Army Must Be Saved"

MONDAY, DECEMBER 19

"Victory!—Sherman at Savannah—Thomas in Tennessee": the main headline in the *New York Times* that morning presided over articles heralding dual triumphs—Sherman's legions closed around the "doomed garrison" at Savannah while Thomas chased Hood's devastated army well away from Nashville, with Forrest being killed in the process.[1]

Near Columbia, however, the supposed corpse of Forrest was as active as ever, deploying his men to support Cheatham's infantry at Rutherford Creek to stop Union forces from crossing. Most of Forrest's cavalry already were in the Columbia area when he arrived since he had sent most of his command ahead to assist Hood. Only Gen. Lawrence "Sul" Ross's brigade of Texans—or at least a portion of it—and the rest of Forrest's artillery battalion, commanded by Capt. John W. Morton, had stayed with the slow-moving column that had reached Columbia the previous night.

Cheatham and Forrest held a strong position at the creek, occupying earthworks along a high ridge in close proximity to, and running generally parallel with, the stream. A four-gun battery was emplaced, and sharpshooters crept in along the bank. A heavy rain had drenched both armies all night, made worse by a numbing cold "beyond the experience of any one in Hood's army." The temperature eased somewhat after sunrise, but the rain now mingled with snow and poured throughout the morning and afternoon, further swelling the creeks and rivers.[2]

Despite the horrible conditions, Forrest's arrival was a reassuring elixir for the army as word spread that he had rejoined Hood. "The inspiring effect of his presence was felt by all," Chalmers related. "At no time in his whole career was the fortitude of General Forrest . . . more strikingly exhibited than at this crisis," added Chalmers's adjutant, Capt. W. A. Goodman.[3] Forrest was upbeat and defiant as usual and spoke of whipping the enemy as he had done on so many other occasions.

Brig. Gen. Edward Hatch's Union horsemen were riding before 6 A.M., splashing south, but the division had not passed Wood's encampment by his 8 A.M. march time. The bulk of the cavalry, however, remained in bivouac because, except Hatch's men, the troopers remained out of rations and almost out of ammunition. Thomas also changed his plans, issuing an order to Wilson at 8 A.M. that the cavalry should remain in camp because of the weather and wait for supply trains to come up, but Hatch was already moving. Thomas also told Wilson to send back ambulances to collect wounded from houses along the route and take them to the hospitals in Franklin.[4]

When he sent these communications, Thomas had not yet received a dispatch sent from Wilson at 6 A.M. saying that Hatch was on the offensive, but the rest of the cavalry was basically grounded without rations. The infantry and their trains clogging the roads had prevented the cavalry's supply wagons from reaching them, Wilson claimed.[5]

Hatch's troopers still were passing when Wood put his infantry on the road anyway. "The ground is in such condition that a wagon cannot possibly move off of the pike, and it is almost impossible to march infantry off of it," related one of Wood's staff officers. Hatch's riders quickly reached Rutherford Creek, finding the pike bridge and two railroad spans had been burned. They were peppered by the Confederate riflemen on the opposite bank and also dodged some cannon shots. A Union officer described the steep-banked creek as "a bold and rapid stream, usually fordable, but subject to rapid freshets, and the heavy rains of the preceding twenty-four hours had swollen it beyond a possibility of it being crossed without bridges."[6]

Wood's infantry began arriving at the creek around 9:30 A.M. and immediately came under fire as well. The rushing water and enemy opposition left the Union men with a few choices: they could wait for the pontoon train to come up over the worsening roads; they could try to construct makeshift spans of their own and fight their way over; or they could attempt to find another crossing point and outflank the enemy. Thomas later lamented that his own pontoniers, mainly Col. George P. Buell's 58th Indiana Regiment, had been assigned to Sherman's army, leaving him with few, if any, troops even remotely familiar with such construction.[7]

Meanwhile, Major Willett's pontoon train was miles to the rear after maneuvering for the better part of two days because of Thomas's erroneous order on the night of the sixteenth. After Thomas had sleepily and mistakenly ordered Willett to move on the Murfreesboro Pike, no one, including Thomas's chief of engineers, Lt. Col. H. C. Wharton, and Willett himself, had noted the discrepancy. On the seventeenth, Willett and the train had marched about fifteen miles toward Murfreesboro before the error was discovered. Willett was then ordered to forge across a nearly impassable country road to reach Franklin, some twenty miles away. The train's 500 horses and mules soon bogged down on this route, and Willett manhandled his bulky wagons back to Nashville on the eighteenth, the day Thomas had expected them to be up with the advance. Willett had finally started down the Franklin Pike on the nineteenth.[8]

Unaware of the pontoon problems, the Federals at the creek quickly realized that they had to rebuild the pike bridge because the boggy ground would not allow their artillery and wagons to cross the stream elsewhere. To do this, they first had to drive off the Confederate defenders. By 10 A.M., Wood had his men working on this assignment. The soldiers built rafts, but it was difficult to maneuver them in the strong current. Other Federals chopped down giant trees on the north bank, hoping that they would fall across the water and allow some men to establish a toehold on the other side. Wood recalled that the "creek was so rapid and the flood so deep that these huge torsos of the forest were swept away by the resistless torrent." Shortly after noon, a message arrived from Thomas that further frustrated Wood. Written at 8:20 A.M., the dispatch stated that because of the bad weather, Thomas had decided that the IV Corps should remain in camp for the day.[9]

While Union soldiers toiled at the creek, Columbia was a hive of activity as the Confederates continued to cross the Duck. The operation lasted through the night, throughout the day on Monday, and into the next night. During the day, Hood ordered all wagons "not actually necessary with the troops" to be sent at once to Pulaski, thirty miles to the south. Only brigade ordnance wagons were to remain with the men. By sending most of his trains ahead, he hoped to allow them a sufficient head start for the Tennessee.[10]

Forrest had orders from Hood to stave off the Federals until 3 P.M. and then pull back across the Duck into Columbia. By 4 P.M., Cheatham and Forrest were withdrawing from their creekside positions; Union forces were initially unaware of their departure. Some confusion, aggravated by raw nerves, exhaustion, and combat fatigue, resulted in a potentially lethal confrontation between Forrest and Cheatham at the river. Cheatham's infantry had been supposed to cross earlier in the day, but had been delayed. Now they were about to move onto one of the bridges when Forrest and some of his troopers rode up. Forrest insisting on going over first. "I think not, sir," Cheatham replied. "You are mistaken. I intend to cross first and will thank you to move out of the way of my troops." Forrest drew his revolver and snarled, "If you are a better man than I am, General Cheatham, your troops can cross ahead of mine." The argument heightened, and nearby soldiers were caught up in the tension. Some of Cheatham's boys cocked muskets and vowed to shoot Forrest "into the middle of Duck River in a minute." The volatile generals were finally separated after Stephen Dill Lee emerged from his ambulance to diffuse the situation. In actuality, Hood's orders were for Cheatham to cross ahead of Forrest, but it is unclear who finally went first. At least one account states the two cooled down enough to apologize to one another. Forrest camped in Columbia that night.[11]

At the creek, the afternoon dragged. The Federals, still frustrated, were running out of options. Most of the large trees capable of spanning the creek already had been cut down and carried away by the rushing water, just as the makeshift rafts had been. The troops also did not have tools to build a bridge capable of supporting artillery and wagons. By 3 P.M., Wood ordered Elliott and Kimball each to try to drive off the enemy with concentrated musketry and construct a foot bridge under cover of darkness. Elliott would operate above the pike crossing and Kimball below it. In the meantime, the rain continued in buckets, raising the creek level to over fifteen feet in most places.[12]

Wood's two division commanders were veterans who had handled much worse adversity than this. A steely-eyed Indianan, the forty-four-year-old Kimball had taught school, practiced medicine, and served as a captain of volunteers in the Mexican War. He had seen action from the early Virginia campaigns and had the rare distinction of defeating Stonewall Jackson at the First Battle of Kernstown, one of the few setbacks sustained by the famous Confederate general. Kimball also fought at Antietam, Fredericksburg (where he was badly wounded), Vicksburg, and Atlanta. Elliott, a thirty-nine-year-old from Pennsylvania, was the son of a U.S. Navy commodore and had seen action in Mexico and on the frontier. His war resume included New Madrid, Corinth, Second Bull Run (where he was wounded), Chancellorsville, and Gettysburg. He led Thomas's cavalry at Atlanta—indeed, most of his career had been spent with mounted troops—and had been in this infantry command less than two weeks, but Thomas had great faith in him.[13]

Late in the afternoon, Hatch ordered Coon's 2nd Brigade to try to send over some dismounted troopers on the charred remnants of one of the railroad bridges, about a mile upstream

Nathan Kimball.

from the pike. Coon managed to cross some men of the 6th Illinois Cavalry, but the stress was too much on the ruined span, which disintegrated and floated away. The remainder of Coon's brigade had to ride some distance farther upstream before finding a ford. The Illinois troopers were involved in some skirmishing and pushed back a portion of the Confederate defenders about two miles before withdrawing to the north bank as night settled.[14]

Wood's men struggled well into the night on their bridge project before Elliott sent word around 11:30 P.M. that the creek's condition made it impossible to span. The rain tapered off by midnight, but a cold wind kicked up, adding to the troops' discomfort. By 1 A.M. on December 20, Kimball also had done all he could. Troops of Brig. Gen. William Grose's 3rd Brigade had failed, at least temporarily, in their construction efforts because of the deep, swift water. Grose's men had built two rafts, but both had been swamped in the torrential current, and two soldiers drowned.[15]

Prisoners brought to Wilson's headquarters eight miles north of Columbia, along with a Union sailor who had escaped from the Confederates, said that Hood had left the town and that Forrest and 7,000 cavalrymen were posted between the creek and the Duck. But Forrest had withdrawn, unbeknownst to Wilson, who, at 4:30 P.M., told Thomas that Forrest "could be dislodged quite easily by crossing a division of infantry on the pike and Hatch by the ruins [of the other railroad bridge]." Thomas replied that he would order Wood to advance on the main road in the morning, if possible, while Hatch's troopers crossed on the second ruined span. With no pontoons at hand, Wood's soldiers would be left up to their ingenuity as to how to proceed.[16]

As if Wilson and Wood were not enough for Hood to deal with, thousands of other Union infantry also were toiling south after him. Schofield's and Smith's corps crossed to the south bank of the Harpeth at Franklin that day, with Smith advancing to Spring Hill and Schofield encamping at Franklin. If the Confederates made an unexpected stand, these Union soldiers were battle tested and ready enough to shove Hood into the Tennessee.[17]

Thomas continued to try to snare the Confederates. Camped near Spring Hill again that night, he updated Halleck about the day's progress: "The infantry has not been able to march to-day in consequence of the heavy rain. . . . The cavalry, however, was enabled to advance somewhat, driving the enemy whenever they came upon him without much difficulty." He added that the railroad from Nashville had been repaired to the Big Harpeth and that engineers were working on the bridge there so that supply trains could reach his advancing troops.[18]

TUESDAY, DECEMBER 20

"They are passing all night, going south," a Columbia resident wrote in his diary regarding the Confederate columns. "They are the worst looking, and most broken down looking set I ever laid eyes on." The main Confederate army was over the Duck by early morning, the river by now having crested at about fifteen feet. During the three-day operation, Hood had gotten across the bulk of what remained of his supply trains and artillery, followed by Lee's Corps, then Cheatham's and Forrest's cavalry late on the nineteenth. After covering the bridge sites since the morning of the eighteenth, Stewart's Corps began crossing around 11 P.M.; the last of it did not clear the river until almost sunup on Tuesday, when the Confederate engineers dismantled the dual pontoon bridges. Charles Quintard described the exodus as "a day of gloominess," adding that he felt he "was parting with my dearest and most cherished hopes."[19]

Hood's new objective was Bainbridge, Alabama, basically a dried-up village and forgotten ferry on the Tennessee's south bank about six miles east of Florence. The river narrowed there somewhat, and the current was usually not as strong as at points above or below. Hood had sent some troops across there when he occupied Florence in November. Now it was the most important point on his line of retreat. From Columbia, the army's immediate destination would be Pulaski.

Before leaving Columbia that morning, Hood made a monumental decision to try to save his army. He reorganized his rear guard, based on Forrest's suggestion, in what was a daring and desperate move necessitated by the near presence of an aggressive, highly motivated enemy. In one of the war's most dramatic moments, the army's dire circumstances forced Hood to piece together the remnants of eight infantry brigades from his corps with Forrest's 3,000 cavalry to form this new force and keep the enemy at bay. Edward Walthall of Stewart's Corps, whom Hood described as "one of the most able division commanders in the South," was chosen to lead the infantry while Forrest held overall command.[20]

Hearing that Forrest was to lead the rear guard, a number of soldiers rushed to his headquarters to volunteer—a testament to his popularity. Other than newspaper headlines, army scuttlebutt, and campfire gossip, Hood and Forrest really did not know each other prior to this campaign. Both were impetuous commanders with fiery personalities, but if there was any friction between them—and it appears there was not—this was not the time for it. To his credit, Hood's formation of the rear guard and his choice of Forrest to command it were among the wisest decisions he made in his wartime career.[21]

Forrest had personally requested Walthall to lead the infantry, and Hood summoned the thirty-three-year-old Mississippian to his camp that morning, shortly after Walthall and his division had bivouacked south of the Duck after their overnight passage. By the time Walthall left his quarters at the Nimrod Porter home to meet with Hood, the main body of the army already was leaving Columbia.

Walthall was Virginia-born, but his family had moved to Holly Springs, Mississippi, when he was a child. An attorney before the war, he became lieutenant colonel of the 15th Mississippi Infantry and fought well in the Confederate defeat at Mill Springs, Kentucky, in early 1862. Elected colonel of the

29th Mississippi in April of that year, he saw action at Corinth and again in Kentucky. Promoted to brigadier general as of December 1862, he distinguished himself in action at Chickamauga and Chattanooga, where he was wounded in the foot. Walthall continued to excel in the Atlanta campaign and rose to major general in July 1864. At Franklin, he had two horses shot from under him, but escaped serious injury other than some severe bruises. Walthall "was an inspiration," recalled one of Chalmers's cavalrymen. "He was courtly and brave, and his tall, handsome form, splendid bearing, and fine, intelligent face will never be forgotten by the men of that army." Since the first day's battle at Nashville, Walthall had led his division as well as that of Maj. Gen. Samuel G. French, who had been relieved of command because of a serious eye problem.[22]

Walthall's command included three of his own brigades: Brig. Gen. Daniel H. Reynolds's; Ector's, commanded by Col. David Coleman; and Quarles's, led by Brig. Gen. George D. Johnston. The other five brigades were Brig. Gen. W. S. Featherston's; Col. J. B. Palmer's; Strahl's, commanded by Col. Carrick W. Heiskell (who had replaced Kellar); Smith's, led by Col. Charles H. Olmstead; and Maney's, led by Col. Hume R. Feild. Walthall immediately issued orders to determine the number of "arms-bearing men" in these brigades and to learn the names and ranks of the regimental and battalion commanders. The results prompted him to combine these eight brigades into four. Palmer would lead his own and Smith's Brigade; Feild would command Maney's and Strahl's; Reynolds would head his own and Ector's; and Featherston was lead his and Quarles's.[23]

Hood earlier had reined up with Col. Luke W. Finlay, who commanded four Tennessee regiments in Strahl's Brigade, and asked if he and his men would serve in the rear guard. The colonel had not hesitated, telling him, "We are soldiers, general." Hood replied that Finlay and the rest of the brigade should report to Feild, adding, "I know no soldiers upon whom I can rely with greater confidence that the work will be done well than you Tennesseans." As Hood talked to Finlay, a private called to him, "General, when are you going to give us a furlough?" Hood looked at him and replied, "After we cross the Tennessee River. The cards have been fairly dealt, for I cut them and dealt them myself, and the Yankees have beat us in the game." Hearing this, another soldier, identified as James Stevenson of the 19th Tennessee, remarked, "Yes, general, but they were badly shuffled." Stevenson's comrades yelled "in appreciation of the comment," as Hood rode off.[24]

Walthall's crazy-quilt brigades totaled approximately 1,800 to 1,900 men—less than half of the infantry Forrest had requested. Of these, Forrest estimated that about 400 soldiers were "unserviceable for want of shoes"; many of them limped along with scraps of blankets, hides, or clothing tied around their feet. The clever Forrest had no choice but to improvise. He ordered wagons emptied so they could carry some of these men, who would then clamber out of the vehicles and fall into line to fight whenever the enemy threatened. He also ordered local oxen gathered and the wagons and artillery of his train double-teamed to pull half of his vehicles as quickly as possible along the awful roads south to the Tennessee. By doing so, he believed that he could at least save half of his train. Eight artillery pieces completed the new rear guard.[25]

Hood informed Stewart of Walthall's assignment around 8:40 A.M., also telling Stewart to have the rest of his corps cook rations and be on the march by 11 A.M. or noon at the latest to cover at least fifteen miles. Years later, a Texan in Ector's Brigade reflected on what was to come: "Of all the hard service poor soldiers ever endured, this is among the worst."[26]

While Forrest took stock of his makeshift force, the Federals at Rutherford Creek also remained busy. Grose's Federals had labored through the night trying to span the stream, as did Col. Emerson Opdycke's 1st Brigade of Elliott's 2nd Division. The exhaustive work finally paid off late Tuesday morning when two foot bridges were completed. Wood's infantry crossed the creek on these bridges. For the Federals, much valuable time had churned away amid the angry water.

Meanwhile, Hatch had dismounted cavalry back across the creek at sunrise to determine if Forrest still was present and had Coon's troopers hard at work constructing a "floating bridge" from the remains of the second burned railroad span, located about two miles downstream. Coon was successful, allowing the rest of Hatch's division, including his Parrotts, to cross and press ahead toward Columbia in the early afternoon. Hatch hoped to have a chance to bring these guns to bear on the Confederate pontoon bridges over the Duck, but he was too late.[27]

Wood had received a note from Thomas around 3 A.M. stating that he should cross the creek "if at all possible" that day and assail Forrest, now believed to be in their front with a strong cavalry force. Hatch's horsemen were to hit the enemy's flank while Wood attacked frontally. Attached to the order, however, was a note from Wilson, who had read Thomas's message and had more updated information than the army's commander. Based on Hatch's reconnaissance over the creek on the afternoon of the nineteenth, Wilson believed—accurately—that Forrest had retreated. Wilson also told Wood that he would have Hatch "push out very early . . . and ascertain in time the true state of affairs to enable you to judge how strongly you ought to push." By 9:30 A.M.,Wood had heard nothing more from Wilson regarding Hatch's movements, but he learned that Grose was nearing completion of his foot bridge and that Opdycke's span was not far behind. By early afternoon, Wood's three divisions were crossing on the rickety wooden bridges. The fact that the bridge-building and troops movements were done without opposition seemed to verify that the Confederates who faced them the day before were gone.

Still, Hatch advanced cautiously, deploying Datus Coon's 7th and 9th Illinois Cavalry on foot to lead his division toward the river. While Hatch moved up, most of the remainder of Wilson's troopers remained in camp, with the commands of Hammond, Harrison, and Croxton (who had rejoined the main column) resting and finally drawing supplies. Also on Tuesday, two dismounted brigades, one each from Johnson's and Knipe's divisions, plus dismounted men from each division's other brigade, were sent back to Nashville to remount and refit.[28]

As expected, Hatch found that the Confederates already were over the Duck; their pontoon bridges were gone as well. The first of Wood's infantry—Kimball's division—reached the Duck around 2 P.M. with Hatch's cavalry. In the distance, the Union troops could see a few enemy pickets and at least one cannon, but it was clear that Hood was already south of Columbia. Like Rutherford Creek, the Duck presented another major obstacle for the Federals: "The river is very much swollen; it is too deep and too swift to bridge with timber, and we will have to wait for the pontoon train to come up," according to Colonel Fullerton. Major Willett's column still was toiling forward somewhere to the rear, and Union forces would need it since the Confederates had destroyed all bridges in the Columbia vicinity.[29]

Hatch's gunners, Battery I of the 1st Illinois Light Artillery, commanded by Lt. Joseph A. McCartney, lobbed some rounds into Columbia. Forrest described it as a "furious shelling" while Coon called it a "light cannonading." Under a truce flag, Forrest, accompanied by Walthall, went down to the river and asked to speak with Hatch about the cannonade. The opposing cavalry generals stood on the ruined remains of the turnpike bridge on their respective sides of the Duck and talked. Forrest told Hatch that there were no Confederates left in Columbia and that the bombardment only threatened harm to women, children, and Union wounded. Hatch agreed to stop the shelling.[30]

Forrest also had about 2,000 Union prisoners to deal with, and he asked Hatch about the possibility of arranging an exchange or parole for them. The Confederates did not have blankets or clothing for their own men, much less these prisoners. Hatch relayed the information to Wilson, and the answer came back two hours later: the Union cavalry did not have any prisoners to exchange, and so the request was denied. Wilson informed Thomas of the prisoner negotiations, and Thomas approved of the way Wilson handled the situation, apparently unaware that Hatch was the point man. This would prove little solace to a number of these captured Federals who died amid the rigors of the Confederate retreat, according to Forrest.[31]

The rest of Wood's corps came up by mid-afternoon after a three-mile march and camped for the night on the Duck's north bank. The infantry bivouacked in woods on the left of the turnpike while Hatch's cavalry encamped on the right. With no way across the river, there was little else to do, and Wood, in a dispatch to Thomas, stewed that his troops were "only prevented by the want of a pontoon train from crossing the river and continuing the pursuit." He also noted the river was high and rising but that there were no signs of the enemy in force on the far bank.[32]

The rain, which had stopped around midnight, began again that afternoon and appeared to have set in for the night, while a strengthening wind added to the chill. Wood received inaccurate information from Thomas shortly before 4 P.M. that the pontoon train would reach the Duck that night, but the delays already suffered because of its absence already galled the Federals. "This corps has already been delayed thirty-four hours waiting for the pontoon train," noted Colonel Fullerton. According to Wilson, the halt at Rutherford Creek "was short, but it gave the enemy a breathing-spell, which was of great value to him. It enabled him to get safely across the last considerable river between him and the Tennessee, to destroy the bridges which he had maintained at Columbia for the purpose of keeping communications with the South, and, what was of still greater importance, to form all of his infantry that had not thrown their arms away into an effective rear guard."[33]

With more and more Union soldiers appearing north of the river, Forrest sent word to Walthall around 5 P.M. to spread 200 men as pickets along the Duck's bank in front of the town, with their line stretching from an abandoned fort to an old mill about half a mile upstream from where the pontoon bridges had been placed. The new rear guard's artillery was camped just south of Columbia on the Pulaski Pike and could be called up if Walthall needed support. By then, Forrest had set up headquarters three miles south of town at Beechlawn, the home of Confederate major A. W. Warfield. The four-columned brick mansion already had been a significant backdrop for the campaign as Schofield occupied it on his retreat to Nashville and Hood established his command post there on November 24 as his army marched north.[34]

Thomas reached Rutherford Creek after dark and sent word to Wood that Schofield was to build a trestle bridge over Rutherford Creek so that artillery and wagons could cross. Meanwhile, General Smith was to assist in hurrying forward the pontoon train to the Duck. Thomas wanted the bridge in place by early on the twenty-first and have the entire army across the river by Wednesday night. Wilson received basically the same information, with the pontoons due at the Duck the next morning if the mules could stand it.[35]

Marching on the Pulaski Pike, Lee's Corps, which led the army that Tuesday, crossed Richland Creek about seven miles north of Pulaski and halted for the night about two miles from the town, with Cheatham next and Stewart last. The troops had done well, covering almost thirty miles on the turnpike despite the conditions. The afternoon's rain had turned to sleet and snow as Lee's men went into camp, and there was nothing for fires except green beech and gum trees. Some men used wooden rails and "soon got comfortably warm." Others "could neither build fires to warm ourselves and dry our clothing, nor obtain . . . little sleep, while our rations of the plainest food were extremely scanty." A Missouri artillerist under Stewart observed the "mark of destruction on every side" of the route, including dead horses and mules as well as live animals "stuck in the mud, but too weak to get out."[36]

Hood himself reached Pulaski and established his headquarters in the home of Thomas Jones, where he "entertained but little concern in regard to being harassed by the enemy." Hood related after the war, "I felt confident that Walthall, supported on his flanks by the gallant Forrest, would prove equal to any emergency which might arise." Chaplain Quintard met with the general and baptized four of the Jones children that

Tuesday. During a prayer service at the home that night, Hood seemed to bare his soul regarding the crushed expectations of the campaign and the army's present predicament: "I am afraid that I have been more wicked since I began this retreat than for a long time past," he said, according to Quintard's account. "I had so set my heart upon success—had prayed so earnestly for it—had such a firm trust that I should succeed, that my heart had been very rebellious." After a moment of reflection, Hood added, "But let us go out of Tennessee, singing hymns of praise."[37]

From Thomas's field headquarters at Rutherford Creek that night, a telegraph operator, with a lantern and six orderlies, set out to find the telegraph line along the railroad, hook into it, and send updates to Nashville and Washington. In the rainy darkness over unfamiliar terrain, one of the party's mules broke a leg struggling over the ice-slick ground. The men eventually found the line, but it was dead, and they trudged north seeking a possible break in the wire. When the lantern went out and no one had a dry match, the cold, drenched little band turned back to Thomas's bivouac. Amazingly, this would be the first—and last—telegraph failure of the pursuit.[38]

The line was restored by 8 P.M., and Thomas managed to dispatch a message to Halleck detailing the day's events. Despite his delays, Thomas told Halleck, "I feel almost confident that I will be able to overtake him [Hood] before he can reach and cross the Tennessee." With the Confederates believed to be heading back to the Florence crossing point, Thomas added that if Steedman's force could get there from Decatur, "I am confident we shall be able to capture the greater part of Hood's army." Also that night, Thomas ordered his chief quartermaster in Nashville to send three trains of forage and two trains of "subsistence stores" to Spring Hill early on Wednesday. Miles behind Thomas, Major Willett and the sixty-boat pontoon train passed through Spring Hill around 6 P.M. and camped about two miles to the south, the teams exhausted and almost out of forage. Willett dispatched Thomas that he would start at daylight on the twenty-first, but that his 500 mules and horses would need food by Wednesday night.[39]

Henry W. Halleck.

CHAPTER 9

"To Pursue and Destroy the Enemy"

WEDNESDAY, DECEMBER 21

The mercury dove again overnight on December 20–21, and the frigid temperatures lingered into the day, made even crueler by more snow and blustery winds. Several inches of ice and snow fell, blanketing the ground by sunup and coating the Confederates who had tried to sleep through it in the open. The winter continued to be the bitterest of enemies to both sides during the race. "Rain fell for four successive days, and when this ceased the weather grew severely cold," a Union surgeon wrote. "This was followed by rain, rain, rain, and as a sequence mud. Probably in no part of the war have the men suffered more from inclement weather than in . . . December, 1864." Forrest's chief gunner, John Morton, wrote: "The coating of ice on the roads gave way to mud, and the continued rainfall froze on the guns and pistols, making it agony for the numb fingers to fire them."[1]

As the race entered its fifth full day, the Union troops "were still buoyed up with the hope of bagging the one-legged chief and his army," a Northern correspondent wrote. This was true, but the cold reality of damp, numb, and blistered feet prompted Wood that morning to send an urgent request to Thomas for 15,000 pairs of shoes and socks to be brought up by railroad and wagon train as soon as possible. "The men are not barefooted, but traveling on the pike in the wet will, in a very few days, ruin their shoes and disable many."[2]

At Pulaski, Hood issued orders to his corps commanders to try to keep the troops together. He ordered that strong details under "energetic officers" be placed with the trains and that "in cases of necessity, animals will be taken from the wagons to draw the artillery, and the loads of any wagons will be partially or entirely thrown out to preserve the wagons and teams." As this was being done, Pulaski's pro-Southern residents gathered as many shoes as they could for the destitute soldiers.[3]

With the three infantry corps in the vicinity that day, the town was crowded with wagons, disorganized units, and railroad cars jammed with wounded men, munitions, ordnance, and other military hardware. Since the rail line remained closed south of Pulaski, these trains were stranded. Another grim picture was slowly coming into focus for Hood that day as he tried to restore the army's composure. He had lost many guns at Nashville, but did not yet know how many. A preliminary tally taken at Pulaski showed the army had 59 cannon, compared to 124 when the Confederates crossed the Tennessee. (By the eighteenth, Thomas was reporting 60 guns captured.) A large number of artillery horses had been killed, and caissons had been destroyed or abandoned.[4]

Among Hood's other worries was the lack of forage for his horses, mules, and oxen, and the general ordered, "Every possible exertion will be made to collect forage at this point, that teams may leave here with a supply, which will be used as sparingly as possible." With the rear guard, Walthall, now headquartered at the Orr residence in Columbia, was making his own beleaguered effort to feed his horses and mules, ordering his brigade commanders to unload their tool wagons and send them out along the Pulaski Pike to "search diligently for forage, and return with the least delay."

Knowing that the enemy was stranded north of the Duck, and how much ground the men had covered the previous day, Hood allowed the bulk of his army to rest or march only a few miles on Wednesday. He instructed Stevenson to move out at first light on Thursday, the twenty-second, in rear of the pontoon train, "making as good a day's march as possible without pushing the troops too much."[5]

The Confederates' concern about forage was mirrored by the Federals. Wood received a note from Thomas around 12:30 P.M., ordering him to gather a two-day supply for the animals of the much-anticipated pontoon train, which, even then, was nearing Rutherford Creek. Wood immediately ordered his division commanders to send forage parties out into the countryside. He warned Thomas that very little food should be expected to be found for the teams since the cavalry and other troops from both armies had pretty well picked the countryside clean. Wood also noted that the infantry advance was hindered by a lack of wagons and horses and requested that three of his batteries be allowed to cross Rutherford Creek as soon as the bridge was laid. The Confederates had "a party of observation" behind stone fences south of the Duck and he wanted to batter them down. The gunners also would assist in laying the pontoon span.[6]

At Columbia, Forrest kept a watchful eye for any signs of enemy activity on the Duck's far side, but there was nothing of significance other than the shared misery from the weather. Amid the snow and biting cold, Colonel Finlay of Strahl's Brigade had roused from his campfire around 3:30 A.M. and led 200 men to relieve infantry pickets guarding the river. As his men settled into their rifle pits along the Duck, Finlay was told that the Confederates they were relieving had made a deal with the Federals not to fire without giving a warning. Finlay would honor the unofficial agreement—at least for most of the day.[7]

In their camp near Columbia, men of the 54th Georgia in Olmstead's Brigade of the rear guard were jolted by a freak accident that morning. Needing firewood to make such breakfast as they had, the regiment's cooks had cut down a tree—which fell on and killed a sleeping soldier named Frank Bourquin. The rattled Georgians watched as a detail carried their friend's body to a local cemetery and tried to carve a hole deep enough in the frozen earth for a grave. Some wondered aloud how a man could journey this far from home and survive the deprivations of war only to meet such an inglorious end. The death aggravated an already upset Olmstead, frustrated since an orderly had sent two of his blankets to the rear with the baggage train, leaving him with only a threadbare overcoat. Still, the colonel had been luckier than most as he had managed to rent a room from a local family for at least two nights. "I had a warm room with comfortable beds," he recalled. "I can remember feeling as I snuggled down into the blankets on the first night and listened to the fierce wind howling outside, that I would be quite willing to have the war come to an end right then and there."[8]

Near the Duck, Wood's infantrymen recuperated in their muddy camps throughout the morning, still waiting for the pontoon train to arrive. "The day was bitterly cold, and the rest which the command gained by laying in camp was much needed after their arduous and laborious service of the many preceding days," Wood reported. At Rutherford Creek that morning, an irritated Thomas learned that the railroad bridge at Franklin still was not repaired as he had ordered, thus hampering his ever-extending supply line. In a telegram to L. H. Eicholtz, a division engineer of U.S. Military Railroads, who was supervising the work at the Harpeth, Thomas said that he "must finish it today" and have trains running at least as far south as Spring Hill by the afternoon. "The army is suffering for forage, which it was expected the railroad would bring before this." Eicholtz responded promptly, telling Thomas that it was "utterly impossible" to complete the span that day. The work had been slowed by the horrid weather, high water, and the mass of iron and other wreckage in the river. "Our ropes freeze and stiffen, and the men are scarcely able to hold themselves on the scaffolding on account of the ice," Eicholtz said. "We cannot possibly cross the bridge before tomorrow noon, unless the water falls and [the] weather moderates. We are doing all that can be done under the circumstances."[9]

Increasing the Union men's frustration, word began to spread about the headquarters error that resulted in the tardiness of Willett's pontoon train, which was finally trundling into the line at Rutherford Creek around 1 P.M. Initially expected by Thomas on the eighteenth, Willett's column was four days late, and most of the blame rested with the army commander himself. Still, Hood remained within grasp, and plans called for Union forces to bridge the creek quickly and rush ahead pontoon sections to span the Duck, likely sometime overnight. At the river, Wood's forage parties trickled in during the afternoon with what amounted to twelve wagonloads of food for the pontoon horses and mules, but irritation about the lateness of Willett's column continued to simmer.[10]

Soldiers began laying the pontoon bridge over the creek even as the weather worsened. Rain alternated with snow, and temperatures grew even rawer. The conditions hindered the work, but the task was finally completed after dark. Smith's infantry went over, along with some wagons with material to bridge the Duck. Almost blinded by the elements, the drivers whipped their teams toward the river.[11]

While Thomas's troops struggled ahead, they had no way of knowing that some 500 miles to the southeast, Sherman's army was celebrating a significant triumph. Savannah had fallen, its Confederate garrison evacuating during the night of December 20–21. Sherman had essentially ended his march to the sea on December 13 with the capture of Fort McAllister on the coast a few miles south of the city. Savannah's seizure would allow him a base of operations for a possible strike into the Carolinas.

Meanwhile, Henry Halleck reminded Thomas of "the vast importance of a hot pursuit." Telling Thomas that "[e]very possible sacrifice should be made," he continued, "If you can capture or destroy Hood's army, Sherman can entirely crush out the rebel military force in all the Southern States. . . . A most vigorous pursuit on your part is therefore of vital importance to Sherman's plans. No sacrifice must be spared to attain so important an object."[12] Despite arguably the greatest triumph of his career, Thomas found himself playing second fiddle to Sherman. In his reply to Halleck a few hours later, he wrote,

William T. Sherman.

General Hood's army is being pursued as rapidly and as vigorously as it is possible for one army to pursue another. . . . I am doing all in my power to crush Hood's army, and, if it be possible, will destroy it; but pursuing an enemy through an exhausted country, over mud roads, completely sogged with heavy rains, is no child's play, and cannot be accomplished as quickly as thought of. I hope, in urging me to push the enemy, the Department remembers that General Sherman took with him the complete organizations of the Military Division of the Mississippi, well equipped in every respect as regards ammunition, supplies, and transportation, leaving me only two corps, partially stripped of their transportation . . . to oppose the advance into Tennessee of that [Confederate] army.[13]

Later in the day, after learning of some successes against Lyon's raiders in Kentucky, Thomas sent another message to Halleck to update him on his own operations: "The progress of the force under my command is impeded by the high state of water in Harpeth River, Rutherford Creek, and Duck River; but, with the assistance of pontoons, just up, I hope to continue the pursuit in the morning."[14]

The soldiers of Lee's Corps trudged through Pulaski, again crossed Richland Creek where it looped in an arc just south of town, and went into camp for the night, with Cheatham's and Stewart's commands bivouacking north of the stream. Sumner A. Cunningham of the 41st Tennessee recalled, "Almost every step tore and bruised their feet, whilst many did in reality leave a bloody track every time they put their feet down from Columbia to the Tennessee River. We saw numbers of privates and some officers trudging along with feet as bruised and bloody almost, as of beef steak and swollen twice their natural size. That they could even stand was a mystery to us. Others had wounds bleeding and sore, with nothing to eat."[15]

In their trenches south of the Duck, Luke Finlay's Tennesseans honored the agreement with the Union pickets not to fire without notice until they saw some black soldiers starting to kill some sheep just over the river. The Confederates sprayed them with musketry, prompting a shout of "All right!" from other Federals on the line, according to Finlay's account.[16]

Wilson's cavalry had for the most part remained inactive on Wednesday, but there was some minor glory for Hatch's boys north of the Duck. The Federals received word that a small force of Confederates was trying to escape to the southeast with two cannon. Coon, who was camped two miles northeast of the river, sent a battalion of the 2nd Iowa, led by Capt. Samuel Foster, down the Lewisburg Pike to try to reach these Southerners. Foster made a day's march before falling on the enemy column on Wednesday evening, seizing the guns, six ambulances and a few spindly wagons without much resistance from a "rear guard of Texas cavalry" about 200 to 300 in number, who fled into the darkness. The Federals also snatched some hogs and cattle, and the escaping Confederates left the road strewn with small arms. With no bridges, these Confederates likely were forced to swim the river, Hatch surmised in a dispatch to Wilson that night.

The little victory helped Hatch observe a cheerful thirty-second birthday on Thursday, but the Maine native had earned a reputation for reliability well before this campaign. After two years at Norwich University in Vermont, he had gone to sea before moving to Iowa, where he was working as a lumberman when the war came. Commissioned as captain of the 2nd Iowa Cavalry, he became its colonel ten months later. Hatch had seen action at New Madrid, Island No. 10, and Corinth and in raids through Mississippi and Alabama in 1863 and 1864. Recovered from a wound sustained in a Tennessee skirmish the previous December, he was intent on riding down Hood.[17]

Thomas established his headquarters about two miles north of the Duck on Wednesday night, expecting Willett's pontoon train to arrive from Rutherford Creek within a few hours. The portion of the pontoons at the creek, meanwhile, were left in place so that the rest of Thomas's pursuing forces could pass. The rain and wet snow that had tormented the soldiers since

Edward Hatch.

Saturday was still falling while the Duck brimmed to overflowing, and it would be another miserable night of waiting. Instead of forming battle plans to wrap Hood in an iron maiden's embrace, Thomas found time to respond to Wood's request for shoes and socks, stating that they would be brought south by rail as far as possible and then by wagon to the army.[18]

About 220 miles southwest of Columbia that day, a Union cavalry force under Brig. Gen. Benjamin H. Grierson trotted out of camps in and around Memphis, intent on wreaking havoc on Hood's tenuous railroad supply line in Mississippi. Grierson already had established himself as a cyclone in the saddle with his 600-mile, sixteen-day raid during the Vicksburg campaign, which was already considered one of the finest Union cavalry operations of the war. Organized into three brigades—3,500 troopers total—his horsemen now were aiming at the Mobile & Ohio and the Confederate supply base at Tupelo. These Federals also could swing down and try to free Union prisoners held in a prisoner-of-war camp at Cahaba, Alabama, if the operation went well. But the primary objective was the Mobile & Ohio, and if Grierson's raiders captured Tupelo or at least severely damaged the ever-fragile Confederate railroad in the region, Hood's already stricken army would be strung out, stranded, and possibly ripe for annihilation.

THURSDAY, DECEMBER 22

Scattered musket fire along the Duck greeted sunrise as the rival skirmishers dueled across the silvery water. With the temperature hovering in the teens and a treacherous north wind, this would be one of the worst days of the retreat for the Confederates, whether Forrest and the rear guard at Columbia or Hood and the main army thirty miles to the south.

In Pulaski around 7 A.M., Hood issued orders to his corps commanders to send pioneer troops out to work on the Lamb's Ferry Road from Richland Creek to a ridge some five miles out, "corduroying well all bad places. The senior engineer officer present will direct the whole." The bad places would be myriad since the turnpike ended at Pulaski, the rural dirt roads south of town already churned into mud pits by the passing of the army's main wagon train. Within the hour, the rest of the army was ordered to march as well "while the ground is frozen," Hood stated. The Confederate pontoon column, commanded by Lt. Col. Stephen W. Presstman, the army's acting chief engineer, already was moving on the Lamb's Ferry route.[19]

Stevenson's troops would follow Presstman's column, with Stewart next, and Cheatham would take the Lawrenceburg Road, which led west from Pulaski, allowing Cheatham to reach the main road to Bainbridge at Lawrenceburg, a route not as chewed up by the armies. It also meant that Cheatham would be isolated from the other two corps if attacked, but it was a gamble Hood had to take to expedite the army's progress. Still, the condition of the roads out of Pulaski meant the Confederates would have to leave behind or destroy more wagons and guns as they bogged in the slush. Other vehicles were abandoned or torched so their animals could be used as double teams to pull the heavy pontoon train. The main wagon column was a few miles ahead of Stevenson and Stewart, having moved at daylight on the Powell Road toward Lexington, Alabama. This route forked to the west from the Lamb's Ferry Road about twenty-two miles south of Pulaski and was on the way to Bainbridge.[20]

As the Confederates prepared to leave Pulaski, Samuel Foster, the wounded Texas cavalryman, still had not found a mount and was unable to walk. Around noon, however, a soldier arrived, saying that he had found a horse, bridle, and saddle for sale by a doctor who was to remain behind at one of the hospitals. The horse would cost Foster $800, which he "considered cheap." The captain and those accompanying him soon started south. "Very cold, ground covered with snow, and the wind whistles," he noted. They made about eight miles before halting and building fires; the other men made Foster as comfortable as they could.[21]

The lead wagons of Willett's pontoons had started to creak into the Union lines at the Duck around 11 P.M. on Wednesday night, with the strung-out column continuing to come up before dawn on the twenty-second. Wood already had Col. Abel D. Streight's 1st Brigade of Beatty's division camped near the river, ready to lay down the bridge as soon as possible, but there were armed Confederates on the far bank who had to be dealt with. At first light, around 5 A.M., the 51st Indiana Volunteers, led by Capt. William W. Scearce, used some of Willett's canvas pontoon boats to cross the Duck and try to clear out these Confederates. The 15th Ohio of Streight's brigade was deployed to cover this assault, which took place about a mile and a half upriver from the town. The Hoosiers went over under fire and, upon landing, immediately found themselves in a brisk firefight with Forrest's cavalrymen, but by about 8 A.M., they had secured the south bank. Streight's men went to work on the bridge shortly thereafter in fifteen-degree conditions. It would be a grueling task.[22]

From Forrest's headquarters at the Warfield house, one of the cavalry chief's staff officers sent word to Walthall around 9 A.M. about the Federal foothold on the south bank, estimating the Indianans' force at about 200 men. Troopers commanded by Lt. Col. William F. Taylor of the 7th Tennesee in Rucker's Brigade were fighting them, along with dismounted Texas cavalrymen from Ector's Brigade who had gone on picket duty that morning. Walthall was already aware of the threat, having been notified by one of his officers on picket. In response, he had dispatched Feild's troops to bolster the right of his line and was readying the rest of his men when Forrest's messenger arrived. Forrest's information was that Union forces had completed a pontoon bridge—which was inaccurate, although there was no denying that the enemy was across the river in some numbers. Forrest himself reached Walthall shortly afterward and, after discussing the situation, ordered Walthall to pull back on the Pulaski Pike.[23]

When he first learned of the enemy crossing that morning, Forrest sent a messenger, J. P. Young, to order up Armstrong's Brigade in support. A mere boy, Young rode six miles through the cutting wind, and upon reaching Armstrong's headquarters, he was nearly frozen and unable to dismount. As soldiers carried him into the house, he murmured, "Boots and saddles." Armstrong's men were soon in the saddle, heading to the front, but by then, Forrest had already decided that he had to evacuate. There was street-to-street fighting in the town as the rear guard sparred with Scearce's Hoosiers, who soon withdrew with a few prisoners, including two officers. The strike cost Scearce twelve men killed and wounded while Confederate casualties tallied about 50.[24]

By 1 P.M., Presstman and Hood's pontoon train were about six and a half miles south of Pulaski. Presstman had sent an engineer officer to examine the ford at Sugar Creek and was prepared to pontoon it if conditions warranted. Also encouraging for Hood, Presstman noted that the pontoon train had "already passed the worst portion of the road, and will make better speed tomorrow." The colonel also said his train would camp about sixteen miles from Pulaski, meaning it had done incredibly well on the bad roads.[25]

Stevenson, with Lee's Corps, halted about eight miles south of Pulaski, just after the Confederates negotiated the unmercifully steep slope of Anthony's Hill. Stewart's troops were next, bivouacking some two miles behind, while Cheatham made only five miles, barely getting out of town and camping near Richland Creek. Stewart—and likely the other corps commanders—had received orders from Hood to march eight or ten miles on the Lamb's Ferry Road, gather his artillery and wagons at that point, and try to collect forage and rations. Under the conditions, they had done as well as could be expected. The deeply rutted route, worsened by the pontoon train's passing, was laced with icy mud chuckholes so big that a mule could get lost in them, a wag drawled to his buddies. Many of the soldiers found it easier to walk on the edges of the woods and fields than on the road itself.[26]

At the Duck, the Federals' bridge work went slowly because of the swift current and floating ice, not to mention that there were only three pontoniers present to direct Streight's inexperienced soldiers in their task. "The troops that are to lay the bridge know nothing about the work," Colonel Fullerton wrote in his journal. "It will, therefore, be necessarily slow." Complicating their efforts, the water fell rapidly during the construction, causing the pontoniers to have to make changes and further delaying the work.[27]

Finally, the span was completed around 6:30 P.M., and Wood's corps, with Beatty's division (including Scearce's blood-ied Hoosiers) in the lead, began crossing half an hour later. Kimball's division followed. It was well after midnight when the last of the corps, elements of Washington Elliott's division, reached the Duck's south bank. Before dawn, the infantry inched through Columbia to see what awaited them on the turnpike beyond. By then, Forrest was a few miles to the south after supervising the town's evacuation hours earlier. Leaving Columbia, Chalmers's cavalry moved on the Bigbyville road while Buford's and Jackson's cavalry protected the rear. By now, the losses to Chalmers's division in the campaign were so great that he had consolidated his troopers into a 500-man brigade.[28]

Meanwhile, Walthall's infantry withdrew to within three miles of Lynnville, a village about halfway between Columbia and Pulaski, and based on Forrest's orders, he went into posi-tion to act as a support for the cavalry. "The sufferings of the troops were terrible," Walthall's assistant adjutant, D. W. Sanders, wrote of this time frame. "Without protection from the severity of the weather, without blankets, and many without shoes, and nearly all indifferently shod, the horrors of the retreat were to be seen as the bare and frost bitten feet of the soldiers, swollen, bruised, and bloody, toiled painfully . . . over the frozen pike."[29]

Thomas was riding toward Columbia on Thursday when he decided to continue the chase, despite all his men had endured thus far and the lost opportunities. The soldiers had fought two pitched battles in forty-eight hours and then been on the march for six days amid dreadful conditions and dwin-dling rations, but the job was not yet finished. With no other major rivers before the Tennessee, perhaps his troops might still bring the Confederates to bay. More than likely, Thomas also wanted to prove all the doubters—Grant, Halleck, Sherman, or anyone else whispering behind his back—that he had the aggressiveness to land a knockout punch. More than likely, as well, he would have been relieved immediately, despite his success at Nashville, had he suspended operations and not taken his best shot at catching Hood at the Tennessee.

Wilson's cavalry, supported by Wood's corps, would continue to be Thomas's bayonet point while the infantry corps of Smith and Schofield would follow and be "used as the occasion demanded." Wood's men would march on the pike while the cavalry moved on each flank across the countryside. As it had the previous day, the bulk of Wilson's cavalry rested on Thursday, but had to be ready to spearhead the pursuit south of the Duck on Friday.[30]

With winter's early sun setting over Pulaski, Hood sent Stewart a message regarding the retreat route. When his men reached the Lamb's Ferry and Powell road intersection, Stewart was to decide "which will be the best road for you to move by. Push forward as far as you can tomorrow." Hood also instructed Stewart that after crossing Sugar Creek, about twenty miles south of Pulaski, he was to send back his best teams to assist in getting the ordinance trains over the stream.[31]

CHAPTER 10

"The Gallant Hood of Texas Played Hell in Tennessee"

FRIDAY, DECEMBER 23

Nathan Bedford Forrest needed to buy some time; his currency would be blood, sabers, and gunpowder. With much of the main army still within a few miles of Pulaski, he had to delay the Federals near Columbia. Forrest and most of his cavalry were about three miles north of Lynnville when he sent a 7 A.M. dispatch to Chalmers, stating that "it is important that we hold the enemy in check as long as possible." Chalmers was to move back toward Columbia, meet the enemy, and "demonstrate strongly upon him, as if you intended to reoccupy the town." Jackson's and Buford's cavalry were to advance north on the pike. "The major-general [Forrest] will not leave here to-day unless forced back," the cavalryman's orders read, adding that Forrest "will go in person to the front this morning."[1]

After crossing the Duck during the night, some units of Wood's infantry had encamped before dawn on the Pulaski Road a mile or so south of Columbia, amid works the Federals had constructed earlier in the campaign. The corps' artillery and baggage train began trundling across the pontoon before sunrise, intent on clearing the unstable span so that Wilson's cavalry could cross starting at 5 A.M. It had been another freezing night, and the coming day would offer little respite from the cold. Thomas had issued orders that the pursuit would continue as soon as the cavalry was across, with the horsemen on the flanks, while Wood's soldiers marched on the pike. Colonel Fullerton doubted that the lone span would hold up under the heavy traffic even before Wilson's boys arrived to cross: "The pontoon bridge is a very poor one, and may break down before all of our artillery and trains pass over it." Sure enough, by 5 A.M., only three of the IV Corps' batteries and a few wagons had managed to reach the other side because of the fragile condition of the structure and the slippery, muddy approaches. The rest of the wagons were held up so that the horsemen could begin crossing before sunup.[2]

At Columbia, Wood issued orders for his divisions to be ready to march as soon as the horsemen had cleared the pike south of town, but by 2 P.M., the cavalry still was passing. Finally, about thirty minutes later, there was a gap in Wilson's column, and the infantry began to move. Kimball's division led, followed by Beatty and then Elliott.[3]

Probing out of Columbia, Wilson's lead units encountered Confederate cavalry pickets along the pike near the Warfield house. There was only light resistance, but Forrest's reputation seems to have stymied their advance much more than a few soldiers with carbines and revolvers. According to Wilson, "Hood's reorganized rear guard, under the redoubtable Forrest, was soon encountered by the cavalry advanced guard, and he was a leader not to be attacked by a handful of men, however bold." The Union men opened artillery fire on these horsemen, who fell back and endured this sporadic shelling for about two miles before they reached a strong defensive position where the road passed through a gorge between two high ridges.[4]

The Federal riders banged into Forrest's main force and recoiled, with Kimball's infantry coming up at 4 P.M. and preparing for action. Based on orders from Wood, Kimball deployed two regiments as skirmishers, with a third in support, and brought up a section of Capt. Theodore S. Thomasson's battery of the 1st Kentucky. Thomasson's gunners unlimbered about 800 yards from the enemy and began blasting away. Wood ordered Kimball to dislodge the Confederates from the pass, which was "handsomely and quickly performed." The Confederates withdrew less than an hour later, leaving behind a mortally wounded cavalry captain, one dead, and four privates captured. Forrest reported simply that from this position, Union forces were "held in check for some time" before he retreated. With darkness looming, the IV Corps bivouacked, and Kimball's men camped in the pass they had seized from the enemy. Beatty's 3rd Division was nearby, and Elliott's infantry brought up the rear.[5]

Wilson still had some cavalry to cross the Duck and informed Wood that they would be over by dark. He also told Wood that his troopers would be ready to take the advance again at 5 A.M. on December 24. By Friday night, Wilson had established headquarters at the Warfield house, the same mansion used by both Hood and Forrest before they evacuated Columbia, and sent orders for the next day's movements. Croxton would lead the cavalry corps on the Pulaski Pike. In thirty-minute intervals, he would be followed by Hammond's brigade, Hatch's division, and Harrison's brigade. The entire cavalry corps would pass Wood's infantry to resume the lead. "It is expected that the infantry . . . will be close enough to make all direct attacks, and leave the cavalry to operate on the flanks and rear." Wilson ordered.[6]

After spending his third night at the Jones home, Hood had left Pulaski on Friday morning, riding south. As the general caught up with his columns, Confederate infantry on the road shuffled aside for his mounted entourage to pass. One old soldier raised his voice in song, so the general could hear what many in the ranks had on their minds. To the tune of the popular "Yellow Rose of Texas," the soldier sang altered—but certainly appropriate—lyrics:

> So now we're going to leave you, our
> hearts are full of woe;
> We're going back to Georgia to see
> our Uncle Joe.
> You may talk about your Beauregard
> and sing of General Lee,
> But the gallant Hood of Texas
> played hell in Tennessee.[7]

Meanwhile, Thomas had heard from two scouts who had returned to him after crossing the Duck and reconnoitering the enemy. Their information was outdated by now, but still of some value. The scouts told him that Hood's army was heading toward Pulaski, where it would divide, the infantry going to Lamb's Ferry, eighteen miles below Florence, and the wagon trains and artillery taking the road to Decatur (present-day U.S. 31). The men also reported that the Confederate artillery horses were "all given out" and that the guns were being pulled by oxen. Forrest's cavalry was described as being "in fair condition" despite a majority being dismounted "and very much out of spirits." Thomas forwarded the information to Wilson in the hope that "If the guns are hauled by oxen, your cavalry may be able to overtake them, and add them to those we already have."[8]

Much of the Confederate army was just south of the Tennessee-Alabama border late in the day, and there were nervous rumors among the soldiers that Federal gunboats had sealed the river, trapping them. Hood camped for the night on the Powell Road about six miles from the village of Lexington, Alabama. Stevenson, with Lee's Corps, bivouacked some two miles to the east, near the intersection of the Lamb's Ferry and Powell Roads. Stewart's command was to the rear on the Lamb's Ferry route; both Stewart and Stevenson had crossed Sugar Creek without major problems. Cheatham's Corps remained on the Lawrenceburg Road, halting after a march of about twenty miles. All three corps had made better progress than the previous day, but the men wondered if they were marching into the gun maws of the Union navy.[9]

The soldiers had struggled mightily in the hilly terrain of Giles County around Pulaski, where the snow and ice made even the slightest slope treacherously slick. Major Porter of Cheatham's staff told of an instance at an especially steep hill where Cheatham ordered him to get a hundred well-shod men from his command to help push the wagons up the incline. Porter dismounted and began his search among the infantrymen. "The fellows soon found out that I was after men with shoes on, and they were highly amused. They would laugh and stick up their feet as I approached. Some would have a pretty good shoe on one foot and on the other a piece of rawhide or a part of a shoe made strong with a string . . . some of them would have all rawhide, some were entirely barefooted, and some would have on old shoe tops with the bottoms of their feet on the ground." From the entire corps, the major found about twenty-five men who had whole shoes.[10]

Leaving the gorge fight, Forrest's troopers rode toward Lynnville as night descended, camping in the vicinity of the village, where Walthall's infantry had been bivouacked since Thursday. The delayed Union pursuit had allowed Forrest's double-teamed trains of oxen and horses to reach the Tennessee with half of his wagons and guns and return to retrieve the other portion of his train. At Lynnville, he hoped to "hold the enemy in check and to prevent any pressure upon my wagon train and the stock then being driven out."[11]

In Charleston, South Carolina, that morning, Beauregard still remained unaware of Hood's plight. He had not yet received Hood's December 17 dispatch from Spring Hill about the Nashville defeat. In any event, he was more focused on Sherman's occupation of Savannah, especially how he could gather enough manpower to block the enemy's expected advance north into South Carolina. Hood's earlier request for reinforcements from the Trans-Mississippi and elsewhere would have to wait, given Sherman's more imminent threat, at least in Beauregard's opinion. Every available man in Georgia and South Carolina was needed to oppose Sherman, and Hood's troops should be sent east as well if no progress was being made in the campaign.[12]

Gen. George Thomas was in Columbia that Friday evening when he wired Halleck to give him an update. The troops were still crossing the Duck and were in close proximity to the enemy rear guard on the Pulaski Road. "I hope to get the whole force across tomorrow and continue the pursuit," he told Halleck. Crews also were hard at work rebuilding the five destroyed railroad bridges between Spring Hill and Columbia, and Thomas hoped they would be completed in four or five days. Thomas also told Halleck again about McCook's defeat of Lyon and that he expected McCook's cavalry to soon rejoin Wilson. These additional troopers would "enable me to completely destroy Forrest, if I can overtake him, which I shall make every exertion to do."[13]

Unlike Sherman, who did not allow journalists to accompany his army on its march through Georgia, there were newspapermen with Thomas who were beginning to document the vast hardships of the chase. "The reader must picture to himself one vast avalanche of mud in which the army floundered," one correspondent wrote, "the cavalry up to their horses bellies, the infantry up to above their knees, while the only glimpse one could get of the artillery was an occasional view of the guns and the tops of the wheels. For miles all that was visible of the wagon trains were the canvas tops."[14]

SATURDAY, DECEMBER 24

From generals to teamsters, the Confederates were not only uneasy about the menace of enemy gunboats, but also about whether the army had sufficient pontoon boats to span the river and continue the escape. "Every mind was haunted by the apprehension that we did not have boats enough to make a bridge," Col. W. D. Gale, Stewart's assistant adjutant general, later wrote to his wife. The war debris on the road from Pulaski included "dead horses and mules, broken wagons and worse than all, broken pontoons," he said. "We counted as we passed them, one, two, three to fifteen."[15]

A decision Hood made a few days before the Nashville battle might yet help with the army's pontoon shortage. Capt. Robert L. Cobb and a company of the 3rd Confederate Engineers had been dispatched to Decatur to replace the pontoon bridge there, using approximately fifteen pontoon boats seized by Brig. Gen. Philip D. Roddey's cavalry after the Union's evacuation of the town. Cobb and his men were in Decatur by December 16, but their mission would change within days as they learned of Hood's disaster. After Hood decided to re-cross the Tennessee, Roddey, who was in command at the place, was ordered to try to float the boats about forty miles downriver to Bainbridge. Cobb would be the man to make the effort. "The whole corps of engineers felt that upon his success depended the fate of the army," recalled Capt. Henry N. Pharr of the engineers, who was with Presstman.[16]

The few Confederates in and about Decatur—Roddey's brigade, one battery, and the engineers—were unaware that Steedman's Union force was headed toward them. If these troops reached the town before the pontoons were away, Cobb would fail in his mission, and Hood, unable to span the Tennessee, would be left to battle Thomas again, this time with the Union navy to his back.

Not completely counting on Cobb and Roddey to come through, Hood had ordered Stewart on the twenty-third to send back 200 men "under energetic officers" early on Christmas Eve to retrieve damaged and abandoned pontoons the army had left behind since leaving Pulaski. Loring and Brig. Gen. Charles M. Shelley, leading Cantey's Brigade, each assigned 100 soldiers for this task. Hood also had told Stewart to send all of his pioneer troops to report to Presstman before daybreak and to load all empty wagons with "plank for decking, gathering it from buildings on the road" to be sent to the bridge site. A party of engineers under Maj. John W. Green was trailing the main army, but was expected soon with some wagonloads of planking.[17]

Near Lynnville that morning, Forrest decided to make a surprise foray against the enemy to try to give his wagons and livestock more time to reach safety. The fact that he had held off the enemy the previous day and the ever-increasing desperation of his assignment likely emboldened him, a cornered wildcat baring his fangs. He ordered his cavalry back toward Columbia, advancing along the pike. Walthall's infantry, a bit refreshed by their Friday rest, shouldered muskets at sunrise with orders from Forrest to march south to Richland Creek, north of Pulaski, and entrench there. Walthall noted that he was to "prepare to hold the crossing should the cavalry, which was retiring slowly, be so pressed as to make it necessary for them to pass over before night." He posted his men along the creek in a strong position.[18]

Meanwhile, Forrest's troopers rumbled north, heading toward the gorge where they had fought the previous day and where the Union advance had spent the night. The Confederates had ridden about three miles when they encountered Croxton's cavalry riding south along the pike and leading Wilson's van. Croxton's men had not been in serious action since the first day of the Nashville battle, but this quickly changed. A Michigan officer noted that the troopers realized they were battling an enemy emaciated by defeat, stragglers, and desertion. The rivals sparred over the broken countryside; carbines and revolvers popped in the cold air. Forrest described the delaying action as a "severe engagement," which seems exaggerated, but the Confederates slowed the bluecoats for several hours in a fighting withdrawal that stretched south past Lynnville to Richland Creek, where Walthall's men awaited.[19]

There were some anxious moments amid this phase of the retreat when Gen. Lawrence Ross's brigade of Jackson's Division, then guarding Forrest's rear, was attacked by a heavy force near the village, threatening "to break over all opposition," according to Ross. With Jackson's other troopers in motion and unprepared to meet the enemy, the situation had the potential for disaster, but Ross's 6th Texas formed up hastily. The Texans "hurled them back, administering a most wholesome check to their ardor." If the 6th had failed to stop the enemy, "probably the entire division . . . might have suffered severely," said Ross. "Sul" Ross was only twenty-six years old but had earned a reputation as a Comanche fighter and had been a captain of Texas Rangers before the war. He entered Confederate service as a private and had fought in well over 100 battles and engagements while rising through the ranks prior to Nashville.[20]

Amid the Lynnville fighting, Wilson reined in beside Capt. Walter H. Whittemore of the 2nd Michigan, impatient for the advance to proceed into the town. "The rebels are going too slow; can't you push them faster?" Wilson implored. Whittemore, rightly concerned that he was confronting Forrest and could be ambushed, told the general that he did not have enough troopers on hand and needed support to attack. When Wilson assured him that he would bring up more men, Whittemore charged the village with three companies, shearing through light resistance. The troops plunged into the hamlet, surprising some exhausted Confederate troopers who were resting with legs thrown over their saddle pommels. Whittemore and others dashed among them, and the captain snatched a baby-faced Confederate by the shoulders and sent him to the rear as a prisoner. Later, the youngster laughingly told Whittemore of his "poor selection," since he was a mere orderly and Forrest himself had been only a few feet away. The Federals, however, soon had possession of the town as the Confederates fell back.[21]

"I am driving the enemy rapidly, without much fighting," Wilson said in a 2 P.M. dispatch to Thomas. At the time, Wilson was just south of Lynnville, the terrain now becoming more flat and open, certainly more conducive for the cavalry to spread out. To this point, Union forces had been hindered by the rough and rocky hill country, which prevented them "from getting forward fast enough on the flanks of the enemy to seriously engage it," according to Wilson. At 2:30 P.M., Forrest was about two and a half miles south of the village and stated that he was heavily engaged, sending word to Walthall to occupy the Richland Creek position "with all possible haste." Walthall also was to "halt all cavalry stragglers, with guns, going to the rear, and form them with your line and make them fight." Unknown to Forrest, the infantry already was in place along the south bank.[22]

By about 4 P.M., Forrest's horsemen had rejoined the rearguard infantry, the Confederates steeled for a more determined stand at the creek. John Morton, Forrest's artillery chief, had six guns positioned on both sides of the stream to sweep the road. The pike bridge remained intact for them to make their escape, when necessary, although they had had to replace floor planking pulled up by the retreating army. Armstrong's cavalry supported the artillery while Chalmers and Buford were drawn up on the left flank and Ross on the right, just east of the railroad and in the vicinity of Buford Station.

Approaching Forrest's position about an hour before dark, Croxton dismounted some of his men, sending them ahead to probe the enemy line, while the Union artillery clattered forward. In what Wilson later described as "a spirited affair," Croxton attacked along the main road while Hatch's men moved to the left, trying to get around Forrest's right flank. There was some artillery dueling, and Forrest claimed that two Union guns were dismounted, although no Federal accounts corroborate this. A Michigander recalled how "shot and shell came and went crashing through the tree tops or bounding along the road," sending tree limbs flying in all directions. "The affair at Richland Creek was for a time quite severe."[23]

Datus Coon's troopers of Hatch's command tried to maneuver through the woods and fields to wrap around the Confederate rear, but were halted by the creek's high water. Coon dismounted his men and for the next half hour they peppered the enemy on the other bank with carbine slugs.

Croxton was having more success. His 1st Tennessee, 2nd Michigan, and 4th Kentucky Mounted Infantry bored into the Confederates who held the pike and Forrest's left flank. In danger of losing his guns posted north of the stream, Morton pulled back to the bridge. There he blasted away, giving his men time to put down enough planks so they could carry the cannon across by hand and lead the battery horses over.[24]

Buford and Chalmers were pressured heavily by Croxton, and there was a brief blitz of hand-to-hand fighting. Amid the melee, a Spencer round tore through Buford's right leg; an unidentified trooper of the 7th Illinois was later credited with the shot. As the combat roiled, Union corporal Harrison Collins of the 1st Tennessee's Company A, saw a Confederate major and standard bearer trying to rally some retreating soldiers. Collins led a few men in a charge, killing the officer, routing the enemy, and capturing the battle flag. The action would earn Collins the Medal of Honor.[25]

Meanwhile, Forrest had learned of Hatch's thrust toward his right and withdrew Jackson's Division—the brigades of Armstrong and Ross—to meet this menace. These troopers also crossed the pike bridge, based on Forrest's account, and went into position to contest the enemy threat.[26] With Chalmers's and Buford's men under duress, with Buford himself down, and with Hatch's Union men threatening his right, Forrest ordered a withdrawal toward Pulaski just after sundown. Ross's Texans covered the rear from a hill near the railroad. Forrest reported his losses at the creek fight as one killed and six wounded while the enemy "lost heavily." The most important result, however, was that the Confederates, so closely pressed by Croxton and Hatch, did not have time to destroy the pike span.[27]

Despite holding the field and capturing some prisoners and an enemy flag, Croxton was frustrated by the performance of Col. Joseph B. Dorr's 8th Iowa Cavalry, which was assigned to cover the brigade's right flank. Croxton stated that he sent for the Iowans several times during the fight, but got no response. Hammond's brigade, slogging through fields on Croxton's right, was not involved in this action, nor were Walthall's troops, according to various accounts. As "the gloom of night compelled 'peace' between the combatants," as one of Croxton's men described it, the cavalry camped along the creek.[28]

That night, Wilson wrote Thomas that he had "driven Forrest all day without bringing him to an engagement" before the Confederates made a "short stand" on both sides of the creek. Croxton had taken a few prisoners. The Federals also were learning more about the makeup of the enemy rear guard; Wilson reported that it included Walthall's infantry as well as Buford's and Jackson's cavalry. Wilson also noted that the Confederates had burned all the railroad bridges to that point, including the one at Richland Creek, but that his proximity prevented them from torching the pike bridge there.[29]

Still, Forrest was managing to stall Wilson while the rest of the army lengthened its lead. "We marched very slowly and whenever the enemy came too near [we] would form line of battle faced to the rear," Charles Olmstead wrote. "This would oblige him [the enemy] also to deploy from column into line and feel his way by throwing out skirmishers, all of which took time and caused delay, the thing we aimed at."[30]

In keeping with Thomas's schedule, Admiral Lee's flotilla of four or five gunboats anchored at Chickasaw, Alabama, west of Florence, on December 24 and prepared to move upstream to try to stop Hood's escape. Lee's vessels blasted a recently built Confederate fort and magazine on the river near Chickasaw, neither of which contained troops or guns. The navy captured two cannon with caissons at Florence and destroyed some flatboats and pontoons at Garner's Ferry, twelve miles below the town. From a handful of enemy stragglers picked up along the river, Lee learned that the Confederates had crossed some of their prisoners at Garner's Ferry on December 19. Most importantly, the admiral was told that Hood's crossing point was about six miles above Florence and that the Confederates were still north of the Tennessee. Now, however, Lee and his tars faced Muscle Shoals, a dangerous and unpredictable stretch of the Tennessee River between Florence and Decatur noted for its shallows, rapids, and sandbars. If he was to reach Hood, Lee would have to navigate this tricky part of the river, putting his gunboats at risk.[31]

Wood's IV Corps had orders to march that morning as soon as the last of Wilson's strung-out cavalry column passed. Elliott's division was to assume the lead, followed by Beatty and Kimball, each division accompanied by a battery. The slow procession of Wilson's horsemen left the infantrymen waiting until almost noon, but they expected to move rapidly with the horsemen out of the way. With his troops on the march around 1 P.M., Wood received a dispatch from Wilson: the cavalry could not operate on the sides of the pike because of the ground's softness, and it had been slowed by constant skirmishing. Wood's men covered twelve to sixteen miles in about five hours of marching this day, with the head of his column reaching a point about two and a half miles south of Lynnville by 5 P.M. The infantry camped there that night, and Wilson's troopers bivouacked less than two miles ahead of them.[32]

Behind Wood, his wagons were among many held up at the Duck because the bridge had broken down several times during the night and that morning. By afternoon, the span had been bolstered enough for Smith's troops to cross, and the cavalry train was passing at 4 P.M. Wood's wagons, with six days' rations, were waiting their turn. Knowing that the soldiers were running low on food, Wood's assistant adjutant general, W. H. Sinclair, readied a three-day ration supply to be hastened ahead as soon as the IV Corps train could move. According to Sinclair, Thomas believed that the IV Corps was "better off for rations than the rest of the troops" and had to wait its turn and refused a request for the IV's wagons to cross ahead of other trains.[33]

By sundown, Wilson had set up his headquarters near Richland Creek in the home of a family who claimed to be relatives of the wounded General Buford. In a dispatch to Thomas at 5:30 P.M., he wrote, "I will push out at an early hour in the morning and try to get in on their flanks if possible." In camp that night, Wilson weighed information from a Confederate deserter about Hood's movements and about news of Sherman's army in Georgia. "The stories of the rebels in regard to Sherman's situation are ludicrous," Wilson wrote to Thomas that night. "They say he offered to surrender his whole command, provided they were paroled. The Confederates refused to take them on these terms. They say they have 'gobbled' him."[34]

Wilson issued orders for the cavalry's Christmas Day onslaught against the enemy. Harrison's brigade would ride at 5 A.M., followed in order by Hammond (of Knipe's division), Hatch, and Croxton. If and when the terrain allowed, the horsemen would advance off the road, while the guns, ambulances, and other wagons moved on the pike. "Every effort should be made to push the enemy as rapidly as possible," Wilson reiterated. The pace of the pursuit was exacting an awful toll on the cavalry horses, which slipped about or crunched through the ice on the roads, churning them into quagmires as they struggled to advance. "The horses' legs were covered with mud, and this, in turn, was frozen, so that great numbers of the poor animals were entirely disabled, their hoofs softened and the hair of their legs so rubbed off that it was impossible for them to travel," Wilson stated. Wilson's marching orders had already been issued when he received Thomas's answer to his 5:30 P.M. dispatch some five hours later. Thomas approved of Wilson's continued pressure, adding, "Your progress is not considered slow, under the circumstances, but on the contrary, is quite satisfactory."[35]

The infantry also was ready to continue on Christmas. "The march will be resumed in the morning as soon as the cavalry get out of the road for us," Wood said in a report to Thomas. "I hope we will yet be able to strike the enemy before he reaches the Tennessee River, provided we can be supplied with subsistence. I therefore respectfully urge that my wagons be allowed to move up, as we will be out of subsistence to-morrow night." Thomas answered that night, stating that while Wood should continue to "push on," Thomas would "do everything in his power to get up your train and that of the cavalry." Also that day, Thomas ordered Schofield to send a brigade to Columbia to act as a temporary garrison and set up provost guards.[36]

Hood made his headquarters that night at the Joiner family home on the Bainbridge Road near Blue Creek, which he reached at 4 P.M. The lead elements of his army, primarily Lee's Corps, were within about two miles of the Tennessee by nightfall, camping at Shoal Creek, while the engineers pressed ahead to the river. Stewart bivouacked behind Stevenson; their two corps had passed through Lexington and reached the Bainbridge Road. Cheatham's Corps had yet to come up from the vicinity of Lawrenceburg; it covered about fourteen miles that day and camped ten miles from the river. One Confederate recalled that the men were "making tracks for the Tennessee River at a quickstep known to Confederate tactics as 'double distance on half-rations.'"[37]

Hood's engineers, aided by infantry squads, immediately began preparing to build the pontoon bridge. One of the first tasks involved lashing together several pontoons to use as a makeshift ferry so that some artillery and horses could be crossed. In the meantime, three of Stewart's guns were emplaced in earthworks on the north bank near Florence to protect the span from the Federal gunboats, which the Confederates were anticipating. These guns were all that remained of two Mississippi batteries, Capt. James A. Hoskins's command and Cowan's Battery, a Vicksburg unit led by Lt. George H. Tompkins. Some gray infantry, including sharpshooters, were also sent over in boats to help protect the artillery posted south of the river, which included Phillips's Tennessee battery of Cheatham's Corps.[38]

Wading Shoal Creek was yet another in a seemingly endless series of frigid experiences for the troops. Rain had swollen the stream to about 200 yards, but it was still shallow enough to ford, although it was near freezing. The water was "clear as a crystal and looked beautiful, and the large boulders looked as if they were right at the surface," related W. A. Manning of the 56th Georgia in Lee's Corps. "After leaving the creek and walking about 50 yards, our clothes froze and you could hear the ice crack as we walked along." Robert Jarman, the Mississippian, described how his brigade, ordered to wade across, was reluctant to do so when their commander, General Brantley, tried to ride over, but his horse stepped on a slick rock and sent Brantley into the cold stream. This broke the impasse, and the Confederates took to the water, laughing as they went.[39]

One of Holtzclaw's soldiers, J. A. Dozier, recalled that the troops forded the creek in rushing water up to their armpits in some places, their uniforms stiff when they reached the other side. Thawing themselves by fires made of cedar rails, Dozier and other men of the 18th Alabama watched their regimental surgeon navigate the stream on a small mule. The animal was doing well enough before it stepped into a hole or crevice, stumbling and pitching the doctor into the creek. A Louisianan in Gibson's Brigade recalled how he stripped off his clothing, tied it to his musket, and used a pole to help keep his balance in the swift water. He kept his shoes on to protect him from the sharp rocks.[40]

Charles Quintard, the Tennessee chaplain, spent his Christmas Eve night at the roadside headquarters of his friend, Henry Clayton. After supper, the general assembled his staff and couriers for prayers. Meanwhile, Samuel Foster, the wounded Texas captain, had not fared well since leaving Pulaski two days earlier on his $800 horse. Intense pain caused fainting spells that prevented him from mounting, and he was forced to ride in an ambulance. Some of his men dressed his wound, but they could pour water through the bullet hole, indicating that he was healing very slowly, if at all. The Texans obtained some whiskey and bread which helped them celebrate Christmas Eve.[41]

Thomas was still near Columbia when he received a Saturday dispatch from Stanton announcing that Lincoln had approved his nomination for a major generalship in the army. At Thomas's field headquarters, surgeon George E. Cooper, the Army of the Cumberland's medical director, watched the general sit motionless and quiet with Stanton's telegram in his hand, apparently reflecting on the previous times he had been passed over for promotion. Thomas also by now was aware of the rumors that he was to be replaced even as he had been assembling his army at Nashville. Thomas then turned to Cooper, handing him the message and saying, "What do you think of that?" The doctor pondered the dispatch for a few moments, choosing his words, before replying, "It is better late than never." "I suppose it is better late than never but it is too late to be appreciated," Thomas answered testily. "I earned this at Chattanooga."[42]

After leaving the Federals in possession of the north branch of Richland Creek, Forrest and the rear guard reached Pulaski "without further molestation," as he described it. Abraham Buford's leg wound was not serious, but Forrest had no choice but to give Chalmers temporary dual command of Buford's Division as well as his own troopers. Some of the cavalry, including Ross's Texans, passed through the town and encamped that night just to the south while Walthall and the infantry bivouacked amid an outer line of earthworks north of the village. Pulaski remained stocked with an immensity of ammunition and other military stores that Hood's main army had left behind. Forrest knew he had to destroy as much of these supplies as possible to prevent them from being captured. He also realized that he had mere hours to do so, since Wilson's hell hounds likely would be pounding down his throat by early Christmas morning.[43]

From his Blue Creek headquarters around 6:20 P.M., Hood sent word to Stewart to be on the lookout for Major Green's engineers and to let these wagons pass if they caught up to the infantry. Green was expected in Lexington that evening with the rear of his train. Stewart was to cross Shoal Creek on Christmas, select a defensive position to protect the ford, and "fortify it as well as possible, having special reference to a good abatis." Hood meant to try to stave off the enemy here, if he had to—anything to give his bridge-builders more time.[44]

On his plantation near Columbia, seventy-three-year-old Nimrod Porter reflected in his diary about the day's events and the overall fortunes of war. His home had been victimized by marauders on both sides during the conflict's course and had that day been visited by Union cavalry—Croxton's boys, Porter believed—who stole his last turkey, all his chickens, and even boots and money from his farm hands and servants. "Tomorrow is Christmas day, a bitter one for us, black or white," he wrote. "A gray fox ran under the kitchen walk. I shot it for dinner. We have a little parched corn." Porter had tried to remain neutral, and that night, he scrawled a final entry conveying the weariness of many. "I wish there were a river of fire a mile wide between the North and South that would burn with unquenchable fury forevermore and that it could never be passable to the endless ages of eternity by any living creature."[45]

CHAPTER 11

"Boys, This Is All My Fault"

SUNDAY, DECEMBER 25

Pulaski trembled.

Forrest spent much of the early morning blowing up munitions that Hood's men and wagons could not carry and that could not be removed by two southbound trains. At least one locomotive and two trains of cars were demolished amid massive explosions that shook the ground, rattled windows, and sent orange flames licking into the predawn sky. A huge bonfire was lit in the town square, and soldiers fed it with supplies that had to be destroyed, including bacon, clothing, and boxes of ammunition. Watching the spectacle, Charles Olmstead was shaken by another sight that he would long remember: "I noticed women and children in their night dresses at the windows of some of the houses—many of the former sadly weeping and wringing their hands. So the day of 'Peace on earth and good will to man' was ushered in by us. God grant that none whom I love may ever see another like it."[1]

Amid the thunder and flashes of detonating ordnance, Forrest ordered Gen. "Red" Jackson to hold the town with his little division of cavalry—Armstrong's and Ross's brigades—as long as possible and then to torch the covered bridge over Richland Creek just south of town when the last Confederates were over. From the point where Wilson and Forrest had clashed the previous day, Richland Creek wound to the west and then curled back to the east at Pulaski's southern outskirts, where the covered bridge would be Jackson's escape route. Walthall's soldiers marched at daybreak, passing through the smoke-filled town and leaving the pike to take the churned-up

Lamb's Ferry Road. Marching through the streets, men of the 1st Tennessee Infantry passed near the spot where Sam Davis, a member of the regiment, had been hanged as a spy by the Federals about a year earlier. The Confederates believed the execution was an atrocity and Davis a martyr to the cause.[2]

In the Union camps about ten miles north of Pulaski, Harrison's 1st Brigade of Johnson's division had the advance, riding out around 5 A.M. Harrison advanced some two miles when he smacked into Jackson's rear guard, either Ross's troopers or Armstrong's Mississippians; these brigades were alternating as rear guard that day. Lt. Col. Harlon Baird's 5th Iowa led Harrison's units and drove back the enemy amid heavy skirmishing. The Confederates were driven from several positions and, by 8:30 A.M., were falling back into the town itself. Baird did not hesitate, charging through the streets as the last of the Confederates were leaving. Pressed by the Iowans and with the covered bridge already afire, some of Jackson's troopers had little choice but to ride through its flaming gauntlet, a few singeing their hair, beards, and eyebrows in their flight. There was a brief fight here as Harrison brought up two guns and deployed a line of troopers along the creek, with their fire driving off Confederates on the opposite bank who unsuccessfully tried to delay them until the span was consumed. But Harrison's men were able to extinguish the flames, and the cavalry poured across without delay. The 5th Iowa lost three killed and three wounded in charging the bridge.[3]

Hatch's division was also descending on Pulaski by now, and troopers of Lt. Col. Robert H. Carnahan's 3rd Illinois Cavalry surprised Confederates on the railroad as they were about to burn two locomotives. The engines were saved and the Confederates scattered, a number being captured.[4]

After his troopers drove out the Confederates "on the keen jump," Wilson himself rode into Pulaski at 10 A.M. From there, he sent a dispatch to Thomas: "Forrest . . . is scarcely out of sight. Everything has gone on the road to Lamb's Ferry, the original intention of going to Decatur having been abandoned for fear they would be intercepted." Wilson continued: "They are trying to reach Florence. I will crowd them ahead as fast as possible. They are literally running away, making no defense whatever." This last assessment would change a few hours later.[5]

In Pulaski, Union forces seized a Confederate hospital containing about 200 men and also found four guns the enemy had dumped in Richland Creek. About a mile south of town, the Federals discovered the burning remains of twenty ammunition wagons belonging to Cheatham's troops; the Confederates had destroyed the train and took the mules to pull the pontoons. "The road from Pulaski to Bainbridge, and indeed back to Nashville, was strewn with abandoned wagons, limbers, small arms, blankets, &c., showing most conclusively the disorder of the enemy's retreat," Thomas later described it.[6]

Slogging out of Pulaski, the Federal cavalry soon brushed with Walthall's men on the Lamb's Ferry Road. "The enemy, with a heavy mounted force . . . began to press us with boldness and vigor," according to Walthall. But like the Confederates, the Union troopers quickly found themselves trying to wade the mud of the country road, the route marked by the smoke of the gutted wagons and discarded artillery shells, among other war debris. The rain resumed about 1 p.m., worsening the already morose conditions, and a slight thaw turned the road into "rivers of slush," a Confederate officer noted.[7]

Meanwhile, Forrest was preparing to ambush his antagonists and soon found the spot to do just that—Anthony's (also known as King's) Hill, about seven miles southwest of Pulaski. There, the Lamb's Ferry Road twisted into a ravine between steep, thickly treed ridges, crowned by Anthony's Hill at the south end, basically a U-shaped rock formation. Hood had sent word to Forrest to hold this position until the army was over Sugar Creek, about fourteen miles farther south. John Morton's guns—his "Bull Pups," as they were known—were hidden among trees on the hill summit, while Featherston's and Palmer's infantrymen were posted along the crest and on the ridges. They were joined by about 800 dismounted cavalrymen, 400 or so each from Armstrong's and Ross's brigades. The remainder of Jackson's troopers protected both flanks.

The soldiers built defenses of fence rails, logs, and tree limbs. Reynolds's and Feild's brigades were held in support, and a "line no thicker than a strong line of skirmishers" was the only Confederate force in the open.[8]

General Chalmers, who had been moving on a another road, was halted to support the Confederate right flank, if needed. "The situation now seemed desperate," Chalmers recalled. "Forrest, with his forty five hundred, as undaunted as Zenophon [*sic*] with his celebrated ten thousand, calmly awaited their approach, and his men gathered courage from their leader."[9]

Nearing Anthony's Hill around 2 P.M., Harrison's Federals encountered the visible skirmishers, whom they quickly brushed aside. "The country was so difficult . . . that the men of Harrison's brigade were necessarily in weak order," Wilson reported, "but nothing daunted, they pursued the enemy's skirmishers back to their fortified position." The Confederates had retreated from previous positions when the cavalry outflanked them, and Harrison had no reason to believe this encounter would be any different. Besides, he had other cavalry coming up from Pulaski to support him. Still, Harrison apparently sensed danger or at least was cautious. He held up his column and dismounted Israel Garrard's 7th Ohio and Maj. Charles H. Beeres's 16th Illinois to probe up the hill in their front.[10]

It was now about 3 P.M., and these Union troopers worked their way up the slope until they were within fifty paces of a hidden line of skirmishers. Forrest then sprung his trap, and the wooded slopes suddenly rumbled with cannon blasts, musketry, and the rebel yell. Ripped by Morton's double canister and angry swarms of minies, Harrison's two regiments melted back down the hill. The Ohioans and Illinoisans had "moved upon the enemy most gallantly, when suddenly he opened from a masked battery of three guns and charged over his works, in two lines of infantry with a column of cavalry, down the main road," said Harrison. "Before this overpowering force my men were obliged to fall back," he stated. "Over the breastworks flashes a line of grey and down the slope they sweep, yelling at every step," recalled Walter Clark of the 63rd Georgia in Olmstead's Brigade. Hammond's horsemen, coming up to support Harrison, were swept up in this withdrawal. Hammond had thrown his lead regiment, the 4th Tennessee, into action dismounted when the 7th Ohio piled into them, running for the rear. The Ohioans sliced through Hammond's column, and the Confederates temporarily poured into this gap between the 4th Tennessee's lead horses and the rest of Hammond's units.[11]

The Confederates overran and captured a 12-pounder Napoleon from Lt. Frank G. Smith's Battery I, 4th U.S. Regular Artillery, in the center. "The enemy retreated in disorder, and my command, by prompt pursuit, captured a number of prisoners and horses and one piece of artillery," Walthall related. In the Confederate defenses, Olmstead's 63rd Georgia had missed out on the initial charge because a captain leading the regiment was unsure if he should join the attack or remain in support of the artillery. The officer decided the Georgians should stay with the guns, but was soon overruled. General Featherston galloped up and asked who the regiment was and what it was doing. When the captain replied that they were supporting the battery, Featherston boomed, "Battery the devil! Get over them breastworks and get quick!" The Georgians hurtled down the slope.[12]

Hatch's troopers were feeding their mounts, many of which had their bridles off, when the disorganized brigades of Hammond and Harrison tumbled back toward their position. An obviously excited Wilson also rode up, telling Hatch, "There they are, hurry up!" The Confederates were still coming on while others wheeled the captured gun up the hill. Hatch quickly ordered the 9th Illinois Cavalry to attack on foot since the terrain was unsuited for a mounted charge. "Too much cannot be said in favor of this regiment," Hatch later reported. "Undismayed by the rapid retreat of the commands going to the rear, Captain [Joseph W. Harper] threw his regiment to one side to let the flying mass pass, and then with a cheer charged the enemy."[13]

Hatch also hurled his 1st Brigade, under Col. Robert R. Stewart, against the Confederates on the left. Stewart thwarted an enemy attempt to turn the Federal right. Hatch also ordered Datus Coon's always reliable 2nd Brigade to move to the right and forward. Harper's men blazed away with their carbines, blunting the assault and allowing Harrison to regroup about half a mile to the rear. Meanwhile, Hammond had withdrawn his Tennesseans to save his horses and remount the troopers. Some of Harrison's and Hammond's troopers joined Hatch's men in this counterstroke, driving the Confederates back to their defenses, while Hatch's other units were unable to flank the enemy position because of the heavy timber, according to Union accounts. The Federals made several thrusts to try to retake the cannon, but failed.

The Confederate version of the battle's climax is that Forrest recalled his jubilant but jumbled attackers, knowing that they were well out of position and ran the risk of running into advancing Federal infantry. Whatever the case—and both sides could have been right in this instance—Forrest withdrew from Anthony's Hill around sundown as Union forces pressed both flanks. General Ross, who had been posted on the right of the Confederate position, stated that the Confederates' surprise offensive was "such an effectual check that he [the enemy] did not again show himself that day. This done, we retired leisurely."[14]

The cannoneer John Morton told of an incident late in the fight in which Armstrong asked to pull back after his troopers had used all of their ammunition, but Forrest told him to hold on a bit longer. Shortly afterward, Armstrong again requested that his men be taken out of their exposed position, but Forrest again denied him. Finally, Armstrong had no choice but to withdraw because of enemy pressure. Riding past Forrest and Walthall, Armstrong, with tears streaming down his cheeks, said to Walthall, "Won't you please make that damned man [Forrest] on the horse see that my men are forced to retreat?" According to Morton, "Forrest, with unusual gentleness and understanding, told him he was gaining time for Hood's main body to get across Sugar Creek. He then checked his watch and said, 'It is about time for all of us to get out of here.'"[15]

Forrest reported that he inflicted losses of 150 killed and wounded and took "many prisoners" in addition to the captured gun. Chalmers, however, "estimated" the casualties as 150, stating that 50 prisoners also were taken, along with about 300 cavalry horses. A quantity of Union overcoats also was seized. Chalmers added that this fight, "which General Thomas treats as a mere skirmish," was highlighted by the Confederate charge which "astonished the Federals so much that they attacked no more that day." As the seized Napoleon was wheeled through the Confederate lines, "it caused great, good cheer," according to an officer in Strahl's Brigade.[16]

Southern losses were about fifteen killed and forty wounded at Anthony's Hill, based on a Confederate account, although Forrest did not report any losses. Still, Forrest likely would have grudgingly agreed with Wilson's postwar assessment of the engagement: "At this stage of the game nothing could resist our onset. The enemy apparently realized that, and again took up his line of retreat."[17]

Some forty-two miles from Anthony's Hill, Hood's main army was filtering into camps and defensive positions across the river from Bainbridge, and the troops were beginning to work on the pontoon bridge. Reaching the Tennessee the previous day, Presstman's engineers had been uneasy, knowing they did not have enough pontoons to reach the south bank and waiting to hear whether Captain Cobb and his pontoniers had secured the boats at Decatur. According to one engineer, Captain Pharr, "We approached the river . . . with that grand old army disheartened, disorganized, wrecked, behind us, and the broad Tennessee river before, while the roar of artillery in the distance told plainly that the rear guard was being pressed by the victorious foe." Shortly thereafter, cheers rent the air as an officer spread the word: "Cobb has come! Cobb has come!" The captain and his men had successfully floated the captured pontoons down the Tennessee, passing the treacherous shoals with little trouble due to the flooded conditions. "A wild cheer for Cobb went up . . . for all felt that the army was saved."[18]

The loss of the pontoons at Decatur rankled the Federals. According to Union brigadier general Jacob D. Cox, who led one of Thomas's divisions, Hood "was favored by a gleam of good fortune" by the boats' arrival, the pontoons having been lost by "some blunder" when Union forces evacuated the town in November. When the Federals left town, the pontoon bridge had been cut loose with the expectation that it would be towed to safety by Union gunboats, Cox claimed after the war. He added that he was unable to "trace the responsibility for the failure either to take it up or destroy it." Instead, the pontoons fell into Confederate hands and likely saved Hood's army from destruction.[19]

Waiting to cross the Tennessee or fight while jammed against the wide river, the Confederates tried to make themselves comfortable and fill their bellies. The river flats and the bluffs above "looked like a hard place to forage at," Robert Jarman recalled, but four men from his regiment, one of whom was barefooted, set out anyway. Raiding a cavalry bivouac, these troops returned in the night with their bounty. The barefooted soldier had boots, and the men also lugged a fifty-pound sack of flour and "a camp kettle of beef off the fire."[20]

"Christmas day dawned bright and beautiful but upon what a scene did that morning's sun arise," wrote Capt. Samuel Cooper of the 20th Tennessee of Cheatham's Corps, which had marched at daybreak, reaching Shoal Creek. "A poor half starved, half clad band of ragamuffins fleeing in disgrace from their last chance for freedom and independence. We thought the Yankees would catch us at last." Soldiers of Granbury's Brigade in Cheatham's ranks were nearing the creek when Hood rode up, "looking worn and tired, but with kindly words for all," remembered W. G. Davenport of the 6th Texas Infantry. "Boys, this is all my fault," the general remarked before heading off. Like the rest of the army before them, Cheatham's men had much difficulty in getting over the creek

Jacob D. Cox.

because of the high water and rough ford. Their struggles were accompanied by the distant thunder of the Union gunboats from the direction of Florence as Admiral Lee probed upstream. Still, completing the crossing later in the day, Cheatham went into position between the creek and the river and, that night, built defenses to protect the bridge "in case the enemy should move on us from below, which was thought not improbable," reported Maj. Henry Hampton of Cheatham's staff.[21]

The Missouri cannoneer Samuel Dunlap and his comrades had marched that morning amid "mud, rain & a repetition of all the vicissitudes which had been our almost constant companions during the retreat." They knew it was Christmas, but this brought them scant comfort from their daily ordeal. "Of course we were aware of the fact—that another anniversary of the birth of our Savior had come around—& also that it was impossible to pass it as in by gone days—but to 'grin & bear it' was all we could do," Dunlap wrote.[22]

W. A. Manning of the 56th Georgia was one of the soldiers sent over the Tennessee to guard Cheatham's artillery, reaching the south bank on Christmas after his icy crossing of Shoal Creek. After navigating the "high and swift" river, Manning and his companions built a fire but were soon told to extinguish it. When orders reached them that they would camp there that night, the fire was rekindled and the men set about gathering rails, bark, and other wood for the blaze and for makeshift beds to keep them out of the water and off the cold, soggy turf. "We went to our couches and slept peacefully, thus spending our Christmas cold and hungry, having left all our baggage at Nashville," Manning related. "Though we had marched all day in frozen clothes and then slept in them, frozen stiff, it seemed a comfortable night, so utterly weary were we."[23]

Also assigned to these guns were the barefooted Lt. Isaac Shannon and his Whitworth Sharpshooters of Cheatham's command. With nothing to eat, these soldiers luckily discovered a cache of corn in a nearby mill and ground about three bushels of meal. They traded some of it for salt, and after a nighttime foray netted "a hog belonging to our army," they cooked their supper in two frying pans made by halving a Union canteen. "We were then comfortable," Shannon remembered.[24]

Meanwhile, Hood had reached the Tennessee by 11 A.M. and issued orders throughout the rest of Sunday "on the riverbank." Hood ordered Stewart to remain beyond Shoal Creek, guarding the roads on that side of the stream. Stewart was to keep a battery with him and send his other guns and his wagons across the creek. "Don't let this work stop, night or day, till you get everything to this side" of the stream, Hood ordered. Stewart would receive instructions about when to withdraw his infantry to the south bank. That afternoon, Hood informed Stewart about two creek fords above the one the rest of the army had used.

Still later in the day, Hood sent orders to Stewart to ford Shoal Creek as soon as his guns and wagons were over, regardless of which ford was used. Based on previous instructions sent to him on Saturday, Stewart was to dig in south of the creek and hold the position. By nightfall, the army was spread in a defensive arc to guard the bridge-construction site. Cheatham was on the right, Stevenson on the left, and Stewart somewhat in advance, protecting the intersection of the Bainbridge and Powell roads. "The pontoon was being laid across the river as rapidly as the arrival of the boats would allow," one of Hood's staff officers wrote.[25]

During the day, Hood wrote the barest of identical dispatches to Secretary of War Seddon and Beauregard: "I am laying a pontoon here to cross the Tennessee River." To Beauregard, he added, "Please come to Tuscumbia or Bainbridge." Incredibly, this was Hood's first attempt to update his superiors about his situation since his December 17 message from Spring Hill, which still had not been received.[26]

The Union IV Corps was some two miles out from Pulaski at 3:30 P.M. when Wood received a dispatch from Wilson, calling for infantry support at Anthony's Hill. Wilson said he had met "a slight check" and added, "If you bring up your infantry, we may get some prisoners, and I think shall be able to drive Forrest off." The troops plunged ahead. The IV Corps had started the day about two and a half miles south of Lynnville on the Pulaski Pike. Wood issued orders around 7 A.M. that Samuel Beatty's division would lead the advance, followed by Kimball and Elliott. Much more dire, however, was the lack of food. "Our supply train is on the other side of the Duck River, and the pontoon bridge is constantly breaking," Wood wrote to Thomas the night before, requesting that the supply train be sent over as soon as possible. Wood was still waiting for the cavalry to move at 8 A.M. on Christmas when he received a reply from Thomas, saying that the train would be hurried ahead. The infantry was able to move about an hour later. The head of Beatty's division reached Pulaski around 1 P.M. after covering eleven miles and was now only a few miles behind the cavalry.[27]

Leaving the pike at Pulaski, the infantry slogged along the Lamb's Ferry Road, which had been rendered "next to impracticable from the depth of the mud," Wood recalled. He ordered that all but four batteries of his artillery be left in the town, using the horses from the guns left behind to bolster the teams of the cannon and caissons still with the columns. Wood also reduced the number of ammunition wagons, each to carry only ten boxes of rounds, to proceed with the infantry. "These arrangements were necessary on account of the conditions of the road on which the enemy retreated," Wood noted. "Without extra teams to the artillery carriages and lightening of the usual load of an ammunition wagon, it would have been impracticable to get the vehicles along; a vigorous pursuit would have been impossible."[28]

Civilians at Pulaski told Union soldiers that the Confederate pontoon train had passed there on Friday and that Hood intended to cross the Tennessee at Lamb's Ferry or Florence. Still, the Federals could not be sure of Hood's objective until they reached the Lamb's Ferry–Powell Road intersection. Beatty's infantry reached the vicinity of Anthony's Hill around 5:30 P.M. after sloshing about four miles in two exhausting hours on the Lamb's Ferry Road. By then, the fighting was over, and Wilson was pushing cautiously after Forrest. With no rations, Wood decided to bivouac there after a hard day's march of sixteen miles.[29]

Thomas reached Richland Creek north of Pulaski late in the day and that night sent a dispatch to Halleck with news of Wilson's recapture of the town and the cavalry's other early morning progress. He also told Halleck that the railroad from Nashville to Pulaski would be repaired and open soon and that Admiral Lee was doing a good job. "I have my troops well in hand and well provided with provisions and ammunition, and close upon the heels of the enemy, and shall continue to press him as long as there is a chance of doing anything," he reported. On the mud-clogged roads, his troops might have disagreed with his claim that they had ample provisions, especially Wood's troops, who had nothing to eat.[30]

After leaving Anthony's Hill, Forrest and the rear guard pulled back to Sugar Creek, their hard-won victory disappearing in the muck and misery as darkness fell. The fourteen-mile trek was made in heavy rain, sleet, and a hard north wind; conditions worsened as the night wore on. The mud was knee-deep to the men, some of whom were barefooted, and in other places up to the horses' bellies. The Georgian Walter Clark wrote that "if there was ever a darker or more starless one [night] I can not place it." Regiments and companies became intermingled, and the men walked "by faith and not by sight" and followed the whistles of the 63rd Georgia's color bearer, Elmore Dunbar. If not for Dunbar's "occasional whistling imitations of the bugle call to let us know 'where he was at' our regiment would have lost all semblance of its organization," Clark said. "I can not well conceive how a larger share of unadulterated physical discomfort could have been compressed into the five solid hours for which we kept it up."[31]

Walthall's infantry and most of the cavalry sagged into their camps at Sugar Creek between 11 P.M. and 1 A.M. The icy stream was clear, and by the light of fires, the men washed themselves and their filthy rags before falling to the ground for a few hours of rest. Nearby was a large section of the army's ordnance train.

Many of the wagons were without draft animals in their traces as the mules had been taken forward to assist in getting the pontoon wagons to the river. Olmstead's Georgians, "weary to exhaustion, dead for sleep," tried to find places to sleep but the farm fields on both sides of the road were plowed, the furrows filled with water. Many of the men plopped down on the fields' ridges. Fortunately for Olmstead, he found an empty ambulance by the road and crawled into it.[32]

Wilson appeared unruffled by the Anthony's Hill ambush, stating that "a few hundred of the enemy's infantry, for the first time since the battles of Nashville, sallied from their breastworks and drove back Harrison's attenuated skirmish line and captured one gun. . . . They were promptly driven back." Thomas wrote that the enemy, showing "something of his former boldness," had a minor gain and took a cannon, but that "the ground lost was almost immediately regained." Realizing the Confederates had left Anthony's Hill, the Union cavalry was slow to advance, wary of another ambush.[33]

Wilson also claimed he was not displeased about the gun, stating that Lieutenant Smith, the battery commander, and his men had been especially "active and aggressive" in keeping up with the advance and that "no reflection rested upon them for the loss of the only gun ever taken from the cavalry corps." Several months later, the piece was recaptured in fighting near Selma, Alabama.[34]

In Montgomery, Alabama, Colonel Brent of Beauregard's staff had received a puzzling telegram from the wounded Gen. Stephen Dill Lee and notified Beauregard in Charleston on Christmas. Lee reported that he was in Florence, Alabama, and that he would "be glad to have General Beauregard's views in regard to recent events in Tennessee." Baffled, Brent wrote Beauregard that "There are no advices whatever from that quarter, and I do not understand General Lee's telegraph." Brent added that he was "apprehensive that some reverse may have occurred." Sensing that disaster had befallen Hood, Beauregard telegraphed Jefferson Davis that same day, recommending Lt. Gen. Richard Taylor as a replacement for Hood "should circumstances require another commander."[35]

At his department headquarters in Meridian, Mississippi, Taylor received a note from Brent that day that Union troops had gone ashore from boats at Chickasaw, Alabama, on the morning of Christmas Eve. The lieutenant of engineers who had seen this could not determine if the vessels were gunboats or transports. More importantly, Taylor still was trying to determine what had happened to Hood in Tennessee, although the sparse information he had painted a bleak picture, based on Union reports published in the papers and rumors "from above." Believing that Hood had suffered a "serious reverse," Taylor wired Maj. Gen. Dabney Maury, commander of the District of the Gulf, that Mobile likely would be attacked. The threat was not immediate but would arise as "soon as the enemy, having pressed his pursuit of our army as far south of the Tennessee as the condition of the roads will permit" could regroup and prepare for a strike. Maury was to strengthen his fortifications and brace for the onslaught. Taylor sent basically the same instructions to Maj. Gen. Franklin Gardner, another of his district commanders, adding that if Hood recrossed the Tennessee, the enemy might push him fifty miles south of the river, if the roads allowed, and then assail Mobile.[36]

From Tuscumbia on Christmas, Isham G. Harris, the Confederate governor of Tennessee who had accompanied Hood since the campaign began, also sent a dispatch to Davis, giving some details of the setback and defending Hood's handling of the campaign: "disastrous as it has ended, I am not able to see anything that General Hood has done that he should not, or neglected anything that he should have done which it was possible to do. Indeed, the more that I have seen and known of him and his policy, the more I have been pleased with him and regret to say that if all had performed their parts as well as he, the results would have been very different."[37]

In their miserable camps atop Anthony's Hill, Wood's infantrymen settled in for the night, their stomachs growling.

A train with three days' rations had reached Pulaski at 7 P.M., and officers had been sent back to hurry it forward, but the wagons might as well have been thirty miles distant rather than seven, based on the terrible roads. The supplies were not expected before almost noon the next day. Nevertheless, Wood also received a message from Thomas around 10:15 P.M. ordering him to issue rations and then follow the cavalry on the twenty-sixth.

After a feint toward Corinth, Grierson's Union cavalry struck Verona, Mississippi, a key Confederate supply depot on the Mobile & Ohio a few miles south of Tupelo, on Christmas night. Col. Joseph Karge's 1st Cavalry Brigade attacked, and his 7th Indiana romped through the camp, scattering the few surprised defenders and igniting the destruction. Karge's troopers destroyed two trains, thirty-two cars, and eight warehouses filled with various stores. They also found and torched about 200 army wagons, most marked "U.S.," which were filled with supplies for Hood's army. Amid the flames and exploding ordnance, the Indianans pulled out, camping at Harrisburg, some five miles distant, near daylight. "The bursting of shells which were contained in this immense depot continued until the afternoon of the next day," Grierson noted. More significantly, Hood's lone railroad supply line had been severed.[38]

CHAPTER 12

"The Widest River in the World"

MONDAY, DECEMBER 26

As Grierson's raiders were silhouetted by the flames at Verona, some 120 miles away, Presstman's exhausted engineers toiled by torchlight, finally completing the pontoon bridge before dawn. By sunrise, the Confederate wagon trains were trundling over in a cold drizzle, but the unwieldy span, consisting of about eighty boats, was far from being sturdy. The river's strong current created a crescent-like bulge in it, causing the Confederates to allow only a few vehicles and guns on it at a time. Around 8 A.M., some wounded soldiers crossed, followed by artillery and other wagons. Everyone remained edgy about the Union navy, which was believed to be nearby. If these vessels slipped past Stewart's and Cheatham's batteries downriver and caught the troops on the bridge or massed to cross, the slaughter could be horrific.

Hood watched the procession from the riverbank, his mind further clouded by the terrible news about the Union cavalry rampaging along the Mobile & Ohio and possibly threatening Corinth. If the railroad was heavily damaged and if Corinth fell, what was left of his already fragile army could face starvation or disintegration within weeks. Hood's inspector general, Col. E. J. Harvie, was already in Mississippi, preparing for the army's arrival, and Hood sent him two late-morning dispatches about the crisis. The enemy had to be driven off the railroad, using troops from Corinth if they could be spared. Harvie also should ask for assistance from General Maury at Mobile. Another message was wired to Harvie within half an hour. The colonel had to "take immediate steps to repair the damage . . . done our

215

railroad. This work should be pushed forward at once and with great energy." Harvie also had to help prevent Hood from being surprised on the Tennessee: "Keep this river well watched by good scouts" from Florence to Chickasaw.[1]

Meanwhile, Wilson's men were in the saddle and on the rampage early, still struggling on the impossible roads, the region getting "wilder and more desolate as we pushed into it," he recalled. Since leaving Pulaski, the cavalry had traveled on "the worst sort of dirt roads through a thinly settled and barren country." Abandoned wagons, broken-down or dying mules, and other assorted flotsam and jetsam continued to be common signposts of the Confederates' passing. Of great concern, the Federal horsemen also were basically out of food. "The country . . . was the worst we had yet seen," Wilson said. "It was entirely stripped of forage and supplies. Our own trains were far to the rear, our haversacks and forage bags were empty."[2]

In the Confederate bivouac at Sugar Creek, the mule teams had returned overnight and were hitched to the remaining ordnance train wagons, which moved south in the foggy predawn. It was still dark about an hour later when Walthall learned from Forrest that Federal cavalry was pushing Ross's pickets not more than a mile or so away and that the infantry should prepare to repel them. Wilson's advance was led by Hammond's brigade of Knipe's division. Wilson later described Sugar Creek as "a clear beautiful stream of limpid water running through an unbroken forest to the river," but it is doubtful that soldiers on either side could relate to such literary flair as they squinted into the cold, thick fog this morning.[3]

Around sunrise, Walthall stationed Reynolds's and Feild's troops in a ravine about 200 yards south of the creek ford, where they hastily erected makeshift defenses of fence rails and logs. Deep sedge grass also helped conceal their position. Armstrong's cavalry held the left of this line while Ross's troopers were stationed on the right. Featherston's and Palmer's brigades were aligned about a half mile to the rear, constructing similar works augmented by the ruins of some old outbuildings "to guard against disaster in the event the troops in front of them were overcome," Walthall stated. Chalmers's horsemen were situated on a parallel road leading to the creek. The Confederates also intentionally exposed a small force that was to withdraw and pull in the Federals.[4]

On a little knoll at the front line, Forrest conferred with Feild, Reynolds, and other officers, including Colonel Finlay of Strahl's Brigade in Feild's command. Forrest told them that when "the infantry broke their line," he would throw Ross's cavalry at them, but Feild misunderstood. "We have got no such infantry, general," Feild stammered. "They will not break our lines." Forrest replied with a laugh, "I don't mean when they break our lines, but when we break theirs." Feild answered instantly, " That's the kind of infantry we have, general," drawing "a big laugh all around," Finlay remembered.[5]

The cacophony of Spencers and Colts to the front soon shook everyone back to reality. Ross's pickets offered token resistance before hightailing to the main body at the creek, pressed by Lt. Col. William R. Cook's 2nd (U.S.) Tennessee of Hammond's command. Both sides would be almost blind because of the milky mist, and this worked to the Southerners' advantage at the outset. Around 8:30 A.M., these Confederates heard Hammond's horsemen splashing across the ford. Cook's men, supported by the 4th (U.S.) Tennessee Cavalry and led by Lt. Col. Jacob M. Thornburgh, formed up on the south bank in their "vigorous pursuit" of Walthall's exposed troops. Hearing officers' orders in the fog, the Confederates soon realized that some Federals were dismounted and closing with them. They waited until the Union men were within thirty to fifty paces of their defenses before a signal shot from Morton's artillery resulted in an infantry volley, "causing the wildest confusion," according to Forrest.[6]

The volley disorganized the dismounted Union soldiers, who fell back as Walthall's infantry sprung forward on the attack. The retreating Federals mixed with their horse holders and the remaining mounted troopers at the creek, adding to the confusion. Two of Ross's cavalry regiments, the Texas Legion and the 9th Texas—about eighty men in all—charged

along the east bank while Col. Edward Dillon's 2nd Mississippi
Cavalry of Armstrong's Brigade attacked the other flank.
Chalmers's horsemen also were in the fray, with the counterat-
tack "producing a complete rout." With the Confederates
swarming after them, Union men scampered back over the
stream, which was saddle-skirt deep. In their excitement,
Walthall's men also plunged into the cold water and continued
across. "The enemy were severely punished, but more fright-
ened than hurt," Chalmers said of the clash.[7]

The Confederates pursued the enemy for 300 yards up to
about two miles before being recalled—again, like at Anthony's
Hill, because of the supposed threat of Union infantry coming
up. Forrest estimated enemy losses in this engagement as about
150 killed and wounded, "many" prisoners and horses captured, and some 400 horses killed. The Confederates got "a
good Yankee breakfast" from the saddlebags of the dead and
captured Union horses, noted an up-till-then dismounted
Texas cavalryman in Reynolds's consolidated brigade. The Confederates seized so many horses that most of the brigade was
mounted for the final push to the Tennessee. Forrest held this
position for two hours more, but with Union forces showing no
signs of resuming the attack and concerned that he might be
outflanked in the lingering fog, he began his withdrawal.
Indeed, some of Walthall's infantry had pulled back as early as
9 A.M.[8]

Hammond eventually brought up some guns of the 14th
Ohio Light Battery to shell the Confederate positions, but by 4
P.M., all that remained there were a few mounted pickets who
soon galloped away. Hatch's cavalry also had reinforced Hammond by late afternoon.

Walthall's soldiers marched to within sixteen miles of the
Tennessee before bivouacking that night. "It had now become
evident that no effort on the part of my command could again
bring Forrest to risk another engagement," Wilson said. Not
surprisingly, the Confederates had a different view. Chalmers
wrote that the "grand result" of Sugar Creek "was that the pursuit was permanently checked and the enemy came no more."

Sugar Creek also would be the last significant combat of the Army of Tennessee on the soil of its namesake state.[9]

In the IV Corps' encampment at Anthony's Hill, Wood's hungry infantry waited through the early morning for the expected supply train to arrive from Pulaski. Around 8 A.M., Wood learned that the lead wagons had advanced only about three miles south of town and were "moving very slowly." Optimistically, he told his division commanders to march as soon as the train came up and the three-day rations were issued, adding that the men should make them last five days.[10]

On the Tennessee, Hood's wagons and artillery took much of the day to reach the south bank, but most of the trains were over by nightfall as the infantry waited its turn. During the afternoon, the Confederates were startled by the boom of heavy guns from several miles downriver as Admiral Lee's gunboats steamed into action. Clouds of gun smoke over the trees confirmed that the Union navy was coming. Despite claims from his pilot that the river was too swift for the Confederates to lay pontoons near Bainbridge, Lee had proceeded upriver past Florence with two lighter-draft gunboats. Some two miles past the town, he encountered Stewart's gunners dug in on the north bank. There was a brief flurry of artillery fire before the vessels backed away minutes after engaging. At the pontoons, the Confederates listened as the cannonading stopped and then heard a steamboat whistle, apparently signaling the enemy's retreat. Lee had come within two or three miles of his objective, but the Confederate artillery and the hazards of Muscle Shoals prevented him from reaching Hood's pontoons.[11]

Hood was at Bainbridge that night. Frank Cheatham also crossed, leaving orders for his troops to move over the bridge at 3 A.M. on the twenty-seventh. Lee's Corps, under Stevenson, was the first infantry over, followed by Cheatham's men; Stewart's Corps brought up the rear of the main army. Because the span remained so fragile, this was an extremely slow process, with the soldiers in single file and three paces apart. It would take two days for the Confederates to complete the crossing.[12]

Among Stewart's troops, the Missourian Samuel Dunlap and his battery mates awoke that morning in a ramshackle log stable near Lexington where they had spent Christmas night. Dunlap wrote that the "frail structure was a great protection, & while we could not have a table filled with choice viands—we could sit in the horse trough & eat buiscuits [sp] & pork." Amid a cold, slow rain and thick fog, the artillerymen had started south again, "whipping the poor horses through the stiff mud," making for the river, Dunlap recalled.[13]

Thomas remained at Pulaski on Monday, monitoring developments and apparently realizing that his odds of catching Hood were dwindling. Wood's IV Corps remained in its camps throughout the day before the supply wagons finally arrived and rations were distributed. By then, it was 5 P.M.—too late to march—so the troops stayed put for the night. Around 7 P.M., Wood received a message from Wilson sent six hours earlier. The cavalryman was at Sugar Creek, some twenty miles from Pulaski, and reported that the Confederates had made a brief stand there before retreating. As soon as he crossed the creek, he would send a brigade to chop down trees and float them down the Tennessee in an effort to smash Hood's pontoon bridge.[14]

From civilians that night, Wilson learned that the bulk of the Confederate army was already across the Tennessee. If true, this was a disappointment, but Wilson still had an opportunity to scoop up Forrest and the enemy's rear guard, which would be a great consolation prize. Overnight on December 26–27, he and Hatch sent out a detachment of 500 picked men led by the ever-dependable Colonel Spalding to harass the Confederates south of Pulaski and try to intercept Forrest north of the river. The troopers were the best mounted men among regiments that had seen the least amount of work during the chase. Spalding would lead the column despite suffering a left knee wound in the December 16 cavalry fight with Rucker's force on the Granny White Pike. A Scottish immigrant who had come to America with his parents in 1843, he had been a school teacher in Monroe, Michigan, before the war. Now he was in the spotlight, trying to pin the notorious Forrest at the Tennessee until reinforcements could come up.[15]

TUESDAY, DECEMBER 27

Still waiting to hear from Hood, the Confederate high command was learning of Grierson's devastation at Verona and desperately trying to communicate with the lost Army of Tennessee. With Union cavalry knifing the Mobile & Ohio and now possibly aiming for Corinth, Hood had to be warned that his Mississippi supply lines were in peril and that he had to arrange for alternatives. The high command had no way of knowing that Hood was already aware of this peril.

After his Christmas night raid at Verona, Grierson continued his railroad wrecking over the next week, focusing on the line from Tupelo south to Okolona. A sharp little fight near the village of Egypt on December 28 highlighted this phase; Union forces overwhelmed a smaller Confederate force before resuming their destructive path to the southwest. By the time Grierson's men eventually reached Union-held Vicksburg on January 5, they had destroyed about 20,000 feet of bridges and trestles, ten miles of track, twenty miles of telegraph lines, four locomotives, and almost 100 railcars, and thirty warehouses packed with supplies, as well as factories, wagons, machine shops, depots, and military ordnance. This was a potentially crippling blow to the already tenuous Confederate rail system in the region, the huge loss of supplies multiplying the many obstacles Hood faced. The Confederates had bit on Grierson's feint toward Corinth and, on that Tuesday, still believed it was one of the Union's main objectives. At this point, however, there was little Hood could do, other than rely on reserve and garrison troops to repel the marauders.[16]

After resting—and finally eating—in camp the previous day, the IV Corps stepped off at 6 A.M., with Kimball's division leading Elliott's and Beatty's divisions. Wood had received a message that morning from Thomas stating that he should "push on and support the cavalry as fast as you can and drive the rebels into the Tennessee." By 10 A.M., the corps had reached the intersection of the Lamb's Ferry and Powell Roads and followed the cavalry toward Lexington. By early afternoon, Wood and his staff reached the cavalry chief's headquarters at Pinhook Town, about two miles beyond another branch of Sugar Creek. Wilson told Wood that he believed Hood's army—or at least most of it—had crossed the river at Bainbridge and that he had sent out patrols, in addition to Spalding's raiders, to determine if this was true.[17]

After conferring with Wilson, Wood sent a dispatch to Thomas at 1:30, telling him that the Confederates were likely over the river. Cavalry patrols had been sent out on various roads, and if this was accurate, the infantry would halt and await orders. Within the hour, the main column of infantry had reached Sugar Creek after a day's march "over the worst road that, perhaps, an army ever marched," according to Colonel Fullerton. The cavalry was camped on the south side of the stream, preventing any further movement.[18]

Meanwhile, Spalding's force was nearing Lexington and closing fast on the enemy. A few miles away, Walthall's infantry reached Shoal Creek after noon and waded over, taking positions to guard the ford there until ordered to withdraw. The rear-guard cavalry passed them there later in the day, moving on toward the Tennessee River. While at the creek, command of Walthall's two divisions reverted to Stewart in line with Hood's instructions.[19]

From Tuscumbia at 3 P.M., Hood sent word to Stewart that General Bate had established batteries south of the river to protect the bridge, thus allowing Stewart to withdraw the artillery posted north of the Tennessee. Also near the river about this time, Cockrell's Brigade of French's Division in Stewart's command rejoined the army. In the advance on Nashville after Franklin, Hood had ordered this brigade, commanded by Col. Peter C. Flournoy, to the mouth of the Duck River near Johnsonville, thus inadvertently sparing it from the disaster. Among Stewart's units that had *not* been spared disaster was the 1st Missouri Battery. Samuel Dunlap and his comrades had camped by the roadside overnight to rest their worn-out horses and moved out in the rain early Tuesday—the road as rough and muddy as ever. But the men were rejuvenated by the fact that they were only a few miles from the river.[20]

Elsewhere, the Federal navy regrouped at Chickasaw and was joined that day by transports with provisions for Thomas's troops. Admiral Lee made another effort to reach the Confederate army, but had to back off again, this time because of the river's dropping water level. Aboard his flagship, *Fairy*, Lee dispatched Thomas that he had been unable to reach Hood's pontoons.[21]

During the day, Wilson sent a rider under a truce flag to try to reach Hood with a copy of a dispatch from Washington about Sherman reaching the Georgia coast and preparing to capture Savannah. Annoyed by Confederate prisoners and deserters who boasted of Sherman's rumored destruction, Wilson wrote to Hood, "This is done that you may furnish the troops of your command more recent, as well as more reliable intelligence concerning operations in Georgia than that imparted to them during the late campaign in Tennessee." Based on time, distance, and road conditions, the messenger would not have had enough time to reach the Confederate army before it completed its crossing.[22]

Meanwhile, Spalding's strike force clattered through Lexington before 2 P.M., sending word to Wilson that the Confederate rear guard had left the hamlet about four hours earlier. Hatch's cavalry also rode through Lexington that day, still in need of rations. A civilian told Spalding's Federals that the Confederates were at Bainbridge, but had not completed the pontoon bridge by Christmas night, and were fortified to hold the crossing point. Union gunboats also were reportedly shelling Florence. Spalding was on the move toward the river shortly thereafter. When this information reached Wilson at Pinhook Town at 6 P.M., he updated Thomas and Wood, telling the latter, "At all events we had better push on as far and as fast as possible. I shall move everything, beginning at 5 A.M." Based on this, Wood sent word to Thomas that he would follow Wilson's advance on the morning of the twenty-eighth as fast as road conditions allowed. He again emphasized the necessity of bringing up rations and forage and asked for instructions if and when the infantry reached the Tennessee.[23]

From the IV Corps artillery park that night, Maj. Wilbur F. Goodspeed, Wood's artillery chief, sent word to headquarters that his horses would eat their last forage the next morning, having only been issued a ten-day supply (six pounds per animal per day) when operations began at Nashville on December 14. Certainly, the quartermaster could not have anticipated such a strung-out pursuit, but the artillerists had been unable to gather much fodder along the way. Wood dispatched a courier to Thomas with this information, adding that if he pushed ahead to the river, he would do so without artillery or ammunition wagons as the cavalry had exhausted the scant provisions in the area.[24]

A. J. Smith's veterans had reached Pulaski that day, and Thomas sent Wilson a dispatch at 5 P.M. that Smith would move southwest early on the twenty-eighth to try to reach the Tennessee at Eastport, Mississippi, in an attempt to cut off the Confederates. Despite being well behind the advance, Smith's men had continued to pass the Confederates' wreckage between Columbia and Pulaski. "All along the route were strewn the numerous evidences of the hasty and panic-stricken manner in which the demoralized rebel army retreated," an officer in the 95th Illinois observed. "Broken firearms, knapsacks and burdensome clothing had been abandoned by the foe in his precipitous flight, and were the sure indications of his terrible discomfiture."[25]

Still, Thomas's chase was running out of time and steam. Admiral Lee's effort had fizzled. Steedman's division had reached Decatur that Tuesday, occupying the town after a brief fight ousted the few Confederates holding the place. He was a few days too late, however, to recapture the vital pontoons that Cobb's engineers had floated downriver. Steedman immediately prepared to march west toward Tuscumbia and assail Hood, but he also had heard rumors that the Confederates were already over the river.

A. J. Smith.

With most of the army over the Tennessee, Cheatham's men trudged through Tuscumbia and camped in the mud that night near Cane Creek, about ten miles from town. Leaving Reynolds's Arkansans to hold Shoal Creek, the rest of Walthall's brigades moved out at about 10 P.M., marching to the Tennessee and occupying defensive works covering the bridge that "the rear division of the army had just withdrawn." Around midnight, Forrest's bedraggled cavalry began to cross the buckling bridge, with orders to dismount and lead the horses over. The span was "a frail looking affair," noted Trooper Charles G. Joy of the 14th Tennessee, "as if it were nothing but inch boards laid on top of the water." Among Ross's Texans was Sergeant John Long, who had been shot through both thighs. Refusing to leave him behind, his comrades had bandaged his wounds with a sack, fed him honey, and rigged a makeshift sidesaddle so that he could stay with them. Nursing a sprained ankle, A. C. McLeary of the 12th Tennessee Cavalry remained in the saddle, the crossing surpassing any of his earlier experiences: "The river was bank full, the bridge in a swing, jumping up and down. My eyes being up above the rest, the lights on the bank in front blinded me like a bat. It seemed to be the widest river in the world."[26]

WEDNESDAY, DECEMBER 28

Spalding's rough-riding raiders had spurred hard for the Tennessee through the night and early morning, but were a few hours too late. The Union men reined up on the north bank just as the pontoon had been swung to the south bank and the last Confederates disappeared in the distance.

Forrest had crossed the rest of the rear guard overnight on December 27–28, and Walthall's infantry had started over the bridge at daybreak, led by Featherston's troops. The brigades of Feild and Palmer followed Featherston; Reynolds's soldiers left their positions at Shoal Creek in time to reach the river by sunup and went across after Palmer. Some of Feild's infantry, Tennesseans from Strahl's Brigade, approached the bridge proudly riding Union cavalry horses they had taken at Sugar

Creek Their glee met reality when stoic guards at the span stopped them, asking to what command they belonged. Answering that they were with Cheatham, one of the sentries grumbled the reply, "Get down off that horse." The men complied with this "woeful order," as one of them described it, returning to their roles as foot soldiers.[27]

Reynolds left some skirmishers in place at the creek for about half an hour in case any Federals appeared, but these men withdrew before Spalding arrived. Ector's Brigade, led by Col. David Coleman of the 39th North Carolina, covered the rest of the rear guard's crossing before going over as well. As the last of Coleman's skirmishers trotted across, Presstman's engineers—with about 200 soldiers whom Walthall had assigned to assist them—retrieved the bridge. "Every wagon, every cannon, every horse, every mule, the hogs, beeves, cavalry, infantry, and finally every scout crossed over," Colonel Gale of Stewart's staff wrote to his wife. Tired and disappointed, Spalding still had lived up to his reputation along the way, bedeviling the Confederates, who abandoned more ambulances, wagons, and caissons, and taking more prisoners, most of them stragglers.[28]

South of the Tennessee, the rear guard was almost immediately dissolved without pomp or circumstance, and the infantry brigades returned to their respective corps. Forrest turned his worn-out cavalry toward Corinth, with Hood's approval, since that region offered the best chance of getting forage and rations. "The campaign was full of trial and suffering, but the troops under my command, both cavalry and infantry, submitted to every hardship with an uncomplaining patriotism," Forrest later reported.[29]

Wilson was at Blue Water Creek when he received the disappointing dispatch from Spalding around 4 P.M. with word of the Confederate escape. His troopers had plowed ahead some six miles south of Lexington in their continuing chase, but were still about ten miles from Bainbridge. The bad roads would prevent his couriers from reaching Thomas with the news until almost twenty-four hours later. Like Wilson, the

Union infantry had started the day in pursuit mode. From his bivouac on the Lexington Road, Wood issued orders for the IV Corps to march at 8 A.M. if the horsemen were out of the way, with Elliott leading, followed by Beatty and Kimball. As usual, the infantry had been irritatingly delayed by the cavalry, and when the foot soldiers did step off at 10 A.M., they made slow progress in the muddy mess. Much of the day, the Federals continued to pass the ruins of the foe. "It were scarcely an hyperbole to say that the road from Pulaski to Lexington was bottomless when we passed over it," Wood noted. "It was strewn with the wrecks of wagons, artillery carriages, and other material abandoned by the enemy in his flight."[30]

Still, by 3:15 P.M., Wood's forces had advanced more than a mile beyond Lexington, after marching almost twelve miles and catching up with Wilson's rear echelon. "The country through which we are passing is barren and desolate," Fullerton noted, "there are also many swamp flats. . . . The cavalry has been in our way all day and we now overlap the rear brigade of the same." Unable to proceed further, the infantry encamped. Sundown brought yet more cruel cold, which would become a hard freeze overnight.[31]

At this point, the Union infantry also was suffering greatly from the wearing nature of the chase. "The roads over which, or rather through which, we had been obliged to march, were as bad as the world ever saw," recalled L. W. Day of the 101st Ohio. An Illinois officer in Smith's corps watched men of the 44th Missouri marching barefoot on a frozen road, noting that "there were similar instances in every regiment. . . . Many a soldier could be seen tramping along . . . while the very blood reddened his footprints on the snowy ground."[32]

Hood remained at Tuscumbia on the twenty-eighth, still wary of possible enemy attempts to attack him south of the Tennessee. His army was spread nearby, and there were some instances of looting by the hungry, destitute soldiers. To quell this, the survivors of Granbury's Brigade were posted as a provost guard, rewarded with an issue of fresh pork, which the men washed down with liquor. The Memphis & Charleston

Railroad still had not been extended to Tuscumbia from the vicinity of Barton Station, meaning few, if any, supplies were trickling in; little had changed since the Confederates' grand departure a few weeks earlier.

Desertion continued its feverish plague. General Chalmers complained that his cavalry had been steadily weakened since their stand on the Granny White Pike likely saved the army: "After that time, while there were many who continued to exhibit the same courage and constancy, I regret to say that there were some who so far forgot their duty as to desert their comrades and seek an ignominious safety in flight." Following the rail line, Cheatham's troops left Cane Creek and marched past Barton Station to Bear Creek, which they found too deep to cross without pontoons. They had managed sixteen miles that day.[33]

Thomas was at Pulaski when he finally received word of Sherman's capture of Savannah and the end of his destructive sweep to the Atlantic. He sent orders to Nashville that day to have 100 guns in the fortifications fired in honor of Sherman's triumphs. Still unaware that Hood had crossed the Tennessee, Thomas had much confidence that his pursuit with cavalry, infantry and gunboats also would end in a similarly grand victory: "Nothing but the impassible condition of the roads will prevent us from capturing his entire army."[34]

Thomas also sent a message to Wood, stating that the IV Corps should "keep pushing" in support of the cavalry. At 7 P.M., Wood, headquartered for the night in Lexington, received word that his wagons were stalled some five miles to his rear. Shortly afterward, a message arrived from Wilson, reiterating the information that Hood was across the Tennessee. Wilson also had sent a staff officer to Thomas with the same news. Wood relayed this intelligence to Thomas as well, adding that "it is no use to move farther as a matter of pursuit" and that "we will wait here in our present camp for further orders."[35]

By 10 P.M., Thomas was writing Halleck that Wilson and Wood were still pressing the Confederates' rear guard, although he suspected they were already across the river.

Thomas also had reports that the navy was shelling Florence, and wounded Confederate prisoners at Pulaski had told the Federals that Hood likely would retreat as far as Meridian, in south-central Mississippi. He told Halleck that he would dog the enemy south of the Tennessee "if the roads are at all practicable." At this point, Thomas believed Hood would withdraw toward Talladega, Alabama, where he would be better able to protect Confederate strongholds at Montgomery and Selma.[36]

At some point on Wednesday, Thomas received a dispatch from Steedman regarding Decatur's capture. In response, Thomas told him the Confederate army had reportedly crossed at Lamb's Ferry and Bainbridge "with what force he could get off." He added that the enemy "is represented as being in [the] most deplorable condition" and that he would try to intercept Hood at Iuka, Mississippi, between Tuscumbia and Corinth. Steedman was to push west from Decatur in case the Confederates retreated toward the southeast in the direction of Courtland and Moulton, Alabama. "The roads from here to Florence are in an almost impassable condition, and the country so completely devastated that we can scarcely get any supplies," Thomas told Steedman, "but the enemy has been as vigorously pursued as circumstances will admit." Meanwhile, Steedman had taken the initiative to move toward Courtland that afternoon to try to find Hood. His cavalry, about 600 troopers led by Col. William J. Palmer, banged into a screen of Confederate horsemen less than five miles out, shoving them back about a mile to a position where the Confederates had posted two cannon. It was after dark by then, and the Federals quickly cracked this line. The gunners fired a few shots before fleeing, leaving the two 12-pounders in the hands of a sergeant and fifteen men of the 15th Pennsylvania Cavalry.[37]

While "Old Pap" tried to determine if the enemy had truly escaped, word was filtering slowly back through the Union army that Hood had eluded them. There was some disappointment, despite the crushing victory in the campaign, that the job had not been finished. No commander expressed his frustration more openly than Wilson, who would later blame Admiral Lee for not shutting the trap door. While the desperate Confederates had managed to navigate the captured pontoons downriver from Decatur to Bainbridge despite the Muscle Shoals hazards, Lee had been unwilling to attempt a break-through at the other end to snare Hood. He also lamented the absence of McCook's two cavalry brigades that had been sent after Lyon's raiders in Kentucky; Wilson claimed that the race would have ended in a great victory if these 3,000 troopers had been with him. In reality, with the limited rations and forage available to the cavalry, not to mention the road conditions, these additional troopers and mounts might actually have hindered the chase—unless they had helped close off the turn-pikes in the precious hours after Hood's initial rout.[38]

In Tuscumbia, Stewart issued orders for his corps to move at sunrise on the twenty-ninth, passing through the town and marching for Iuka. Walthall would lead, followed by Loring, who assigned two regiments as a rear guard. The corps trains would move ahead of the troops. "Having the river between us & the enemy [we] felt very much relieved," remembered Samuel Dunlap, whose battery had crossed the Tennessee with other elements of Stewart's artillery. "We 'high privates' could have enjoyed an extended rest—but our officers thought [it] best to move on."[39]

CHAPTER 13

"We Could Eat Our Oysters in Mobile"

THURSDAY, DECEMBER 29

Realizing that its prey likely had escaped, the Union army spent much of the morning quietly resting and cleaning up in its camps strung out for miles along the boggy roads north of the Tennessee, uncertain of what to expect.

With his supply wagons and other trains mired in the muck well to the rear, General Wood, still at Lexington, issued orders at 7 A.M. for his division and battery commanders to send out "large foraging parties to get whatever corn there may be in the country." During the night, his men had found enough subsistence in the area to feed the corps' horses and mules for one day, but much more would be needed based on present circumstances. Around noon, Wood received a dispatch from Thomas, written the day before, to send his artillery back to Pulaski so that the animals could be fed. Wood also was instructed to hold his infantry in position, "ready to move in whatever direction they may be required." Wood sent his pioneer troops out to try to repair the road behind him so that his guns could reach Pulaski. Still, since the campaign situation had changed dramatically in such a short time and Thomas's order was a day old, Wood wanted clarification from his commander. He sent a message to Thomas at 3 P.M., asking whether, in light of developments, he should still return his artillery to Pulaski. If he had heard nothing by the following night, he would start the guns to the rear.[1]

That afternoon, Thomas finally verified that the Confederates were over the river and that the navy had been unable to reach the bridge. He ordered the pursuit to cease immediately. Hood had slipped the noose, but there was still no other way to describe this campaign except as a monumental Union triumph that had vanquished one of the Confederacy's two principal armies. If he was disappointed at all, Thomas did not reveal it, instead focusing on all that had been accomplished. In orders issued later in the day, he announced the end of the campaign—at least temporarily—because of the Confederates' exodus. In General Orders, Number 169, Thomas told his soldiers that the "flying and dispirited enemy" had been driven beyond the Tennessee and that the "impassable state of the roads and consequent impossibility to supply the army" compelled a halt of operations.[2]

Thomas also responded that day to Admiral Lee's report about being unable to reach Hood's crossing point, but there were no harsh words for the navy: "Your efficient cooperation on the Tennessee River has contributed largely to the demoralization of Hood's army." From the *Fairy*, the admiral updated Thomas that Confederate work parties were building a battery on the heights overlooking Eastport and that he was "annoying" them. Lee added, "The river has fallen so low that Hood can cross above without interruption from [the] navy."[3]

With his army seemingly out of immediate danger beyond the Tennessee, Hood still faced the catastrophe of the widespread railroad destruction wrought by Grierson's marauders. This was a potentially severe setback to feeding and clothing his army, and his staff frantically explored the remote possibilities of having supplies brought up by wagon train from northern Alabama. An already terrible situation was prevented from worsening, however, by two industrious officers, Col. J. C. Cole, who commanded infantry reserves in northeastern Mississippi, and Maj. George Whitfield, who was responsible for military rail traffic in the region. Bridges on the Mobile & Ohio were still smoldering from Grierson's torches when Whitfield and Cole impressed work gangs to rebuild them, pushing the men at a torrid pace. Within six days of Grierson's strike, supply trains, though few in number, were again able to reach Corinth.[4]

Hood decided to leave Tuscumbia for Corinth on Thursday, but he and his staff were forced to remain at the railroad's terminus west of town late into the night until a train arrived on the Memphis & Charleston. The last of the army, Stewart's rear guard, left the town around 1 P.M., heading west. Hood's cars reached the hamlet of Burnsville, Mississippi, the next evening, December 30, passing a cheerless New Year's Day there before leaving by rail for Corinth early on January 2. In the mud along Bear Creek, Cheatham's weary men readied timbers for a pontoon bridge and crossed some wagons on the railroad span as they watched for the boats to come up. It would be a long wait.[5]

At Lexington, General Wood was concerned about reports of a guerrilla band, about 100 strong, operating near Wise's Mill, along Blue Water Creek, six miles west of the town. These marauders were said to be well mounted and well armed and could cause trouble. Wood sent word to Wilson about this force, adding that he would send some infantry to deal with it the next morning. Also that day, Wood received orders from Thomas "that the pursuit cease" and that he should prepare to march to the vicinity of Huntsville and Athens, Alabama, where he would go into winter quarters and gird for a spring campaign. Most of the cavalry was being sent there for the winter. Schofield and the XXIII Corps received orders that day to march to Dalton, Georgia, where they would winter, while the objective of Smith's corps was still Eastport. Wilson that afternoon dispatched Thomas that all his information led to the conclusion that Hood's army was headed for Corinth.[6]

Despite being unable to pocket Hood, it had been a dazzling, if exhausting, few weeks for Union arms in Tennessee—and much worse for the Confederates. Henry Stone of Thomas's staff wrote after the war, "About a month before, General Hood had triumphantly begun his northward movement. Now, in his disastrous retreat, he was leaving behind him, as prisoners or deserters, a larger number of men than General Thomas had been able to place at Pulaski to hinder his advance—to say nothing of his terrific losses in killed at Franklin. . . . At so small a cost, counting the chances of war, the whole Northwest was saved from an invasion that, if Hood had succeeded, would have more than neutralized all Sherman's successes in Georgia and the Carolinas."[7] According to an Illinois officer, "The history of the war will not present an army worse beaten, cut up and disorganized then was Hood's army at that time."[8]

It had been some three months since that September day in Macon when Jefferson Davis predicted a Union debacle and retreat resembling Napoleon's withdrawal from Moscow. Now there *had* been such a military disaster—on a smaller scale certainly—but Davis had picked the wrong army. "The prediction of Jefferson Davis had indeed come to pass," stated one Northern account. "There was a Moscow retreat. But it was of the Confederate, not of the national army."[9]

The Army of Tennessee had been shattered, its leadership as well as its ranks, decimated by casualties and desertion, its blood nourishing the landscape of Franklin, Nashville and the torn-up roads from Shy's Hill to Bainbridge. That night, Thomas sent a telegram to Washington, informing his superiors of the end of the chase. Within hours, Grant and Halleck agreed that the pursuit should resume as quickly as possible.

FRIDAY, DECEMBER 30
While the Union brass digested the news of Thomas's decision, at least one of Hood's tormentors remained eager to resume the hunt south of the Tennessee. Realizing the enemy's dire condition, Wood pressed for an extended offensive to regain the rest of Alabama, using the river as a base of operations before the frazzled Confederates could regroup. From Lexington that day, he wrote Thomas that he was "confident that his [Hood's] command cannot be reorganized for service for some weeks, perhaps not before spring" and that "the whole country from the Tennessee River to Mobile is open to us. . . .

I have no hesitation in saying that we could eat our oysters in Mobile in forty days from the date of departure."[10]

Wood had formed an accurate description of the Confederate rank and file based on his own observations, descriptions from civilians during Hood's retreat, and reports from two Federals who had escaped from the Confederates near the Tennessee. One of these soldiers stated that he had been among Lee's troops, not more than half of whom were still armed, and that "there was no organization at all in the corps." He said that from Pulaski to the point where he escaped, the enemy had nothing to eat but parched corn. The other Union soldier had traveled with Cheatham's Corps and saw only "occasionally a musket or two to shoot cattle, &c., along the line of retreat." Wood concluded that "for rout, demoralization, even disintegration, the condition of his [Hood's] command is without parallel in this war."[11]

In Lexington, the first of the mud-caked wagons bearing three days' rations for the IV Corps' infantry creaked into town just after 11 A.M. Wood immediately ordered his division commanders to stretch the food over five days. Serviceable wagons were in such demand that the rations were to be unloaded immediately so that they could be returned to Pulaski to help convey sick and wounded to the rear. At the cavalry camp on Blue Water Creek, a staff officer sent by Wilson to Florence to try to contact the navy had returned without finding Admiral Lee, who had steamed farther downstream. Colonel Spalding also had seen the silent Confederate defenses guarding the pontoon bridge site. Based on all the information he could gather, Wilson believed the Confederates were headed for Corinth and would winter there.[12]

In Richmond that Friday, anxiety heightened over the fate of Hood's army. There had been no official word from Tennessee or the government, and the Northern papers continued to crow over what they described as a paralyzing Confederate defeat at Nashville and the agonies inflicted on Hood in the pursuit south. The *Richmond Daily Dispatch*, however, took issue with the one-sided reports: "For our own part, we have arrived at the conclusion that the bulletins of Thomas are a tissue of lies, such as nobody but a Yankee, unless it be a renegade, could possibly weave together—that Hood has received no serious check, although he has been compelled to relinquish the siege of Nashville as a work above his strength—that his army is not only existent still, but existent in such a condition that it is able to set Thomas at defiance, who dares not attack him upon his retreat."[13]

At Charleston, Beauregard was preparing to head west to find the Army of Tennessee. He had not yet heard back from Jefferson Davis regarding his Christmas Day recommendation of replacing Hood with Richard Taylor if needed. He would send another dispatch to Davis on the thirty-first, this time asking for authorization to appoint Taylor to army command "should I find its [the army's] condition such as to require a change." Beauregard would leave Charleston on January 2 on what would be a circuitous route to Tupelo because of the Confederacy's ramshackle railroads.[14]

In Washington, Halleck was displeased with Thomas for calling the halt. He wrote to Grant at City Point that afternoon: "I think from the tone of General Thomas' telegram that there is very little hope of his doing much further injury to Hood's army by pursuing it. You will perceive that he is disposed to postpone further operations till spring. This seems to me entirely wrong. . . . If Thomas was as active as Sherman, I would say march directly from Decatur" into the Alabama interior, "living upon the country. . . . But I think Thomas entirely too slow to live on the country." As usual, Grant also was not satisfied with Thomas. "I have no idea of keeping idle troops in any place, but before taking troops away from Thomas it will be advisable to see whether Hood halts his army at Corinth," Grant wrote to Halleck. "I do not think he will, but think he is much more likely to be thrown in front of Sherman; if so, it will be just where we want him to go."[15]

That night, Thomas wired Halleck that, based on information from Wilson, it appeared Hood was moving to Corinth. Believing this to be true, Thomas had ordered the cavalry to

Eastport, where it could easily attack the already-devastated Mobile & Ohio and be within close striking distance of Corinth. Indeed, Croxton's troopers were expected to reach Eastport that afternoon and, in the coming days, were to try to destroy the railroad bridge at Bear Creek, where Cheatham's soldiers awoke that morning. Smith also was to concentrate at Eastport, while Wood's corps still would go to Huntsville. Thomas also decided to send Schofield's men to Eastport rather than Dalton, based on the direction Hood had taken. Orders also were sent to have forage for the entire cavalry corps shipped to Eastport, along with shoes and other clothing. Smith's corps was on the move that day in the vicinity of Lawrenceburg, marching south. Thomas sent Smith orders that if he found Hood at Corinth and had sufficient cavalry support, he had permission to launch an attack. Still, the Federals believed, even if Hood halted at Corinth, he would not be able to remain there very long, since Grierson had wrecked much of the railroad south of the town, leaving it all but isolated.[16]

Wilson immediately set about trying to improve and replenish his command. In a lengthy letter to Thomas, he requested a base camp north of the Tennessee, where he could be easily supplied by steamboat and still menace the enemy at various points, and a period of seventy to ninety days to "perfect" his corps. Wilson asked for 15,000 Spencer carbines and 10,000 horses, hoping to strengthen his corps to 25,000 men.[17]

Union forces continued to be hindered by a lack of pontoons. Two spans were in place at the Duck River while a trestle bridge was being constructed there, but there were few boats, if any, at the front, even if Thomas had wanted to make an immediate crossing of the Tennessee. From Nashville, Major Willett sent word that Friday that a pontoon train of sixty boats would be ready to leave on the thirty-first, but Thomas ordered them to remain there until further orders. One of the Duck spans was to be packed up and hurried forward immediately.[18]

Along the mucky banks of Bear Creek, Cheatham's Confederates were stuck in a similar waiting game. With no pontoons forthcoming, Cheatham began moving his corps at daylight on the railroad bridge over the stream. At some point during the preparations or the actual crossing, these soldiers watched the train carrying Hood and his staff chug past en route to Burnsville. The Confederates were across by 2 P.M. and, following the railroad past Iuka, encamped that night about five miles from Burnsville after covering only about twelve miles. "Our movements were very slow—because of rough, mudy [*sic*] road & bad condition of stock," the Missouri artilleryman Samuel Dunlap wrote that day. If the Tennessee presented somewhat of a barrier to any major Union attacks, it did not protect the Confederates from rain, sleet, and snow.[19]

Pontoons also were on the mind of Colonel Palmer, Steedman's cavalry chief, who had located Hood's five-mile-long pontoon train trundling south through the Alabama countryside, apparently well away from the main Confederate army. Palmer was near the village of Leighton, about thirteen miles west of Courtland, and was preparing for an overnight ride to catch the unsuspecting enemy column early on Saturday. He had reports that some of Forrest's cavalry was in the vicinity, however, and sent a request to Steedman that afternoon for infantry support. Steedman, who was at Courtland with the main body, replied before sunset that the infantry could not reach Palmer in time and that Palmer should use his best judgment regarding the strike. If Thomas had halted, the hunt was far from over for Palmer's troopers and the sleepy Confederate teamsters in their carbine sights.[20]

SATURDAY, DECEMBER 31

At Burnsville on a depressing New Year's Eve, Hood issued a circular to his corps commanders with orders for the disposition of the army. Lee's Corps was to march for Rienzi, Mississippi, on the Mobile & Ohio, first repairing a swampy road between Rienzi and Burnsville and then working on the road between Rienzi and Tupelo. Cheatham's objective was Corinth, where he was to repair the dirt road from there to Rienzi, while Stewart was to remain in the Iuka-Burnsville area, upgrading the roads and sending wagons along upper Bear Creek to gather forage. "Keep your pickets out toward the Tennessee," Hood warned Stewart.[21]

Around sundown that day, Palmer's cavalry hit the Confederate pontoon train near Russellville, Alabama, about twenty miles south of Tuscumbia. Yipping Union soldiers galloped along the length of the long column, shooting at startled wagoners and hacking at the traces of spooked teams. Based on orders from Hood, the Confederate wagons had been moving toward Columbus, Mississippi, where, it was hoped, there would be forage for the animals. Palmer's men brushed aside Roddey's Confederate cavalry escort after weak resistance and torched the 200 vehicles and 78 pontoon boats. The destruction lasted until 3 A.M. the next day. Learning that a Confederate supply train also was in the area, Palmer rode to attack it as well, surprising this column in camp the next night in Itawamba County, Mississippi, a few miles across the state line. The Union men burned about 110 wagons and sabered or shot 500 mules. In one of the wagons, they found a wounded enemy colonel, whom Palmer left there with a tent, some supplies, and a prisoner to care for him. Palmer then turned back with approximately 200 prisoners taken during the brief raid, reaching Decatur on January 6 after a round-trip ride of some 250 miles with the loss of one killed and two wounded. Thomas credited Palmer with striking "the last blow of the campaign," "a most crushing defeat—almost an annihilation," while Hood was left to report Roddey's "inefficiency."[22]

From Washington that morning, Halleck fired a verbal salvo at Thomas, telling him that the campaign against Hood was to be renewed in short order: "Lieutenant-General Grant does not intend that your army should go into winter quarters. It must be ready for active operations in the field." Thomas also was to forward information about Hood's line of retreat "so that orders may be given for a continuance of the campaign." In another dispatch to Thomas that afternoon, Halleck informed him of Grierson's raid on the Mobile & Ohio. Thomas replied that night, telling Halleck that he was watching Hood closely and that his men and horses needed time to recuperate, refit, and reorganize. Nevertheless, his troops would soon be assembled at Eastport and Huntsville, awaiting orders. For the next two weeks, the Federals would gird to restart the campaign south of the Tennessee, provided Hood remained in the vicinity of Corinth and did not move farther south.[23]

In the wake of the chase, thousands of Federals were engaged in repairing roads, rebuilding bridges, and caring for the wounded of both sides since the running nature of the fight had presented logistical problems in dealing with casualties. With railroads fragmented at the time, corpsmen used ambulances to collect fallen soldiers along the line of march and take them to hospitals at Nashville, Franklin, Columbia, and Pulaski. In the latter three places, these Federals often were crowded in with numbers of Confederate wounded left behind by Hood. Wood's IV Corps had carried sick and wounded in ambulances until they reached proper hospital accommodations. As the chase lengthened, with the Tennessee & Alabama Railroad broken up by burned bridges, some of these men had been left in the care of medical officers with few supplies. Confederate corpsmen, left behind with the Confederate wounded, assisted their Union counterparts.[24]

CHAPTER 14

"Nothing but Gloom before Us": 1865

On New Year's morning, Richmond awoke to a few inches of snow to welcome 1865. There was little activity along the rival trenches stretching between Petersburg and the capital as church bells tolled. Most importantly that Sunday, there were rumors that Hood had turned on Thomas and defeated him. "This was believed by many," the War Department clerk John Jones wrote in his diary. Even the Northern newspapers seemed to have toned down their reports about the severity of the Confederate debacle. Based on what he knew, Jones believed that "Hood's army was not destroyed and he retreated with about 20,000 men, although he likely lost a lot of guns." By Monday, January 2, the street "croakers," as Jones called the gossips and complainers, were in full throat again with word that Hood was in northern Alabama with a great accumulation of supplies and that Thomas was possibly preparing to march to Virginia.[1]

At Pulaski, Thomas spent New Year's trying to confirm that Hood was marching for Corinth while attending to the details of his own troop buildup at Eastport and Huntsville. He was also dealing with the enlistment expirations for a number of regiments and preparing the Army of the Tennessee's reserve artillery, although it was much depleted in guns and other equipment, to be sent to Sherman if needed. General Steedman and his men were ordered to Chattanooga from Decatur, leaving a garrison at the latter place.

On January 2, Halleck wired Thomas that he was to continue trying to catch or bleed the Confederate army, but a troop concentration on the river would be a building block for a spring offensive, if needed. That night, Grant took a shot at Thomas's logistical planning—again filtered through Halleck—claiming that the Department of the Cumberland had always been wasteful in gathering and using mules and horses for its wagon trains.[2]

The same day, Thomas received reports that tended to confirm that Hood was bound for Corinth, but he telegraphed Halleck, "I can scarcely believe he will attempt to halt" there because of the damaged railroad south of the town. The Federals also mulled information from two civilians who had been in Tuscumbia when the Confederates passed through "in a deplorable condition." Thomas was in contact with Admiral Lee, arranging to have navy transports sent to Eastport "preparatory to a continuance of the campaign." About this time, Lee offered an explanation to Thomas about why he had been unable to reach the enemy's pontoon bridge, writing that "foggy weather and a rapidly falling river" were to blame. The admiral also basically admitted that he underestimated the Confederates and their need for desperate measures: "Bainbridge was not a regular ferry, and my clever pilot thought the water was too swift there for a crossing. Hood must have been sorely pushed to have resorted to such a place on the shoals." By January 4, Thomas had returned to Nashville to direct operations.[3]

Forrest met with Hood at Corinth on January 2 and was told that the Army of Tennessee would soon be sent to Augusta, Georgia, as reinforcements against Sherman, and that his cavalry would be left to hold this section of the country. Knowing the debilitated condition of his command, the frustrated Forrest returned to his headquarters and penned a dispatch to Richard Taylor: "I regret to say that the means at my disposal are not adequate to the task devolving upon me. My command is greatly reduced in numbers and efficiency by losses in battle and in the worn-down and unserviceable condition of animals." Forrest then gave his assessment of Hood's force: "The Army of Tennessee was badly defeated and is greatly demoralized, and to save it during the retreat from Nashville, I was compelled almost to sacrifice my command."[4]

From Corinth on January 3, Hood sent a message to Jefferson Davis asking for the authority to furlough his army's trans-Mississippi troops, one of his rare communications since Nashville. Lt. Col. J. P. Johnson of Hood's staff was on his way to Richmond to "explain to you the campaign in Tennessee." That same day, Hood dispatched a message to Beauregard and Secretary of War Seddon, telling them, "The army has recrossed the Tennessee River, without material loss since the battle in front of Nashville. It will be assembled in a few days in the vicinity of Tupelo." He stressed the need for the troops to rest and be refitted, adding that it was of "vital importance" that his trans-Mississippi soldiers be furloughed by units for 100 days.[5]

Cheatham reached Corinth on January 1 and encamped, trying to reassemble what was left of his corps. Among his troops was Olmstead's Brigade, which had served so well in Forrest's rear guard. "The conduct of men and officers in this trying retreat was admirable," Olmstead reported. "They bore the hardships forced upon them unflinchingly, and were ever ready to show a bold front on the approach of the enemy." Cheatham's men rested at Corinth for the next eight days, during which men combed their hair, shed their clothes, or cleaned them for the first time in weeks. Soldiers of the 63rd Georgia hired a woman to wash their underwear, which had not been changed in a month. They tried to apologize to her about the condition of these clothes, but she would have none of it, telling them, "I have washed some for Forrest's cavalry that was so stiffened with dirt that they were able to stand alone." One Georgian thought he had lost a calico handkerchief somewhere along the march. Peeling off his tattered uniform, he was surprised to find it plastered under the back of his vest.[6]

Lee's and Stewart's troops reached their destinations on January 2—Lee at the village of Rienzi, a few miles south of Corinth, and Stewart at Burnsville. These two corps were ordered to resume their march to Tupelo the next day.

The countryside between Corinth and Tupelo had been crisscrossed by both sides and fought over so much earlier in the war that Hood's men were marching through a grim time capsule, from the earthworks at Corinth to the battlefields of Brices Cross Roads and Booneville. Makeshift graveyards seemed to be everywhere, with most of the crude headboards carved with the names of Southern boys. One somber Confederate described the region as a vast cemetery where much of the Army of Tennessee was now mustered, its miserable survivors staggering toward a seemingly hopeless future. Another soldier, however, was more defiant: "It is true, the enemy has made some black marks through portions of the country, and left many monuments in the shape of smouldering ruins and houseless chimneys to remind us of his vandalism, but we are at Corinth again, and the rebellion is no nearer crushed."[7]

At Rienzi, the lack of forage drove a frustrated General Chalmers to write Forrest on January 3, urging him to move the cavalry farther into the Mississippi interior. One of Chalmers's troopers, Pvt. Emmett Hughes of the 7th Tennessee, wrote home the next day: "I send you these few lines to let you know that I am unwell and barefooted and [have] no chance to get anything. . . . Sister this has been one of the hardest trips that is on record. I am broke down my horse broke down sick & six men left our company last night. Their [sic] is only ten men with the company [Company E] and forty-seven with the regiment. We were expext [sic] to be sent home any day until this morning and we learn the Yankees are crossing Tenn river as we have to stay here to see what they are doing if they advance we are going to fight them."[8]

More than 230 miles from Nashville, Hood established headquarters at Tupelo on January 5 and set about to stitch together his ripped-apart army. But the slaughter at Franklin, the collapse at Nashville, and the inhumane conditions of the retreat to the Tennessee and beyond were too much to bear. Having to deal with the quirky logistics of pontoon crossings at the Harpeth, Duck, and Tennessee Rivers while staving off the Federals and holding together the remnants of a beaten army

Richard Taylor.

were no minor achievements—especially that winter—but none of this mattered as the Confederates tried to get food, rest, shoes, and blankets. In six weeks, the Army of Tennessee had fought two major battles and marched some 500 miles. Amid this surreal fog of fatigue and defeat, Hood oddly still refused to send a detailed report about the disaster, and it would be almost a month after the Nashville debacle before the Richmond government learned of the extent of the calamity.[9]

En route to Hood's army, Beauregard had reached Augusta, Georgia, by January 3 when he received authorization from Davis to replace Hood with Richard Taylor if circumstances justified the change. By the sixth, Beauregard had progressed only to Macon, where he received Hood's messages, sent on the third, about recrossing the Tennessee and regrouping the army at Tupelo. The dispatches offered Beauregard "a gleam of comfort" that rumors of Hood's catastrophe had been exaggerated, but Hood still was providing scant details. And Beauregard was strongly opposed to Hood's intent to furlough the trans-Mississippi troops at a time when all soldiers were needed in the ranks. He sent word to Seddon about the proposal. Even so, with no better idea of Hood's reality, Beauregard continued his trek over the broken railroads and boggy winter roads to see for himself.[10]

Not to be outdone by Sherman, who offered Savannah as a Christmas gift to President Lincoln, Thomas got into the act on January 5 with his Nashville war trophies. "The Army of the Cumberland takes a hand in sending Christmas presents," the *New York Times* reported four days later, "and tenders the President and the people of the United States 10,000 rebel prisoners, and sixty-eight pieces of artillery." Wilson was also in a giving mood. He and the cavalry had been encamped near the hamlet of Pinhook Town since December 28, bored and with little to eat. Some Nashville newspapers reached them with news of Sherman's capture of Savannah. "This suggested to one of the staff that we should present the city of Pinhook, 'with all its dependencies and resources,' to Lincoln as a New Year's gift," Wilson recalled. The staff officers amused themselves with mock dispatches to this effect, anything to relieve the melancholy of being in such a cold, desolate place during the holidays. "It was a grim and cheerless sort of fun, but there were no holiday dinners, no steaming hot punch, and no revelry for those dreary days," Wilson remembered. Troopers found enough corn to keep the horses alive, and Wood's infantry was bivouacked within supporting distance, but the roads were impossible and the countryside too destitute to allow any of them to remain here very long. Wood told Wilson that it took a double team twelve hours to pull an army wagon six miles.[11]

January also saw Thomas officially promoted to major general in the Regular army, to date from the first day of the Battle of Nashville. The old "Rock of Chickamauga" also could enjoy his new nickname, the "Sledge of Nashville," as the newspapers called him. Yet the bickering and animosity still lingered. Sherman had favored a thrust by Thomas into middle and southern Alabama, but Grant did not think Thomas was equal to the task. Thomas himself opposed a winter campaign because of the uncertainty of Hood's intent as well as the terrible road conditions.

If Grant and others believed Thomas had been sluggish in his pursuit, Thomas's proponents contended that the chase was deflated by a lack of supplies in an already war-ravaged countryside, as well as by flooded creeks and rivers and the fact that the pontoniers of Buell's 58th Indiana had been sent to Sherman. Given the conditions, which Grant was not totally aware of at the time, it is hard to imagine any other Union army doing any better to catch Hood, especially with the high-voltage Wilson as the lance tip, looking to slash his own glory in the headlines. Thomas's troops had fought a pitched two-day battle before immediately embarking on an unexpected race to the Tennessee amid some of the worst weather of the war.

Nevertheless, preparations were underway in the first week of January to resume the offensive south of the Mississippi, on the premise that Hood was concentrating at Corinth. In January's first week, the Federals also needed to rest and be refitted with even the most basic needs, such as shoes and clothing. At

Huntsville on January 5, Wood ordered Elliott to send an infantry regiment back to Pulaski to escort the corps' artillery and wagons south. These troops were to take five days' rations with them but "leave behind in camp all barefooted men and those who cannot make the march."[12]

By late December and early January 1865, what was left of a hopeful Confederate public—not to mention the government in Richmond—was still trying to learn exactly what happened to Hood's army, even though Northern newspapers were trumpeting a major Union victory. As days passed without claims of a Confederate victory in Tennessee, the despondency of yet another calamity set in. "We have a hope that it will turn out that Hood, though obliged to retreat . . . did so in good order and without sustaining even as great a loss . . . as the enemy," the *Richmond Daily Dispatch* reported on December 28.[13] The following day, the *Richmond Sentinel* acknowledged that Hood had retreated, based on Northern accounts, but that the Confederates had not been routed as the Union claimed. A panicked army would have moved more rapidly, and Thomas's pursuit would have covered more ground than was mentioned in the Union army reports, the paper reasoned.[14]

By about January 8, it was obvious to the Federals that the Confederates had left Corinth and gone farther south to Tupelo. When it was learned that the remnants of the Army of Tennessee would likely soon be sent east to help oppose Sherman, the Union brass altered its plans for Thomas's forces. In fact, the army that had pulverized Hood would not fight again as an organized force. Schofield and most of his corps were sent to North Carolina in mid-January, and the army's dissection continued into early spring.

Dispersed in northeastern Mississippi, Hood's army tried to recuperate amid wretched conditions little better than on its terrible retreat. "Some of my horses have not had a grain of corn for two days and nights, and none more than six each," General Chalmers told Forrest from the village of Jacinto on January 8. "Some of my men are deserting, and great many horses giving out." The same day, Seddon sent Hood word that his proposed furlough for the trans-Mississippi troops was rejected "as dangerous; compliance would probably be fatal." Some of the barefooted soldiers were issued shoes at Tupelo, but many could not wear them because of their sore or raw feet. Most of Lee's Corps had trudged into Tupelo by January 6.[15]

Taylor arrived there ahead of Beauregard and inspected the army on January 9, even as Stewart's Corps was arriving and settling into their camps that day. He was shocked by what he found: "This was my first view of a beaten army . . . and a painful sight it was. Many guns and small arms had been lost, and the ranks were depleted by thousands of prisoners and missing. Blankets, shoes, clothing, and accouterments were wanting." Leaving Tupelo later that day, Taylor reached Meridian, Mississippi, when he wired Jefferson Davis about what he had seen. "The army needs rest, consolidation, and reorganization. Not a day should be lost in effecting these latter. If moved in its present condition, it will prove utterly worthless; this applies to both infantry and cavalry. Full powers should be immediately given to the commander. For prudential reasons I use one of the former key-words instead of the last." Taylor was inferring that Hood's days were numbered.[16]

From Montgomery, en route to Tupelo that day, Beauregard telegraphed Hood that Davis wanted Hood to send "whatever troops you can spare" to assist Hardee's forces in South Carolina. Beauregard added that he would be in Tupelo to confer with Hood "as soon as practicable." Beauregard also sent a dispatch to Davis that day, stating that when he reached Hood, he would send as many men as possible to Hardee.[17]

While the generals nattered about this, the reality of the awful situation plaguing the Army of Tennessee was most evident in the filthy, stinking camps in and around Tupelo. "The whole army cannot muster 5,000 effective men," E. T. Freeman, an officer on General French's staff, wrote to French from Tupelo on January 10. "Great numbers are going home every day, many never more to return, I fear. Nine-tenths of the men and line officers are barefooted and naked." Walthall's Division—or what was left of it—was nearing Tupelo with the rest of

Stewart's Corps about this time. Walhtall lamented, "The remnant of my command, after this campaign of unprecedented
peril and hardship, reduced by its battles and exposure, worn
and weary with its travel and its toil, numbered less when it
reached its rest near Tupelo than one of its brigades had done
eight months before."[18]

Perhaps spurred by Taylor's visit, Hood sent a report on
January 9 to Beauregard about the campaign. This would be his
most open and informative dispatch since leaving Nashville. He
claimed that after Atlanta's fall, the army was out of position to
stop Sherman from advancing on Augusta or Macon or to prevent Sherman from bolstering his supply and communications
line between Atlanta and Chattanooga, primarily by the construction of railroad blockhouses. Hood stated, "Feeling that
the morale of the army was such as to require some change of
position, I resolved to move to the rear and force him [Sher-
man] to fall back with his entire army to Chattanooga, or divide
his forces and attempt to move with one wing to the Atlantic
and the other to Tennessee, thereby giving me the chance of
crushing one part of his army." Sherman had certainly divided
his army, but the result had obviously been calamitous for the
Confederates in Georgia and Tennessee. Hood concluded his
report with a positive view of the dismal state of affairs: "I
regard, however, our situation far better in having the grand
army of the Federals divided, with one wing in Tennessee and
one in Savannah, than to have had their entire force now lying
in the heart of Georgia."[19]

Still in Montgomery, Beauregard wasted little time in craft-
ing a brief but scalding response. He sent it not to Hood, but
to the War Department, along with a copy of Hood's report.
Beauregard contended that Hood's original plan, "if carried
out without modification," would have compelled Sherman to
retreat into central Tennessee to protect his supply and communications lines before he had the opportunity to gather
himself for the march to the Atlantic. But instead of crossing
the Tennessee at Gunter's Landing, Hood changed course to
Florence and Tuscumbia, where a lack of supplies, the unde-

pendable railroad, and late-arriving cavalry stalled Hood's offensive for three weeks, thus allowing Sherman to rebuild the damaged railroad between Atlanta and Chattanooga and to collect sufficient supplies for his strike to the sea. Beauregard said that since he did not have a detailed report from Hood or reports from Hood's subordinates, he could not express an opinion about the reasons for the campaign's failure. But he went on to say that after Franklin, Hood should have targeted Murfreesboro instead of Nashville with his entire army, likely overwhelming its garrison. Hood then could have destroyed railroad bridges on the Duck and Elk Rivers, possibly forcing the Federals to evacuate Chattanooga and Bridgeport, Tennessee.[20]

At daybreak on January 10, Cheatham put his men in motion toward Tupelo, generally marching along the line of the Mobile & Ohio. They camped near the town of Rienzi that night after a fifteen-mile march during which the impassible roads forced the soldiers to take a "very circuitous" route with their wagons and horses. Soldiers of the 6th Tennessee saw a stoic Cheatham standing at the end of a railroad bridge as they passed, his features seemingly reflecting all that the army had endured. The "grim old warrior . . . stood as motionless as a statue," one Confederate noted, "his gray eyes set with a fixed and vacant look, and his countenance wearing an expression of profound melancholy." By the twelfth, the Confederates had removed all sick, wounded, and supplies from Corinth to Tupelo. Arriving at Saltillo, just north of Tupelo, on the thirteenth, Cheatham's baggage train took a road to the southeast to reach Hood's camps while his infantry trudged through a swamp to rejoin the rest of the army.[21]

While Hood's furlough plan was nixed, Forrest had given most of his troopers a much-needed leave after they reached Corinth in the first week of January. With Roddey watching the Tennessee crossings, Forrest issued a twenty-day respite to his men, retaining only Ross's Texans for scouting, guard, and picket duty. Troopers of the 7th Tennessee Cavalry received word of their furlough on January 5. "Loud shouts of joy burst

William J. Hardee.

from their lips, and with three cheers for their esteemed commander the soldiers turned their horses' heads to their homes
in west Tennessee," stated one account. The furloughed men
were told to harass the enemy at every opportunity while on
leave and to bring in stragglers and any available horses.[22]

The clouds of defeat did not totally overshadow the Confederates. From Corinth on January 12, Ross reported that his
brigade returned from Tennessee with tired horses but "morale
not in the least affected nor impaired by the evident demoralization which prevailed to a considerable extent throughout
the larger portion of the army." An officer of the 1st Mississippi
Cavalry who returned to the army about this time after being
on detached duty wrote that Armstrong's Brigade "was neither
demoralized nor whipped, but it was in bad shape from loss of
men and horses. Some of the bravest men of the command had
been left to sleep their last sleep in the soil of Tennessee."[23]

At Richmond, Jefferson Davis received Taylor's dispatch
about the plight of Hood's army and responded on January 12:
"Sherman's campaign has produced bad effect on our people.
Success against his future operations is needed to reanimate
public confidence. Hardee requires more aid than Lee can
give him, and Hood's army is the only source to which we can
now look." Davis proposed that Hood's cavalry and Stewart's
Corps be added to Taylor's department to "hold Thomas in
check" while the rest of the Army of Tennessee was sent east to
oppose Sherman as soon as possible. "The presence of those
veterans will no doubt greatly increase the auxiliary force now
with Hardee."[24]

CHAPTER 15

"Alas for Hood!"

The magnitude of Hood's failure was beginning to settle ominously across the South, like the last ringing chords of a dirge. "The moral effect of the capture of Savannah has not been as great even as that of Atlanta," the *Richmond Daily Dispatch* said on January 14. "The two together were no such disaster as the defeat of Hood's army."[1]

The shroud of reality now also cloaked Hood himself—finally—amid the woeful conditions at Tupelo. His Tennessee failure caused him to make the most monumental decision of his life: he would request to relinquish command. Hood would later write to General Cooper that with "so much dissatisfaction throughout the country as in my judgment to greatly impair, if not destroy, my usefulness and counteract my exertions, and with no desire but to serve my country, I asked to be relieved, with the hope that another might be assigned to the command who might do more than I could hope to accomplish." From Tupelo on January 13, Hood telegraphed Secretary of War Seddon with his request.[2]

The threat of widespread desertion plagued the army to such a degree that Hood instructed Forrest on January 14 to "keep picked bodies of cavalry near at hand, that they may be ready to pursue and capture any men that may desert from the army. If the first party of deserters can be caught and promptly punished, it will perhaps deter others from doing the same." Orders to his corps commanders the same day stressed vigilance regarding deserters. James Porter of Cheatham's staff claimed that during the retreat there had been "as few desertions as was ever the case with an army under similar circumstances" and that the presumed mass exodus of Tennesseans had not occurred, even though many of these soldiers were within a short distance of their homes. Thomas Head of the 16th Tennessee in Cheatham's Corps contended that the army's Tennesseans left in droves after being demoralized at Franklin "to take care of their families."

Even if Porter's claim is accurate, which seems unlikely, Hood's ranks were thinning in more ways than one. A major factor in sparking desertions was the fact that the army was near starvation. "We are rapidly running out of breadstuffs," Hood's inspector general, Colonel Harvie, wrote to the super-intendent of the Mobile & Ohio on January 14.[4] Hood also was coping with a growing problem of lawlessness by his men in the Tupelo area. He sent a circular to his commanders about the "depredations daily committed in the vicinity of the army by soldiers with arms." In an attempt to prevent these inci-dents, weapons were ordered to be stacked and company rolls called frequently "to ascertain absentees from camp." In a sep-arate circular, sent to Stewart, Cheatham and Stevenson, Hood noted, "Depredations of all kinds are daily increasing" and commanders "should use every means necessary to keep their men constantly employed in camp" while patrols "under good officers" should be sent out to arrest lawbreakers. In the cav-alry bivouacs, rumors abounded that the war was almost over and that the troopers on furlough would not be recalled. For-rest was said to be arranging to take a colony of Confederates into Mexico.[5]

Hood's losses in the retreat and for the entire Tennessee campaign have never been accurately calculated because valu-able documents were lost or destroyed in the war's chaotic final months and events to the east overshadowed the cam-paign in Tennessee. For the rest of his life, Hood remained unwilling to acknowledge the severity of his defeat. He claimed that his total losses in the thirty-four-day campaign were about 10,000. But Hood had crossed the Tennessee with about 35,600 infantry and artillerymen in November and retreated and regrouped with approximately 18,000 to 19,000: the army had been almost carved in half.[6]

Forrest's cavalry losses, not to mention his strength, are even more difficult to pinpoint. Addressing his troopers after reaching Bainbridge, Forrest told them that their ranks "never exceeded five thousand" and that their losses during the past year were 2,000 killed or wounded and 200 captured. Hood believed that Forrest left Tennessee with 2,300 troopers.[7] As for artillery, Hood entered Tennessee with 124 guns but reached Tupelo with only 67, based on a January 20, 1865, inspection report. After the war, Hood admitted to losing 54 guns captured at Nashville (but also capturing and using Union guns).[8]

Still making his way to Hood's army, Beauregard had learned of the grim findings of Taylor's inspection. At Meridian on January 13, he wired Davis that Hardee should not expect immediate help from the Army of Tennessee. Notwithstanding the "disorganization and demoralization" of Hood's forces—at least in Taylor's judgment—the roads and railroads from Mississippi to eastern Georgia were in awful shape, a fact that Beauregard knew from firsthand experience on this trip. Beauregard finally arrived in Tupelo overnight on January 14–15, and Hood told him of his desire to be relieved. By now, Hood had sent a second telegram to Seddon regarding his request to step down because "I felt that my services could no longer be of benefit to that army." He also stated that he had "no other aspiration than to promote the interests of my country" and that "the campaigns to the Alabama line and into Tennessee were my own conception; that I alone was responsible; that I had striven hard to execute them in such manner as to bring victory to our people."[9]

Beauregard quickly saw for himself the pitiful condition of the troops and "could now realize the full truth of the reported disintegration and confusion of the Army of Tennessee," wrote Col. Alfred Roman of his staff. "Very little—if anything— remained of its former cohesive strength. If not, in the strictest sense of the word, a disorganized mob, it was no longer an army." The escape to Mississippi had brought little solace from this unusually brutal winter, and the soldiers were almost out of food and still had scant cold-weather clothing and few blankets.

Beauregard had his authorization from Davis to replace Hood with Taylor but claimed that Hood's visible suffering prevented him from giving the order. According to Roman, "So humiliated, so utterly crushed was he, in appearance, by the disastrous results of his defeat and its ruinous effects upon his army, that . . . Beauregard, whom he had just apprised of his application to be relieved . . . had not the heart virtually to disgrace him by ordering his immediate removal."[10]

Amazingly, Hood apparently held out vague hope that he would retain army command or at least be assigned to lead a corps or division, despite his own request to be relieved. He wrote to Jefferson Davis on the sixteenth, "If I am allowed to remain in command of this army, I hope you will grant me authority to reorganize it and relieve all incompetent officers. If thought best to relieve me, I am ready to command a corps or division, or do anything that may be considered best for my country."[11]

Beauregard decided that it would be best for the army to recuperate and remain where it was rather than be sent east to Hardee. "To divide this small army at this juncture to reinforce General Hardee would expose to capture Mobile, Demopolis, Selma, Montgomery, and all the rich valley of the Alabama River," he wrote to Davis from Tupelo on the seventeenth. Taylor had basically agreed in a dispatch to Davis on the fifteenth, stating that "an attempt to move Hood's army at this time would complete its destruction."[12]

Hood also seems to have persuaded Beauregard that a retooling and ouster of deficient officers was necessary for the army, as if the combat decimation in the campaign had not devastated the command structure enough. "I am fully satisfied the Army of Tennessee requires immediate reorganization and consolidation, removing at [the] same time all inefficient and supernumerary officers," Beauregard told Davis in a separate message on the seventeenth. "Generals Hood, Taylor, Forrest, and corps commanders agree fully with me in that opinion."[13] During discussions with Beauregard on the fifteenth, the generals had agreed on a furlough system for the army. One of every seven men in regiments from west of the Mississippi was given leave while one soldier for every fifteen from units east of the river was furloughed; none of the leaves lasted longer than ninety days. The leaves would ease, though minimally, the immense need for food and supplies, but most of these men never returned to the army.[14]

With rumors already swirling about a change at the top, some officers and enlisted men had begun circulating petitions to return Joe Johnston instead of Taylor to command, but it was too late. On January 15, Davis and Seddon had promptly complied with Hood's wishes: Hood was relieved and Taylor was to take over. Beauregard was to be sent immediately to Georgia and South Carolina with as many troops as possible to help deal with Sherman, Seddon ordered.[15] Davis would later blame Beauregard for the "ill-advised" campaign's failure and try to distance himself from its planning, claiming that he was out of the loop in the decision-making process. But he had offered no protest in November when he learned of Hood's proposal to strike into Tennessee.[16]

The Union buildup at Eastport was in overdrive when Thomas arrived there on the morning of January 15, at which point A. J. Smith updated him of the various locations of Hood's forces. Heavy rains in the region had again turned the roads into mud pits, but also had caused the Tennessee to rise, allowing larger steamships to reach Eastport with supplies. Schofield's troops began embarking on transports for the journey east.[17]

Within a few weeks, the rest of the army was dispersed as well, with Wood's corps posted in eastern Tennessee and Smith's troops transferred to the U.S. Army of the Gulf in Alabama. Portions of Wilson's cavalry were scattered from Alabama to Tennessee to the Carolinas, although, by early March 1865, Wilson's command had been reorganized, retooled, and reinforced to 27,000 troopers, most of them armed with Spencer repeaters. Wilson accurately described the bulk of his corps, then concentrated near Waterloo, Alabama, as "the largest body of cavalry ever collected on the American

Joseph Johnston.

continent." When he unleashed this force on a massive spring raid against enemy munitions centers at Selma, Alabama, and Columbus, Georgia, Wilson acted in independent command, which meant that Thomas, despite his glories and promotion, was again shoved to the back burner.[18]

After Taylor reached Tupelo on the eighteenth, a group of soldiers went to Hood's headquarters, where the embattled commander was being serenaded by the band of Gibson's Louisiana brigade. When the musicians finished, the men called for Hood, who hobbled out on a balcony. He thanked them for their service through the many hardships they all had endured. He told them he hoped they would soon be supplied with new uniforms to strengthen their pride as fighting men and with more bayonets, since "it was the bayonet which gave the soldier confidence in himself, and enabled him to strike terror to the enemy." He hoped they would support Taylor and avenge their comrades "whose bones lay bleaching upon the fields of Middle Tennessee."[19]

Elements of Lee's Corps began leaving Tupelo the next day. Cheatham's Corps followed on the twentieth. These troops were ordered first to Augusta, Georgia, where they would then be sent to oppose Sherman's forces, who were then just beginning to burn north from Savannah into South Carolina. A portion of Stewart's Corps would follow within a few days. Also during this period, some 4,000 troops—units of Stewart's and Lee's Corps—were sent to help defend Mobile.[20]

On January 23, Hood said farewell to what was left of the army: "In taking leave of you, accept my thanks for the patience with which you have endured your hardships during the recent campaign. I am alone responsible for its conception, and strove hard to do my duty in its execution. I urge upon you the importance of giving your entire support to the distinguished soldier who now assumes command, and I shall look with deep interest upon all your future operations and rejoice at your success." Most of his men never read or heard this message since they were already on their way east. It would be at least several days before these troops learned of Hood's exit.[21]

Sam Watkins likely summed up the feelings of a majority of the men who served under Hood. "As a soldier, he was brave, good, noble, and gallant, and fought with the ferociousness of the wounded tiger, and with the everlasting grit of the bull-dog," Watkins remembered, "but as a general he was a failure in every particular." The Alabama private Edward McMorries basically agreed: "Gen. Hood was one of the bravest of the brave, and we do not think his proven incompetency to command the army detracts one jot from his distinguished services to his country."[22]

"Alas for Hood!" his old adversary General Wilson wrote after the war. "He passed out broken-hearted at last by the weight of his misfortunes. His courage and his undoubted ability as a leader and a general deserved better luck. But it was his sad fate to dash his veteran army to pieces against far better leadership backed by the still greater infallibility of numbers." One of Thomas's officers, James Rusling, voiced a similar opinion: "Poor Hood! He was really an able and gallant soldier; and his army was incomparable—the same substantially that was pitted against Sherman all summer. But he ought to have known better than to butt his brains out against 'The Rock of Chickamauga.'"[23]

Richard Taylor criticized both commanders. "It is difficult to imagine what objects he [Hood] had in view," in besieging Nashville since Thomas could still be reinforced from the north, Taylor wrote. Yet "had the Federal general possessed dash equal to his tenacity and caution, one fails to see how Hood could have brought man or gun across the Tennessee."[24]

As a final indignity on the day of his farewell, Hood at last learned of the destruction of his pontoon train almost a month earlier. Before boarding his train for Richmond that day, Hood sent a message to Davis about the ongoing pipe dream of obtaining thousands of recruits from the trans-Mississippi. He wanted to cross the Mississippi and believed that he could bring in 25,000 troops for the Confederacy. "I know this can be accomplished, and earnestly desire this chance to do you so much good service," he told Davis. "Will explain my plan on arrival."[25]

Hood journeyed from Tupelo to Richmond by way of Columbia, South Carolina, where he called on his old friend Mary Chesnut, who described the sad-eyed general who once had been a heartthrob in southern social circles: "His is a face that speaks of wakeful nights and nerves strung to their utmost tension by anxiety. He can stand well enough without his crutch, but he does very slow walking. How plainly he spoke out these dreadful words: 'My defeat and discomfiture'—'My army is destroyed'—'My losses'. . . . He said he had nobody to blame but himself."[26] Before heading north from South Carolina, Hood also tried to rekindle his engagement to Buck Preston. He had written to her from the Nashville lines that he was coming to marry her in January. Now, however, the shock of his appearance and his failures fueled opposition to their marriage by her parents and her sister, which was more formidable than Hood could deal with at this nadir in his life. When he left for Richmond on February 7, there was little sadness about his departure; his lack of fire for her had cooled Buck's enthusiasm.[27]

Hood reached Richmond on February 8, but was all but ignored amid the Confederacy's last gasps of survival and his own battlefield failures. He would never hold active command again, his military career ruined in his six months leading the Army of Tennessee. His arrival was so lackluster that the war clerk John Jones did not note it in his diary until March 15, writing, "General Hood is here, on crutches, attracting no attention, for he was not successful."[28]

By mid-February, Hood had created waves in high circles with his official report on the Atlanta and Tennessee campaigns. He criticized Johnston, Hardee, and others for their actions in the Atlanta fighting, and the allegations were so serious that Johnston would consider charges against him and Hardee and Hood would exchange written insults. Beauregard also weighed in, annoyed by the way Hood had ignored him despite being his superior officer. Of Tennessee, Hood claimed that except for "an unfortunate event"—the initial break of Bate's Division, which allowed the Federals to enfilade the entire line, prompting the rout—"I think we would have gained a complete victory." He continued: "It is my firm conviction that, notwithstanding that disaster, I left the Army in better spirits and with more confidence in itself, than it had at the opening of the campaign. . . . Were I again placed in such circumstances, I should make the same marches and fight the same battles, trusting that the same unforeseen and unavoidable accident would not again occur to change into disaster a victory which had been already won."[29]

Hood's assessment of what happened in Tennessee bore little resemblance to reality. After being shoved backward on Nashville's first day, the Confederates were holding their own on December 16 before Thomas's overpowering assault on the Confederate left dispersed Bate and ignited the army's breakup. This was no "accident": Thomas had outgeneraled Hood, feinting and hurling more troops than the Confederates could handle on that flank. Hood's claim that defeat was seized from the jaws of victory also is wrong. His troops had been hammered on the fifteenth, and the Federals aggressively resumed the offensive on the second day with superior numbers and momentum. Even if Hood had held off Thomas on the sixteenth and been able to implement his planned attack on the seventeenth, the odds of success were slim at best.[30]

The Federals tightened their noose around Richmond, even as Hood recuperated and conferred with Davis about his plan to bring in trans-Mississippi recruits. There was some discussion of Hood being given a command in western Virginia, but Lee favored sending him west. Hood spent almost two months in the capital before embarking for Texas on or about April 1, with orders to marshal troops willing to join Lee in the east. Preparing to depart, he wrote to Davis, "I am more content & satisfied with my own work whilst in command of the army of Tenn, than all my military career in life." Returning to South Carolina on the roundabout trip west, Hood made one last foray to conquer Buck Preston's heart, but their relationship was essentially over. There were gossipy whispers that he lost himself in a moment of passion, kissing her on the throat as she warmed her legs by a fire—outrageous behavior in 1865. Still, Buck later confided to Mrs. Chesnut that if Hood had been more persistent, she would have married him.[31]

Hood had reached Sumterville, South Carolina, by mid-April, when he received the "painful intelligence" of Lee's surrender at Appomattox. Still, he proceeded west with his staff and escort, reaching the Mississippi River near Natchez around the end of April. In the coming weeks, the Confederates vainly tried to get across the "mighty river," as Hood called it, and on several occasions, they evaded Federal cavalry in the swamps and canebrakes. News of Kirby Smith's surrender of the trans-Mississippi forces deflated any remaining hope, and on May 31, 1865, Hood and at least two of his men rode into Natchez to lay down their arms.

In a meeting with Union major general John W. Davidson, Hood offered his sword, but Davidson refused it, almost immediately paroling Hood and the others. The now ex-Confederates were allowed to head for Texas, via New Orleans, reaching that city in June's first week. Continuing west by train, Hood propped himself on boxes and trunks in a baggage car. A fellow passenger, Louly Wigfall, noted his depressed demeanor. Hood "sat opposite, and with calm, sad eyes looked out on the passing scenes, apparently noting nothing. The cause he loved was lost—he was overwhelmed with humiliation at the utter failure of his leadership—his pride was wounded to the quick by his removal from command."

As Hood's party was endeavoring to cross the Mississippi on April 26, some shards of the Army of Tennessee were surrendered with the rest of Johnston's forces near Durham Station, North Carolina, more than two weeks after Lee's Army of Northern Virginia capitulated at Appomattox. In Alabama, the Confederates sent to Mobile from Tupelo fought bravely before Spanish Fort and Fort Blakely, the keystones of the city's defenses, were overwhelmed by Union troops on April 8–9. Mobile fell three days later. Forrest held out a while longer, overmatched but still battling Wilson's cavalry before he surrendered on May 9 near Gainesville, Alabama, after receiving orders to do so.[33]

The Army of Tennessee had died hard, leaving its graves over a territory ten times the size of the area over which Robert Lee fought. No other army on either side had its innards gnawed out so furiously by the often petty, vicious bickering of its generals and the perpetual upheaval of command changes. Gut shot at Franklin, the army had staggered to Nashville, only to have its already fragile spine broken by a rock—Thomas. Wilson's carbines had only aggravated the agony on the retreat through a frozen hell of foot-stabbing ice, high water, and rivers of mud that were once roads.[34]

"Coming generations and historians will be the critics as to how we have acted our parts," the Tennessean Sam Watkins wrote years after the war. "The past is buried in oblivion. The blood-red flag, with its crescent and cross, that we followed for four long, bloody, and disastrous years, has been folded never again to be unfurled. We have no regrets for what we did, but we mourn the loss of so many brave . . . men who perished on the field of battle and honor." In 1907, Luke Finlay, who led three Tennessee regiments as a colonel in Strahl's Brigade, wrote to *Confederate Veteran* about Hood's army during the retreat: "It was in the lion's mouth."[35]

Even before the war's end, the exodus of Hood's army from Tennessee evoked contrasts—at least among Confederates—with the stirring deeds of patriots in the American Revolution. "I shall never forget the passage of the Duck River. Washington crossing the Delaware was insignificant," W. D. Gale of Stewart's staff wrote to his wife in January, 1865. "Valley Forge bore but little comparison to the patient endurance of hardships of the Confederate soldiers who worked and fought their way from Nashville to Tupelo," claimed George Brewer of the 46th Alabama, decades after the war. "When a child we shed tears when reading of Washington at Valley Forge; of his men leaving bloody tracks in the snow," noted Sumner A. Cunningham of the 41st Tennessee. "Little did we dream that we would witness similar scenes. The sufferings and hardships endured by Hood's army on its retreat were greater than any endured by our revolutionary forefathers."[36]

Thus ended the Tennessee campaign, one of the most unique and tragic military retreats in American history. Soon it was relegated to little more than a few paragraphs or pages in most volumes about the conflict, as if its soldiers, blue and gray, had marched into oblivion, vanishing into ice and snow swirled by the mournful winds of time.

APPENDIX A

Gettysburg, Antietam, and Nashville: Contrasting the Confederate Retreats

Antietam, on September 17, 1862, held the gory honor of being the bloodiest day of the war, with almost 13,000 Federals and 10,000 Confederate casualties. The battle forced Lee to abandon his Maryland campaign. Lee stood his ground throughout the day on September 18, defiantly awaiting another attack from George McClellan, which never came. That night, Lee retreated across the Potomac, a few miles away, escaping into Virginia by sunrise on the nineteenth. There was no Union pursuit until later in the day when cavalry and an infantry corps reached the river. The Federals crossed two divisions on the twentieth, and there was insignificant fighting before Union forces withdrew to the north bank. That was the extent of McClellan's chase, and while his victory allowed Lincoln to issue the Emancipation Proclamation, there was much criticism of his failure to hunt down Lee's temporarily wrecked army. In the coming weeks, McClellan's now characteristic hesitancy to move against the enemy resulted in his removal from army command in late October.[1]

After the three-day battle at Gettysburg, Lee's army retreated in a heavy rain on the night of July 4, 1863, staggered by 28,000 casualties. The Rebels withdrew into Maryland, reaching the Potomac River south of Hagerstown, but the river's swollen condition prevented Lee from crossing to the relative safety of Virginia until the night of July 13 near Falling Waters, West Virginia. Maj. Gen. George G. Meade's Army of the Potomac had won a signature victory, but with losses of 23,000 men, Meade—like McClellan at Antietam—did not mount a vigorous pursuit. This changed on the morning of July 14 as two cavalry divisions attacked Lee's rear guard on the north bank. Union forces, including Brig. Gen. George Custer, captured some prisoners and mortally wounded Brig. Gen. James J. Pettigrew before being driven off.[2]

While the Confederate retreats from Gettysburg and Antietam had long processions of ambulances and other wagons bearing thousands of wounded south, Hood's exodus was of a much different dimension. After each of the other titanic battles, the Confederates had time to organize their withdrawal; in both cases, Lee stood fast despite the horrendous bloodletting and allowed his forces some brief rest and reorganization before starting south. Certainly, Hood did not have to deal with the same level of casualties at Nashville, but his retreat was through Franklin, Pulaski, and other places where masses of wounded Confederates had been left behind in the prior weeks of fighting. There is no indication that he tried to evacuate great numbers of these men—or any at all—unless they had recovered sufficiently to move on their own or were ambulatory. Most were left to the care and mercy of Union forces.

The weather was a major difference between Nashville and the other two campaigns. After Antietam, Lee still had weeks of late-summer and early-autumn conditions in which to conduct his retreat. The same is true of the Gettysburg campaign. In contrast, Hood, Beauregard, and, to some degree, Davis disregarded not only the weather but the soldiers' equipment, supplies, and ability to deal with winter conditions in sending the Army of Tennessee north. As always, the Confederates' most reliable quartermaster was the Union government, but not even captured equipment could sustain them through the hardships of this campaign.

Franklin had been fought on November 30—and Hood still decided to move his shredded divisions north into the twin maws of a deepening winter and the equally unmerciful circle of bayonets around Nashville. Even in mild years, December and January in central Tennessee can be relentless, but Hood overlooked this, as well as the daily deterioration of his army, in taking his gamble. Cursed by the weather and the dilapidated state of Confederate railroads, Hood's army waited in the orange mud at Tuscumbia and Florence while the Tennessee River rose and rampaged in November, thus allowing Thomas invaluable time to assemble his troops. Nature eventually benefitted the Confederates in December 1864, when rising creeks, streams, and rivers stalled the Union pursuit. This was scant solace for Hood's survivors, who had suffered a crippling defeat and the most nightmarish retreat in a war painfully renowned for combat butchery and horrid aftermaths.

APPENDIX B

No Appomattox?

Had Thomas and the Union navy bagged Hood's army at the Tennessee River, the whole course of the war would have changed, and thousands of lives on both sides likely would have been saved. Henry Halleck contended that if Hood's forces could be captured or destroyed, Sherman would be able to smash the rest of the Confederate military in his thrust through the Carolinas and beyond. While this is arguably an exaggeration, it is no stretch of the imagination to say that without the shards of the Army of Tennessee, Sherman, having already torched his way through South Carolina by late February 1865, might have avoided battle at Bentonville, North Carolina—or at least had an easier triumph since the veterans from Tennessee would not have been there to provide the backbone of the force opposing him.

With Hood's army off the chessboard, it is also likely that the Union offensive against Mobile, Selma, and other Confederate bases in south-central Alabama would have been accelerated—and less contested. Most importantly, Robert E. Lee would have faced even fewer options than the presence of Joseph Johnston's force ultimately allowed him. When he evacuated the Richmond-Petersburg lines on the night of April 2 after crushing Union attacks at Five Forks and on the South Side Railroad, Lee hoped to join Johnston in North Carolina. If Johnston, without soldiers from the Army of Tennessee as the spine of his force, had been scattered or overwhelmed by Sherman and other Union troops (including Schofield's corps, which arrived on the Carolina coast in mid-February), there might have been no surrender at Appomattox on April 9.

Some will argue, quite correctly, that Johnston fought longer than Lee, not capitulating until April 26, and that he surrendered more troops than Lee did at Appomattox. Others could make the equally justifiable claim that without the skeleton units from the Army of Tennessee, Johnston would never have been able to hold out that long and would have succumbed much sooner. If Johnston had been out of the picture by mid-March, it is not inconceivable that Lee, painfully realizing the daily deterioration of the Army of Northern Virginia, would have surrendered at Petersburg—especially after the costly repulse of his surprise attack at Fort Stedman on March 25.

APPENDIX C

Hood's Retreat and Thomas's Pursuit: The Journey Today

Landing at Nashville's airport, a first-time visitor familiar with the region's Civil War history sees the Brentwood Hills range to the south, silent sentinels for this metropolis. It's an understatement to say that massive urban growth and a web of interstates has greatly transformed the city since Thomas and Hood battled here. Progress often trumps history. Richmond, Atlanta, and Washington have long grown out of—and over— their nineteenth-century roots. Nashville is no different.

Much of the route where Hood's retreat began is unrecognizable from any other swatch of suburbia where office parks and strip malls dominate. Only an occasional silver and black historical marker offers evidence of past events. To understand and explore the battle and the paths of Thomas and Hood amid the aftermath, U.S. Highway 31 is crucial. This was the main avenue of war in the 1864 Tennessee campaign, slicing through Brentwood, Spring Hill, Franklin, Columbia, and Pulaski.

Brentwood, where Hood tried to re-form his splintered army on the night of December 16, has evolved into a ritzy bedroom community for Nashville business gurus, star musicians, professional athletes, and other moneyed elite. Sitting in a barbeque restaurant on the main drag, I see a Walgreen's across the four-lane street and try to imagine the chaos on this stretch of highway that bitter night, with the troops trudging past this place amid the glare of modern-day lights and forgotten deeds.

Franklin is the most tragic place of all for several reasons. The town built over much of its history for no apparent reason. A funeral home, office complex, and farm-equipment store occupy vast swaths of ground bought with more blood than any acre at Gettysburg. Today, a view from Winstead Hill, where the Confederates formed their massive attack against the Union defenses, is a depressing sight of just-any-town development, a sad testament to a succession of municipal leaders with no clue about their historic treasure. Stand in the Target parking lot and try to imagine the sweep of armies over this land.

Preservation groups like Save the Franklin Battlefield have done great work, but have to overcome decades of ignorance and indifference. Home lots are still being sold on the acres where Cheatham's troops closed with the Union earthworks. Franklin is among hundreds of locales across the country to forsake its Civil War legacy, but only a few others are as significant.

Just south of Franklin is the stately William Harrison house, which witnessed not only the epic battle but the running fight on December 17 during Hood's retreat. Two Confederate generals drew their last breath in this house: Brig. Gen. John H. Kelly, who died in September 1864 after a clash with Union cavalry, and Brig. Gen. John C. Carter, who succumbed to wounds after the November battle.

Spring Hill is dominated by its gigantic General Motors automotive plant, the corporation having bought up much other local land and Civil War–era mansions.

Farther south down U.S. 31, Columbia is an historic town most renowned for being the home of future president James K. Polk. The most notable landmark related to the Tennessee campaign is Beechlawn, the home of the A. W. Warfield family located a few miles south of town. It served as headquarters for John Schofield and later Hood as the armies pushed toward Nashville in November 1864. Amid the retreat, Hood returned here when the army was in Columbia, Forrest directed the early actions of his rear guard from here, and Wilson headquartered here as his horsemen pushed south in pursuit of the enemy. Today it is a private home.

Farmland and nice countryside mark the portion of the route from Columbia to Pulaski. No sign of any kind marks the north branch of Richland Creek, the site of the Confederate rear guard action on December 24.

Pulaski, the seat of Giles County, has a population of about 8,000. Its bustling town square makes it difficult to visualize Confederates detonating munitions and other supplies on Christmas morning, 1864. Tennessee Highway 11 (the Lamb's Ferry Road) leading southwest out of town is the route taken by most of Hood's army. Cheatham's Corps took a different road, marching west on what is now U.S. 64 toward Lawrenceburg. Highway 11 close to town would have been where Hood first heard his troops singing their variation of the "Yellow Rose of Texas" as he and they continued to "play hell in Tennessee."

There are no historical markers at Anthony's Hill, where Forrest staged his Christmas Day ambush, but its steep, thickly treed slopes make it easy to see why he chose this position to make a stand.

Sam Davis is among the most popular historical figures in this region. A local Confederate soldier who was captured by the Federals in 1863 and later hanged as a spy, Davis is considered a Confederate martyr and is immortalized by a statue in front of the Giles County Courthouse and by a monument near the site of his execution. The Sam Davis Memorial Bridge crosses Sugar Creek, scene of Forrest's December 26 fight with Wilson's cavalry, near the Alabama border.

From this point, the route crosses the state line as the armies veered west on Alabama 64 (the Powell or Lexington Road). Passing the small town of Lexington, Hood's wagons, pontoons, and two corps of infantry (Lee's and Stewart's), had a straight shot west to reach the Bainbridge Road (present-day U.S. 43) heading south to the river. Cheatham's troops picked up U.S. 43 at Lawrenceburg and hustled to rejoin the army.

The Tennessee River in the area where Hood's army crossed it is much different today, having been transformed by dams and hydroelectric plants that were cornerstones of the Tennessee Valley Authority's projects in the 1930s.

The Wilson Dam, completed in 1924, and the Wheeler Dam—along with the reservoirs of the same names—now cover what once were the treacherous Muscle Shoals, controlling flood levels and providing electricity for hundreds of thousands of people. One dam and lake are named for Confederate major general (and eight-term Alabama congressman) Joseph Wheeler. With construction beginning in 1918, the Wilson Dam and reservoir honor President Woodrow Wilson, *not* the flamboyant Union cavalryman James Wilson, who roamed this region in 1864 and 1865.

APPENDIX D

Orders of Battle

THE HUNTERS

Organization of the Union Army in Pursuit from Nashville, December 17–29, 1864

Maj. Gen. George H. Thomas

IV CORPS, Brig. Gen. Thomas J. Wood

1st Division, Brig. Gen. Nathan Kimball
    1st Brigade, Col. Isaac M. Kirby
        21st Illinois, Capt. William H. Jamison
        38th Illinois, Capt. Andrew M. Pollard
        31st Indiana, Col. John T. Smith
        81st Indiana, Maj. Edward C. Mathey
        90th Ohio, Lt. Col. Samuel N. Yeoman
        101st Ohio, Lt. Col. Bedan B. McDonald.
    2nd Brigade, Brig. Gen. Walter C. Whitaker
        96th Illinois, Major George Hicks
        115th Illinois, Col. Jesse H. Moore
        35th Indiana, Lt. Col. Augustus C. Tassin
        21st Kentucky, Lt. Col. James C. Evans
        23rd Kentucky, Lt. Col. George W. Northrup
        45th Ohio, Lt. Col. John H. Humphrey
        51st Ohio, Lt. Col. Charles H. Wood.
    3rd Brigade, Brig. Gen. William Grose
        75th Illinois, Col. John E. Bennett
        80th Illinois, Capt. James Cunningham
        84th Illinois, Lt. Col. Charles H. Morton
        9th Indiana, Col. Isaac C. B. Suman
        30th Indiana, Capt. Henry W. Lawton

36th Indiana (one company), Lt. Col. John P. Swisher
84th Indiana, Maj. John C. Taylor
77th Pennsylvania, Col. Thomas E. Rose

2nd Division, Brig. Gen. Washington L. Elliott
    1st Brigade, Col. Emerson Opdycke
        36th Illinois, Maj. Levi P. Holden
        44th Illinois, Capt. Alonzo W. Clark
        73rd Illinois, Capt. Wilson Burroughs
        74th and 88th Illinois, Lt. Col. George W. Smith
        125th Ohio, Maj. Joseph Bruff
        24th Wisconsin, Capt. William Kennedy
    2nd Brigade, Col. John Q. Lane
        100th Illinois, Lt. Col. Charles M. Hammond
        40th Indiana, Lt. Col. Henry Leaming
        57th Indiana, Lt. Col. Willis Blanch
        28th Kentucky, Maj. George W. Barth
        26th Ohio, Capt. William Clark
        97th Ohio, Lt. Col. Milton Barnes
    3rd Brigade, Col. Joseph Conrad
        42nd Illinois, Lt. Col. Edgar D. Swain
        51st Illinois, Capt. Albert M. Tilton
        79th Illinois (incl. detachment of 27th Ill.),
          Col. Allen Buckner
        15th Missouri, Capt. George Ernst
        64th Ohio, Lt. Col. Robert C. Brown
        65th Ohio, Maj. Orlow Smith

3rd Division, Brig, Gen. Samuel Beatty
    1st Brigade, Col. Abel D. Streight
        89th Illinois, Lt. Col. William D. Williams
        51st Indiana, Capt. William W. Scearce
        8th Kansas, Lt. Col. John Conover
        15th Ohio, Col. Frank Askew
        49th Ohio, Maj. Luther M. Strong
    2nd Brigade, Lt. Col. Robert L. Kimberly[a]
        59th Illinois, Maj. James M. Stookey
        41st Ohio, Capt. Ezra Dunham

71st Ohio, Lt. Col. James H. Hart
93rd Ohio, Lt. Col. Daniel Bowman
124th Ohio, Lt. Col. James Pickands.
3rd Brigade, Col. Frederick Knefler
    79th Indiana, Lt. Col. George W. Parker
    86th Indiana, Col. George F. Dick
    13th Ohio (four companies), Maj. Joseph T. Snider
    19th Ohio, Col. Henry G. Stratton

Artillery, Maj. Wilbur F. Goodspeed
    Indiana Light 25th Battery, Capt. Frederick C. Sturm
    Kentucky Light, 1st Battery, Capt. Theodore S. Thomasson
    1st Michigan Light, Battery E, Capt. Peter De Vries
    1st Ohio Light, Battery G, Capt. Alexander Marshall
    Ohio Light, 6th Battery, Lieut. Aaron P. Baldwin
    Pennsylvania Light, Battery B, Capt. Jacob Ziegler
    4th United States, Battery M, Lt. Samuel Canby

CAVALRY CORPS, Brig. Gen. James H. Wilson

Escort: 4th United States, Lt. Joseph Hedges

1st Division, Brig. Gen. Edward M. McCook[b]
    1st Brigade, Brig. Gen. John T. Croxton
        8th Iowa, Col. James B. Dorr
        4th Kentucky (mounted inf.), Col. Robert M. Kelly
        2nd Michigan, Lt. Col. Benjamin Smith
        1st Tennessee, Lt. Col. Calvin M. Dyer
        Illinois Light Artillery, Board of Trade Battery,
          Capt. George I. Robinson

5th Division, Brig. Gen. Edward Hatch
    1st Brigade, Col. Robert R. Stewart
        3rd Illinois, Lt. Col. Robert H. Carnahan
        11th Indiana, Lt. Col. Abram Sharra
        12th Missouri, Col. Oliver Wells
        10th Tennessee, Maj. William P. Story

---

a. Kimberly led the 41st Ohio during the Battle of Nashville and assumed command of the 2nd Brigade when Col. P. Sidney Post was wounded seriously on the second day of fighting.
b. McCook and his 2nd and 3rd Brigades were away, chasing Lyon's Confederate cavalry in north-central Tennessee and western Kentucky.

2nd Brigade, Col. Datus E. Coon
    6th Illinois, Col. John Lynch
    7th Illinois, Maj. John M. Graham
    9th Illinois, Capt. Joseph W. Harper
    2nd Iowa, Maj. Charles C. Horton
    12th Tennessee, Col. George Spalding
    1st Illinois Light Artillery, Battery I, Lt. Joseph A.
      McCartney

6th Division, Brig. Gen. Richard W. Johnson
    1st Brigade, Col. Thomas J. Harrison
      16th Illinois, Maj. Charles H. Beeres
      5th Iowa, Lt. Col. Harlon Baird
      7th Ohio, Col. Israel Garrard
    2nd Brigade, Col. James Biddle
      14th Illinois, Maj. Haviland Tompkins
      6th Indiana, Maj. Jacob S. Stephens
      8th Michigan, Col. Elisha Mix
      3rd Tennessee, Maj. Benjamin Cunningham.
    3rd Brigade (on detached duty)
      15th Pennsylvania, Col. William J. Palmer
      5th Tennessee, Lt. Col. W. J. Clift
    Artillery
      4th United States, Battery I, Lt. Frank G. Smith

7th Division, Brig. Gen. Joseph F. Knipe
    1st Brigade, Bvt. Brig. Gen. John H. Hammond
      9th Indiana, Col. George W. Jackson
      10th Indiana, Lt. Col. Benjamin Q. A. Gresham
      19th Pennsylvania, Lt. Col. Joseph C. Hess
      2nd Tennessee, Lt. Col. William R. Cook
      4th Tennessee, Lt. Col. Jacob M. Thornburgh.
    2nd Brigade, Col. Gilbert M. L. Johnson
      12th Indiana, Col. Edward Anderson
      13th Indiana, Lt. Col. William T. Pepper
      6th Tennessee, Col. Fielding Hurst
    Artillery
      Ohio Light, 14th Battery, Lt. William C. Myers.

The following Union forces participated in the pursuit, but most were not actively engaged, except in support roles:

XXIII CORPS, Maj. Gen. John M. Schofield

2nd Division, Maj. Gen. Darius N. Couch
    1st Brigade, Brig. Gen. Joseph A. Cooper
        130th Indiana
        26th Kentucky
        25th Michigan
        99th Ohio
        3rd and 6th Tennessee
    2nd Brigade, Col. Orlando H. Moore
        107th Illinois
        80th and 129th Indiana
        23rd Michigan
        111th and 118th Ohio
    3rd Brigade, Col. John Mehringer
        91st and 123rd Indiana
        50th and 183rd Ohio
    Artillery
        Indiana Light, 15th Battery
        Ohio Light, 19th Battery

3rd Division, Brig. Gen. Jacob D. Cox
    1st Brigade, Col. Charles C. Doolittle
        12th and 16th Kentucky
        100th and 104th Ohio
        8th Tennessee
    2nd Brigade, Col. John S. Casement
        65th Illinois
        65th and 124th Indiana
        103rd Ohio
        5th Tennessee
    3rd Brigade, Col. Israel N. Stiles
        112th Illinois
        63rd, 120th, and 128th Indiana
    Artillery
        Indiana Light, 23rd Battery
        1st Ohio Light, Battery D

DETACHMENT, ARMY OF THE TENNESSEE, Maj. Gen.
        Andrew J. Smith

1st Division, Brig. Gen. John McArthur
    1st Brigade, Col. William L. McMillen
        114th Illinois
        93rd Indiana
        10th Minnesota
        72nd and 95th Ohio
        Illinois Light Artillery, Cogswell's Battery
    2nd Brigade, Col. Lucius F. Hubbard
        5th and 9th Minnesota
        11th Missouri
        8th Wisconsin
        Iowa Light Artillery, 2nd Battery
    3rd Brigade, Col. William R. Marshall
        12th and 35th Iowa
        7th Minnesota
        33rd Missouri
        2nd Missouri Light Artillery, Battery I

2nd Division, Brig. Gen. Kenner Garrard
    1st Brigade, Col. David Moore
        119th, 122nd Illinois
        89th Indiana
        21st Missouri (detachment of 24th Missouri attached)
        Indiana Light Artillery, 9th Battery
    2nd Brigade, Col. James I. Gilbert
        58th Illinois
        27th and 32nd Iowa
        10th Kansas (four companies)
        Indiana Light Artillery, 3rd Battery
    3rd Brigade, Col. Edward H. Wolfe
        49th and 117th Illinois
        52nd Indiana
        178th New York
        2nd Illinois Light Artillery, Battery G

3rd Division, Col. Jonathan B. Moore
    1st Brigade, Col. Lyman M. Ward
        72nd Illinois
        40th Missouri
        14th and 33rd Wisconsin
    2nd Brigade, Col. Leander Blanden
        81st and 95th Illinois
        44th Missouri
    Artillery
        Indiana Light, 14th Battery
        2nd Missouri Light, Battery A

PROVISIONAL DETACHMENT (DISTRICT OF THE
      ETOWAH), Maj. Gen. James B. Steedman

Provisional Division, Brig. Gen. Charles Cruft
    1st Colored Brigade, Col. Thomas J. Morgan
        14th, 16th, 17th, 18th, 44th U.S. Colored Troops
    2nd Colored Brigade, Col. Charles R. Thompson
        12th, 13th, 100th U. S. C. T.
        1st Battery, Kansas Light Artillery
    1st Brigade, Col. Benjamin Harrison
        Three battalions from XX Corps (detached)
    2nd Brigade, Col. John G. Mitchell
        Troops on detached duty from the Army of the
          Tennessee
    3rd Brigade, Lt. Col. Charles H. Grosvenor
        68th Indiana
        18th and 121st Ohio
        2nd Battalion, XIV Army Corps
    Artillery
        20th Battery, Indiana Light
        18th Battery, Ohio Light
    Cavalry, Col. William J. Palmer
        15th Pennsylvania (detached from Wilson's 6th
          Division, 3rd Brigade)

THE HUNTED
Organization of the Confederate Army of Tennessee in
Pursuit from Nashville, December 17–29, 1864

Gen. John Bell Hood

LEE'S CORPS, Lt. Gen. Stephen D. Lee[c]

Johnson's Division, Maj. Gen. Edward Johnson[d]
    Deas's Brigade, Brig. Gen. Zachariah C. Deas
        19th Alabama, Lt. Col. George R. Kimbrough
        22nd Alabama, Capt. H. W. Henry
        25th Alabama, Capt. Napoleon B. Rouse
        39th Alabama, Lt. Col. William C. Clifton
        50th Alabama, Col. John G. Coltart.
    Sharp's Brigade, Brig. Gen. Jacob H. Sharp
        7th and 9th Mississippi, Maj. Henry Pope
        10th and 44th Mississippi and 9th Battalion, Mississippi
          Sharpshooters, Capt. Robert A. Bell
        41st Mississippi, Capt. James M. Hicks[e]
    Manigault's Brigade, Lt. Col. William L. Butler
        24th Alabama, Capt. Thomas J. Kimbell
        28th Alabama, Capt. William M. Nabors
        34th Alabama, Lt. Col. John C. Carter
        10th South Carolina, Lt. Col. C. Irvine Walker
        19th South Carolina, Capt. Thomas W. Getzen
    Brantley's Brigade, Brig. Gen. William F. Brantley
        24th and 34th Mississippi, Capt. Clifton Dancy
        27th Mississippi, Capt. Samuel M. Pegg
        29th and 30th Mississippi, Capt. R.W. Williamson
        Dismounted Cavalry, Capt. D. W. Alexander

---

c. Lee was wounded on December 17 and relinquished corps command
that night to Maj. Gen. Carter L. Stevenson.

d. A sizeable portion of Johnson's Division (except Brantley's Brigade) was
captured on December 16, including Johnson himself. The units and
commanders shown for not only this division, but Hood's entire army,
are based largely on a December 10 organizational return made after the
Battle of Franklin but before the Battle of Nashville. Compiled with battle reports from December 17 through the end of the year, this is the
most complete information available.

e. Hicks was wounded at Franklin, but appears to have retained command
at least through the Nashville fighting. By late March 1865, the 41st Mississippi was serving with Johnston in North Carolina, its commander
listed as Capt. G. W. Spooner.

Stevenson's Division, Maj. Gen. Carter L. Stevenson
    Cumming's Brigade, Col. Elihu P. Watkins
        34th Georgia, Capt. Russell A. Jones
        36th Georgia, Col. Charles E. Broyles
        39th Georgia, Capt. William P. Milton
        56th Georgia, Capt. Benjamin T. Spearman.
    Pettus's Brigade, Brig. Gen. Edmund W. Pettus
        20th Alabama, Col. James M. Dedman
        23rd Alabama, Lt. Col. Joseph B. Bibb
        30th Alabama, Lt. Col. James K. Elliott
        31st Alabama, Lt. Col. Thomas M. Arrington
        46th Alabama, Capt. George E. Brewer

Clayton's Division, Maj. Gen. Henry D. Clayton
    Stovall's Brigade, Brig. Gen. Marcellus A. Stovall
        40th Georgia, Col. Abda Johnson
        41st Georgia, Capt. Jared E. Stallings
        42nd Georgia, Col. Robert J. Henderson
        43rd Georgia, Col. Henry C. Kellogg
        52nd Georgia, Capt. Rufus R. Asbury.
    Holtzclaw's Brigade, Brig. Gen. James T. Holtzclaw
        18th Alabama, Lt. Col. Peter F. Hunley
        32nd and 58th Alabama, Col. Bushrod Jones
        36th Alabama, Capt. Nathan M. Carpenter
        38th Alabama, Capt. Charles E. Bussey.
    Gibson's Brigade, Brig. Gen. Randall L. Gibson
        1st Louisiana, Capt. J. C. Stafford
        4th Louisiana, Col. Samuel E. Hunter
        13th Louisiana, Lt. Col. Francis L. Campbell
        16th Louisiana, Lt. Col. Robert H. Lindsay
        19th Louisiana, Maj. Camp Flournoy
        20th Louisiana, Capt. Alexander Dresel
        25th Louisiana, Col. Francis C. Zacharie
        30th Louisiana, Maj. Arthur Picolet
        4th Louisiana Battalion, Capt. T. A. Bisland
        14th Louisiana Battalion Sharpshooters,
         Lt. A. T. Martin

STEWART'S CORPS, Lt. Gen. Alexander P. Stewart

Loring's Division, Maj. Gen. William W. Loring
  Featherston's Brigade, Brig. Gen. Winfield S. Featherston
    1st Mississippi, Capt. Owen D. Hughes
    3rd Mississippi, Capt. O. H. Johnston
    22nd Mississippi, Maj. Martin A. Oatis
    31st Mississippi, Capt. Robert A. Collins
    33rd Mississippi, Capt. T. L. Cooper
    40th Mississippi, Col. Wallace B. Colbert
    1st Mississippi Battalion, Maj. James M. Stigler
  Adams's Brigade, Col. Robert Lowry
    6th Mississippi, Lt. Col. Thomas J. Borden
    14th Mississippi, Col. Washington L. Doss
    15th Mississippi, Lt. Col. James R. Binford
    20th Mississippi, Maj. Thomas B. Graham
    23rd Mississippi, Maj. George W. B. Garrett
    43rd Mississippi, Col. Richard Harrison
  Scott's Brigade, Col. John Snodgrass
    55th Alabama, Maj. James B. Dickey
    57th Alabama, Maj. J. Horatio Wiley
    27th, 35th, and 49th Alabama (consolidated),
      Lt. Col. John D. Weeden
    12th Louisiana, Capt. James T. Davis

Walthall's Division, Maj. Gen. Edward C. Walthall
  Quarles's Brigade, Brig. Gen. George D. Johnston
    1st Alabama, Lt. Charles M. McRae
    42nd, 46th, 49 th, 53rd, and 55th Tennessee,
      Capt. Austin M. Duncan
    48th Tennessee, Col. William M. Voorhies.
  Cantey's Brigade, Brig. Gen. Charles M. Shelley
    17th Alabama, Capt. John Bolling, Jr.
    26th Alabama, Capt. D. M. Gideon
    29th Alabama, Capt. Samuel Abernethy
    37th Mississippi, Maj. Samuel H. Terrall
  Reynolds's Brigade, Brig. Gen. Daniel H. Reynolds

1st Arkansas Mounted Rifles (dismounted),
  Capt. R. P. Parks
2nd Arkansas Mounted Rifles (dismounted),
  Maj. James P. Eagle
4th Arkansas, Maj. Jesse A. Ross
9th Arkansas, Capt. W. L. Phifer
25th Arkansas, Lt. T. J. Edwards

French's Division, Maj. Gen. Edward C. Walthall[f]
  Ector's Brigade, Col. David Coleman
    29th North Carolina, Maj. Ezekiel H. Hampton
    39th North Carolina, Capt. James G. Crawford
    9th Texas, Maj. James H. McReynolds
    10th Texas Cavalry (dismounted), Col. C. R. Earp
    14th Texas Cavalry (dismounted),
      Capt. Robert H. Harkley
    32nd Texas Cavalry (dismounted)
      Maj. William E. Estes
  Sears's Brigade, Lt. Col. Reuben H. Shotwell
    4th, 35th, 36th, 39th and 46th Mississippi
    7th Mississippi Battalion (no regimental commanders
      available)[g]
  Cockrell's Brigade, Col. Peter C. Flournoy
    sent on detached duty prior to Nashville.

CHEATHAM'S CORPS, Maj. Gen. Benjamin F. Cheatham

Brown's Division, Brig. Gen. Mark P. Lowrey[h]
  Gist's Brigade, Lt. Col. Zachariah L. Watters
    46th Georgia, Capt. Malcolm Gillis
    65th Georgia and 8th Georgia Battalion,
      Capt. William W. Grant
    2nd Georgia Battalion Sharpshooters,
      Capt. William H. Brown

---

f. Walthall led his own and French's Division after French left the army on December 16 because of a serious eye condition.
g. Shotwell assumed command after Sears was wounded at Nashville on December 15.
h. Lowrey assumed division command after Maj. Gen. John C. Brown was wounded at Franklin. Army records do not show who replaced Lowrey as brigade commander, although Lt. Col. R. H. Abercrombie seems to be the likely candidate. The brigade was led by Lt. Col. J. F. Smith in the North Carolina operations.

16th South Carolina, Capt. John W. Bolling
24th South Carolina, Capt. W. C. Griffith.
Strahl's Brigade, Col. Andrew J. Kellar[i] and
    Col. C.W. Heiskell
    4th, 5th, 31st, 33rd, and 38th Tennessee,
      Lt. Col. Luke W. Finlay
    19th, 24th, and 41st Tennessee, Capt. Daniel A.
    Kennedy
Maney's Brigade, Col. Hume R. Feild
    4th (provisional), 6th, 9th, and 50th Tennessee,
      Lt. Col. George W. Pease
    1st and 27th Tennessee, Lt. Col. John L. House
    8th, 16th, and 28th Tennessee, Col. John H. Anderson.
Vaughan's Brigade, Col. William M. Watkins
    11th and 29th Tennessee, Maj. John E. Binns
    12th and 47th Tennessee, Capt. C. N. Wade
    13th, 51st, 52nd, and 154th Tennessee, Maj. John T.
    Williamson

Cleburne's Division, Brig. Gen. James A. Smith
    Govan's Brigade, Col. Peter V. Green
      1st, 2nd, 5th, 13th, 15th, and 24th Arkansas, (no
      known commander)
      6th and 7th Arkansas, Lt. Col. Peter Snyder
      8th and 19th Arkansas, Maj. David H. Hamiter[j]
    Lowrey's Brigade (no known commander)
      16th, 33rd, and 45th Alabama, Lt. Col. Robert H.
      Abercrombie
      5th Mississippi and 3rd Mississippi Battalion,
      Capt. F. M. Woodward
      8th and 32nd Mississippi, Maj. Andrew E. Moody

---

i. Kellar led the brigade in the first days of the retreat, but was replaced by
    Heiskell by the time Forrest organized the army's rear guard.
j. Brig. Gen. Daniel C. Govan, the brigade commander, was shot in the
    throat while engaged along the Granny White Pike on December 16. No
    records show who relieved him, but Green was in command when the
    brigade fought under Johnston in North Carolina in late March 1865.
    Some accounts state that Govan was recovered enough to rejoin his
    brigade during this time. Green had led the fragments of the 1st, 2nd,
    5th, 13th, 15th, and 24th Arkansas prior to Govan's wounding and likely
    continued to lead them during the retreat.

Granbury's Brigade, Capt. E. T. Broughton
  5th Confederate, Lt. William E. Smith
  35th Tennessee, Col. Benjamin J. Hill
  6th and 15th Texas, Capt. Benjamin R. Tyus
  7th Texas, Capt. O. P. Forrest
  10th Texas, Capt. R. D. Kennedy
  17th and 18th Texas Cavalry (dismounted), Capt. F. L.
    McKnight
  24th and 25th Texas Cavalry (dismounted), Capt. John
    F. Matthews
  Nutt's (Louisiana) Cavalry Company, Capt. L. M. Nutt
Smith's Brigade, Col. Charles H. Olmstead[k]
  54th, 57th, 63rd Georgia and 1st Georgia Volunteers

Bate's Division, Brig. Gen. William B. Bate
  Tyler's Brigade (no known commander)[l]
    37th Georgia, Capt. James A. Sanders
    4th Georgia Battalion Sharpshooters, Maj. Theodore
      D. Caswell
    2nd, 10th, 20th, and 37th Tennessee, Maj. H. C. Lucas
  Finley's Brigade, Maj. Jacob A. Lash
    1st and 3rd Florida, Capt. Matthew H. Strain
    6th Florida, Capt. Angus McMillan
    7th Florida, Capt. Robert B. Smith
    1st Florida Cavalry (dism.) and 4th Florida Infantry,
      Capt. George R. Langford.
  Jackson's Brigade (no known commander)[m]
    1st Georgia Confederate and 66th Georgia, Lt. Col.
      James C. Gordon
    25th Georgia, Capt. Joseph E. Fulton
    29th and 30th Georgia, Col. William D. Mitchell
    1st Georgia Battalion Sharpshooters, Lt. R. C. King

---

k. Olmstead, with Smith's Brigade, was with Forrest at Murfreesboro and
   rejoined Hood's army at Columbia after a forced march.
l. Leading Tyler's Brigade, Brig. Gen. Thomas B. Smith was captured and
   wounded (in that order) when the army collapsed on December 16. A
   captain identified only as H. Rice was in brigade command by March
   1865 in North Carolina. Lucas led the Tennessee units after Lt. Col.
   William H. Shy was killed on the sixteenth while defending the hill that
   now bears his name.
m. Brig. Gen. Henry R. Jackson was captured on December 16. His senior
   officer, Lt. Col. James C. Gordon, likely led the remaining troops away
   from Nashville.

ARTILLERY[n]

Lee's Corps, Maj. John W. Johnston, Lt. Col. Llewellyn Hoxton
    Courtney's Battalion, Capt. James P. Douglas
        Dent's (Alabama) Battery
        Douglas' (Texas) Battery
        Garrity's (Alabama) Battery
    Eldridge's Battalion, Capt. Charles E. Fenner
        Eufaula (Alabama) Battery
        Fenner's (Louisiana) Battery
        Stanford's (Mississippi) Battery
    Johnston's Battalion, Capt. John B. Rowan
        Corput's (Georgia) Battery
        Marshall's (Tennessee) Battery
        Stephens's (Georgia) Light Artillery

Stewart's Corps, Lt. Col. Samuel C. Williams
    Trueheart's Battalion
        Lumsden's (Alabama) Battery
        Selden's (Alabama) Battery
        Tarrant's (Alabama) Battery
    Myrick's Battalion
        Bouanchaud's (Louisiana) Battery
        Cowan's (Mississippi) Battery
        Darden's (Mississippi) Battery
    Storrs's Battalion
        Guibor's (Missouri) Battery
        Hoskins's (Mississippi) Battery
        Kolb's (Alabama) Battery

Cheatham's Corps, Col. Melancthon Smith
    Hoxton's Battalion
        Perry's (Florida) Battery
        Phelan's (Alabama) Battery
        Turner's (Mississippi) Battery

n. Maj. Gen. Arnold Elzey was assigned as the Army of Tennessee's chief of
   artillery in September 1864, but apparently was not with the troops when
   Hood entered Tennessee. Elzey was still recuperating from the devastating effects of a head wound sustained at Cold Harbor in 1862, which limited his physical activities.

Hotchkiss's Battalion
Bledsoe's (Missouri) Battery
Goldthwaite's (Alabama) Battery
Key's (Arkansas) Battery
Cobb's Battalion
Ferguson's (South Carolina) Battery
Phillips's (Mebane's) (Tennessee) Battery
Slocumb's (Louisiana) Battery

CAVALRY, Maj. Gen. Nathan B. Forrest

Chalmers's Division, Brig. Gen. James R. Chalmers
Rucker's Brigade, Col. Edmund W. Rucker[o]
7th Alabama
5th Mississippi
7th, 12th, 14th, and 15th Tennessee
26th Tennessee Battalion
Biffle's Brigade, Col. Jacob B. Biffle
9th and 10th Tennessee

Buford's Division, Brig. Gen. Abraham Buford[p]
Bell's Brigade, Col. Tyree H. Bell
2nd, 19th, 20th, and 21st Tennessee Cavalry
Nixon's Tennessee Regiment
Crossland's Brigade, Col. Edward Crossland
3rd, 7th, 8th, 12th Kentucky Mounted Infantry
12th Kentucky Cavalry
Huey's Kentucky Battalion

Jackson's Division, Brig. Gen. William H. Jackson
Armstrong's Brigade, Brig. Gen. Frank C. Armstrong
1st, 2nd, and 28th Mississippi Cavalry
Ballentine's Mississippi Regiment
Ross's Brigade, Brig. Gen. Lawrence S. Ross
3rd, 5th, 6th, and 9th Texas Cavalry
1st Texas Legion.

Artillery: Morton's Tennessee Battery

---

o. Rucker was wounded and captured on the night of December 16. Lt. Col. Rolla R. White of the 14th Tennessee led the brigade thereafter.
p. Buford was shot in the leg on December 24 at Richland Creek. Chalmers led his own and Buford's Division for the remainder of the retreat.

APPENDIX E

Timeline of the Tennessee Campaign

1864

September 25. Jefferson Davis arrives at Palmetto, Georgia, to meet with Hood and inspect the Army of Tennessee.

September 29. Hood's army starts march north; Union major general George Thomas ordered to Tennessee with two infantry division to deal with Forrest.

October 5. Battle of Allatoona Pass (Georgia).

October 19–20. With Hood's army moving into northern Alabama, Sherman calls off his pursuit, deciding to return to Atlanta and prepare for a march through Georgia to some point on the southern coast; Hood's army reaches Gadsden, Alabama, on the twentieth.

October 24. Brig. Gen. James H. Wilson assumes cavalry command in the U.S. Military Division of the Mississippi and immediately begins massive reorganization of the mounted troops; Wilson's appointment and tireless effort will be crucial factors in the campaign.

October 30. Confederate army encamps at Tuscumbia, Alabama, just south of the Tennessee River; rainy weather will delay them there for three weeks as Thomas builds an army to meet them.

November 13–20. Hood's army is finally able to cross the Tennessee despite the weather and begins a general movement toward Tennessee on the twenty-first.

November 15. Sherman torches much of Atlanta and embarks on his march to the sea.

November 22. Cavalry fighting near Lawrenceburg, Tennessee, as Hood's army proceeds north.

November 28. Armies in vicinity of Columbia, Tennessee; Schofield's Union forces retreat north toward Spring Hill.

November 29. Clash at Spring Hill, Tennessee; Hood misses chance to bag Schofield or at least get between his forces and Nashville; Schofield evacuates Spring Hill positions overnight on November 29–30.

November 30. Battle of Franklin; Hood loses more than 7,000 men, including a number of generals and other commanders, vainly trying to batter Schofield's entrenched line; Schofield retreats during the night, reaching Nashville's defenses by December 1.

December 2. Confederate army advances toward Nashville and begins digging in a few miles south of the city along a five-mile-long position.

December 7–8. A worsening winter storm inundates the region, including an ice storm on the eighth that paralyzes the movements of both armies; Thomas is under increasing pressure from Halleck and Grant to attack Hood, despite the frigid weather.

December 10. Thomas plans large-scale assault but is thwarted by bad conditions.

December 15. First day of Battle of Nashville; a thaw and break in the weather finally allows Thomas to attack; his offensive forces Hood to retreat a few miles; Maj. Gen. John A. Logan is en route to Nashville to replace Thomas, whose success is not yet known to the Union high command.

December 16. Second day of Battle of Nashville; Thomas renews assault and eventually crumples the enemy's left and routs the Confederates; Hood's fragmented forces funnel south on the Franklin Pike.

December 17. Wilson's cavalry and Wood's infantry lead the pursuit; fighting at Hollow Tree Gap, Franklin, and West Harpeth River; Confederates camp between Franklin and Spring Hill.

December 18. Federal cavalry pursuit of Hood continues toward Columbia; skirmishing near Spring Hill and action at Rutherford Creek; Union IV Corps crosses Harpeth River at Franklin; Confederate army begins crossing Duck River at Columbia; Forrest and a portion of his command reach Columbia from the Murfreesboro area after earlier sending units ahead to Hood.

December 19. Confederates continue crossing the Duck; more fighting at Rutherford Creek.

December 20. Confederate army completes Duck crossing by early morning; Forrest is ordered to organize a rear guard of his cavalry and picked infantry brigades to hold up the Union advance.

December 24. Fighting at Richland Creek, north of Pulaski.

December 25. Confederate rear guard evacuates Pulaski after destroying supplies and munitions; Forrest makes a stand at Anthony's Hill south of town; at the Tennessee River, engineers continue work on Hood's pontoon bridge.

December 26. Fighting at Sugar Creek near the Tennessee-Alabama border; the rear guard continues to try to delay the Union pursuit; Confederate pontoon bridge is completed before dawn and army begins immediate crossing; Union gunboats try to reach the span but are driven back by enemy artillery and possible concerns about the river conditions.

December 27. Dropping water level prevents the Union navy from making another assault on the bridge; Union cavalry and infantry in pursuit are running out or are low on rations as Confederates continue to cross the Tennessee.

December 28. Forrest's rear guard crosses the span before daybreak; engineers dismantle it shortly thereafter.

December 29. Thomas orders a halt to his pursuit; Hood's army proceeds west and south from area of Bainbridge toward Corinth, Mississippi.

December 31. Union cavalry destroy Confederate pontoon train south of Tuscumbia.

1865

January 1. Union horsemen who burned Hood's pontoon train on the thirty-first waylay a Confederate supply train in Itawamba County, Mississippi, torching more than 100 wagons.

January 3. Hood reaches Corinth, immediately making plans to withdraw the army farther south to Tupelo because of a lack of supplies.

January 5. Hood establishes headquarters in Tupelo, with the army to follow; Thomas offers Lincoln the gift of Nashville as a late Christmas present.

January 13. Hood requests to be relieved of army command.

January 15. Hood is relieved, replaced by Lt. Gen. Richard Taylor, but order does not take effect until January 23; Thomas arrives at Eastport, Mississippi, amid a Union military buildup there to continue the offensive.

January 16. Thomas, a major general of volunteers since April 1862, is promoted to the same rank in the regular Army.

April 8–9. Elements of the now-dismantled Army of Tennessee fight at Spanish Fort and Fort Blakely in the Mobile, Alabama, defenses, before both strongholds are overwhelmed by Union forces.

April 26. Other remnants of Hood's army surrender with Gen. Joseph Johnston in North Carolina.

May 4. Forrest and his cavalry, along with intermingled units fleeing after the fall of Mobile, are surrendered in Alabama; Forrest capitulates on May 9.

Notes

INTRODUCTION

1. U.S. War Department, *The War of the Rebellion: A Compilation of the Official Records of the Union and Confederate Armies* (Washington, DC: Government Printing Office, 1880–1901), part 1, 700 (hereafter cited as *OR*).

CHAPTER 1

1. Hudson Strode, *Jefferson Davis: Tragic Hero—The Last Twenty-five Years, 1864–1889* (New York: Harcourt, Brace & World, Inc., 1964), 93; Edward A. Pollard, *The Lost Cause—A New Southern History of the War of the Confederates* (New York: E. B. Treat & Company, 1867), 581; *Daily Richmond Enquirer*, 29 September 1864; and Thomas L. Connelly, *Autumn of Glory: The Army of Tennessee, 1862–1865* (Baton Rouge, LA: Lousiana State University Press, 1971), 478–79. Thomas Connelly points out that in speeches on this trip and prior, Davis mentioned Tennessee troops triumphantly returning to their state, but this appears to have been merely crowd-rousing rhetoric since he and Hood did not discuss such a move. When Davis left Palmetto, Hood was to focus on cutting the Western & Atlantic.

2. John Bell Hood, *Advance and Retreat: Personal Experiences in the United States and Confederate Armies* (Secaucus, NJ: Blue and Grey Press, 1985), 253–55.

3. *Cincinnati Commercial*, 26 October 1864, reprinted in the *Charleston Mercury*, 7 November 1864.

4. Ezra J. Warner, *Generals in Blue: Lives of the Union Commanders* (Baton Rouge, LA: Louisiana State University Press, 1964), 501.

5. Stanley F. Horn, *The Decisive Battle of Nashville* (Baton Rouge, LA: Louisiana State University Press, 1984), 9; Freeman Cleaves, *Rock of Chickamauga: The Life of General George H. Thomas* (Norman, OK: University of Oklahoma Press, 1948), 242; and Mark M. Boatner III, *The Civil War Dictionary* (New York: David McKay Company, Inc., 1987), 291.

6. *OR*, part 3, 333; and William T. Sherman, *Sherman's Civil War* (New York: Crowell-Collier Publishing Company, 1962), 318. Sherman contradicted himself somewhat in postwar accounts. From a spy who was at Palmetto and from Southern newspaper accounts, Sherman claimed

that he knew Davis had stirred Hood's Tennessee and Kentucky troops with promises that they soon would be back on their "native soil" and that the Yankees would be ousted from Georgia in a catastrophic retreat similar to Napoleon's debacle. "He [Davis] made no conceal-ment of these vainglorious boasts," Sherman noted after the war, "and thus gave us the full key to his future designs. To be forewarned was to be forearmed, and I think we took full advantage of the occasion." At the time of Davis's speech, there was no concrete plan for a Confeder-ate thrust into Tennessee, but Davis, with his well publicized speeches, had inadvertently put the Federals on alert.

7. Jerry Keenan, "The Gallant Hood of Texas," *America's Civil War* 7, no. 1 (March 1994): 46; and William J. Cooper, Jr., *Jefferson Davis, American* (New York: Alfred A. Knopf, 2000), 536.

8. Richard M. McMurry, *John Bell Hood and the War for Southern Independ-ence* (Lincoln, NE: University of Nebraska Press, 1982), 164; and Alfred Roman, *The Military Operations of General Beauregard in the War between the States* (New York: Harper & Brothers, 1884), 2:293. Hood later said he did this in order to be closer to a link with Forrest, who was raiding in western Tennessee. Beauregard claimed Hood told him that he moved farther west because he believed the landing was too heavily guarded. It is beyond the scope of this work to analyze the controversies surround-ing Hood's altered plans and Beauregard's responses.

9. *OR*, part 3, 358, 365, 377–78.

10. Shortly after the war, Thomas claimed that he had proposed a march to the sea to Sherman just after Atlanta's capture but his idea had gone nowhere. Thomas B. Van Horne, *The Life of Major-General George H. Thomas* (New York: Charles Scribner's Sons, 1882), 255–56, 261, 270.

11. McMurry, *John Bell Hood*, 164; and Connelly, *Autumn of Glory*, 486–87.

12. *Recollections and Reminiscences, 1861–1865* (South Carolina Division, United Daughters of the Confederacy), vol. 5, 397.

13. John Allan Wyeth, *The Life of General Nathan Bedford Forrest* (New York: Barnes & Noble Publishing, 2006), 505.

14. Cleaves, *Rock of Chickamauga*, 246.

CHAPTER 2

1. *OR*, part 1, 752; *OR*, part 2, 850–51; Horn, *Decisive Battle of Nashville*, 14, states the linked cavalry numbered about 8,000, which seems high.

2. Van Horne, *Life of Major-General George H. Thomas*, 275.

3. Sherman, *Sherman's Civil War*, 355; *OR*, part 1, 1,242; Roman, *Military Operations*, 2:301; Connelly, *Autumn of Glory*, 488–89.

4. *OR*, pt.1, 1,227–28; Hood, *Advance and Retreat*, 278, 304–5; Connelly, *Autumn of Glory*, 489–91; and McMurry, *John Bell Hood*, 169.

5. McMurry, *John Bell Hood*, 33, 99; Keenan, "Gallant Hood of Texas," 44–45; and Ezra J. Warner, *Generals in Gray: Lives of the Confederate Com-manders* (Baton Rouge, LA: Louisiana State University Press, 1959), 142–43; and Jack D. Welsh, *Medical Histories of Confederate Generals* (Kent, OH: Kent State University Press, 1995), 105–6.

6. Ibid.

7. Strode, *Jefferson Davis*, 84; and Wiley Sword, *The Confederacy's Last Hurrah: Spring Hill, Franklin, and Nashville* (Lawrenceville, KS: University Press of Kansas, 1992), 12; and *New York Times*, 23 July 1864.

8. Warner, *Generals in Gray*, 183–84; Welsh, *Medical Histories*, 136–37; and Horn, *Decisive Battle of Nashville*, 15.

9. Warner, *Generals in Gray*, 293–94.

10. Warner, *Generals in Gray*, 47–48; and Horn, *Decisive Battle of Nashville*, 14; and Peter Cozzens, *No Better Place to Die* (Urbana, IL: University of Illinois Press, 1990), 213.

11. *OR*, part 1, 1,227.

12. *Confederate Veteran* 15 (November 1908), 508; and W. O. Dodd, "Reminiscences of Hood's Tennessee Campaign," *Southern Historical Society Papers* 9 (1881): 519.

13. Sword, *Confederacy's Last Hurrah*, 83–84.

14. Van Horne, *Life of Major-General George H. Thomas*, 272; Arthur Howard Noll, ed., *Doctor Quintard—Chaplain, C.S.A., and Second Bishop of Tennessee—Being His Story of the War (1861–1865)* (Sewanee, TN: The University Press of Sewanee, 1905), 108–9; and Connelly, *Autumn of Glory*, 492.

15. *OR*, part 1, 656–57; and Hood, *Advance and Retreat*, 283–90.

16. *OR*, part 1, 108; and Col. Harry Stone, "Hood's Invasion of Tennessee," *The Century* 34, issue 4 (August 1887): 607–8.

17. Hood, *Advance and Retreat*, 295–96; and Edward Young McMorries, *History of the First Regiment, Alabama Volunteer Infantry, C.S.A.* (Nashville, TN: The Publications Committee, 1904), 87.

18. Dodd, "Reminiscences of Hood's Tennessee Campaign," 523.

19. Stone, "Hood's Invasion of Tennessee," 601–2.

20. Paul H. Stockdale, *The Death of an Army: The Battle of Nashville and Hood's Retreat* (Murfreesboro, TN: Southern Heritage Press, 1992), 35–37; and Dodd, "Reminiscences of Hood's Tennessee Campaign," 523.

21. Sam R. Watkins, *"Co. Aytch": A Sideshow of the Big Show* 236–37.

22. Horn, *Decisive Battle of Nashville*, 43-44.

23. *OR*, part 1, 75, 654; and Wyeth, *Life of General Nathan Bedford Forrest*, 523.

24. *OR*, part 1, 654 (Hood's February 15 report); Connelly, *Autumn of Glory*, 507; and Horn, *Decisive Battle of Nashville*, p 68.

25. Sword, *Confederacy's Last Hurrah*, 302–3; and Stockdale, *Death of an Army*, 45.

26. Stockdale, *Death of an Army*, 12; Watkins, *"Co. Aytch"*, 237; and *Recollections and Reminiscences*, vol. 1, 257.

27. Sword, *Confederacy's Last Hurrah*, 303–4; Watkins, *"Co. Aytch"*, 236–37; and Richard Harwell, ed., *The Journal of Kate Cumming—A Civil War Nurse* (Savannah, GA: The Beehive Press, 1975), 235.

28. *OR*, part 1, 660. Olmstead (1st Volunteer Regiment of Georgia) had assumed command of Brig. Gen. James A. Smith's brigade after the Battle of Franklin, when Smith rose to lead Patrick Cleburne's division after Cleburne was killed. The 1st Volunteers should not be confused with the 1st Georgia Regulars.

29. *OR*, part 1, 658. The Tennessee & Alabama also was known as the Nashville & Decatur because of a consolidation agreement among the lines in the region. Forrest had wrecked many of the bridges and trestles of this line between Decatur and Spring Hill in his September–October raid, but they were soon rebuilt by the Federals.
30. Roman, *Military Operations*, 309–12, 625; Hood, *Advance and Retreat*, 299; and *OR*, part 2, 685.
31. *OR*, part 2, 685; and Sword, *Confederacy's Last Hurrah*, 304.

CHAPTER 3
 1. Gen. Jacob D. Cox, *Sherman's March to the Sea: Hood's Tennessee Campaign & the Carolinas Campaigns of 1865* (New York: Da Capo Press, 1994), 104–5; and Stone, "Hood's Invasion of Tennessee," 608.
 2. *New York Times*, 1 January 1865; Boatner, *Civil War Dictionary*, 836; and Bruce Catton, *This Hallowed Ground: The Story of the Union Side of the Civil War* (Garden City, NY: Doubleday, 1956), 366–68.
 3. Warner, *Generals in Blue*, 500–502; and Cleaves, *Rock of Chickamauga*, 50.
 4. Warner, *Generals in Blue*, 500; and Sword, *Confederacy's Last Hurrah*, 75.
 5. Cozzens, *No Better Place to Die*, 21–22; Warner, *Generals in Blue*, 51–52, 500–502; and Boatner, *Civil War Dictionary*, 606, 836.
 6. Warner, *Generals in Blue*, 501; and Sword, *Confederacy's Last Hurrah*, 77.
 7. Sherman, *Sherman's Civil War*, 380–81; and U.S. War Department, *Official Records of the Union and Confederate Navies in the War of the Rebellion* (Washington, DC: U.S. Government Printing Office, 1894–1922), vol. 2, 639. Sherman did not receive this message until December 16 near Savannah.
 8. Clarence C. Buel and Robert V. Johnson, *Battles and Leaders of the Civil War: Being for the Most Part Contributions by Union and Confederate Authors* (New York: Century Co., 1887), vol. 4, 467–68; Horn, *Decisive Battle of Nashville*, 77; and Jerry Keenan, *Wilson's Cavalry Corps: Union Campaigns in the Western Theater, October 1864 through Spring 1865* (Jefferson, NC: McFarland, 1998), 46.
 9. Warner, *Generals in Blue*, 566–67; *OR*, part 2, 249; and Sherman *Sherman's Civil War*, 337.
10. Sherman, *Sherman's Civil War*, 380–81. Sherman did not receive this message until December 17 near Savannah.
11. *OR*, part 2, 84; and Sword, *Confederacy's Last Hurrah*, 76–79.
12. Stockdale, *Death of an Army*, 35.
13. Stone, "Hood's Invasion of Tennessee," 610; and *OR*, part 1, 108–9.
14. *OR*, part 2, 96.
15. Stone, "Hood's Invasion of Tennessee," 608. Unsure if the message had been dispatched, Grant sent word to Thomas that night that the order was suspended. Thomas would be unaware of the order until years later when Halleck told him about it during a conversation in San Francisco.
16. Horn, *Decisive Battle of Nashville*, 51–52; and Stone, "Hood's Invasion of Tennessee," 608–10.
17. Warner, *Generals in Blue*, 569–70; Boatner, *Civil War Dictionary*, 946–47; Frances H. Kennedy, ed., *The Civil War Battlefield Guide* (Boston:

Houghton Mifflin, 1990), 154–56; and James H. Wilson, *Under the Old Flag* (New York: B. Appleton and Company, 1912), 101.

18. Boatner, *Civil War Dictionary*, 189–90.
19. Buel and Johnson, *Battles and Leaders*, vol. 4, 467.
20. Stone, "Hood's Invasion of Tennessee," 609.
21. Wilson, *Under the Old Flag*, 91and Cleaves, *Rock of Chickamauga*, 260.
22. Stone, "Hood's Invasion of Tennessee," 610–11.
23. Wilson, *Under the Old Flag*, 109, 143–44; and Buel and Johnson, *Battles and Leaders*, vol. 4, 467.
24. Stone, "Hood's Invasion of Tennessee," 609.

CHAPTER 4
 1. Stockdale, *Death of an Army*, 41.
 2. Cleaves, *Rock of Chickamauga*, 261.
 3. John Walker, "Blood on the Snow," *Military Heritage* 8, no. 5 (April 2007): 42; and Horn, *Decisive Battle of Nashville*, 92. Redoubts 4 and 5 had not been completed at the time of attack.
 4. Horn, *Decisive Battle of Nashville*, 93; and Walker, "Blood on the Snow," 42.
 5. Sword, *Confederacy's Last Hurrah*, 341–42; Connelly, *Autumn of Glory*, 508–9, Horn, *Decisive Battle of Nashville*, 76–77; and Hood, *Advance and Retreat*, 302.
 6. *OR*, part 1, 756, 771; and Wyeth, *Life of General Nathan Bedford Forrest*, 531.
 7. Stockdale, *Death of an Army*, 29.
 8. *New York Times*, 1 January 1865; Cleaves, *Rock of Chickamauga*, 254; and *OR*, part 2, 194–95.
 9. *OR*, part 1, 50; and *OR*, part 2, 194–95.
10. Connelly, *Autumn of Glory*, 510; and Stephen Z. Starr, *The Union Cavalry in the Civil War* (Baton Rouge, LA: Louisiana State University Press, 1985), vol. 3, 550.
11. Bromfield L. Ridley, *Battles and Sketches of the Army of Tennessee* (Mexico, MO: Missouri Publishing Company, 1906), 431–32; and *OR*, part 2, 696.
12. *Richmond Daily Dispatch*, 26 January 1865.
13. Horn, *Decisive Battle of Nashville*, 118–20.
14. Horn, *Decisive Battle of Nashville*, 121; and *OR*, part 1, 689.
15. Horn, *Decisive Battle of Nashville*, 121–22; *OR*, part 1, 689; and Walker, "Blood on the Snow," 44.
16. Hood, *Advance and Retreat*, 303.

CHAPTER 5
 1. Watkins, *"Co. Aytch"*240. Various accounts dispute descriptions of the soldiers being panicked.
 2. Ridley, *Battles and Sketches*, 432; Buel and Johnson, *Battles and Leaders*, vol.4, 437; and *OR*, part 1, 660.
 3. Noyes, "Excerpts from the Civil War Diary of E. T. Eggleston," *Tennessee Historical Quarterly* 17 (December 1958): 345; *OR*, part 1, 689; and *Confederate Veteran* 7, no. 4 (April 1899): 154.

4. *OR*, part 1, 695; and Horn, *Decisive Battle of Nashville*, 148.

5. *OR*, part 1, 698; Warner, *Generals in Gray*, 52–53; and Welsh, *Medical Histories*, 40.

6. Watkins, *"Co. Aytch"*, 240; *Confederate Veteran*, 17, no.1 (January 1909): 12–13; and McMurry, *John Bell Hood*, 350.

7. *OR*, part 1, 698, 695.

8. Herman Hattaway, *General Stephen D. Lee* (Starkville, MS: University Press of Mississippi, 1976), 143–44; Stockdale, *Death of an Army*, 88; *Confederate Veteran* 12, no. 7, 350; and *OR*, part 1, 689.

9. *OR*, part 1, 698–99; Hattaway, *General Stephen D. Lee*, 143–44; and Stephen D. Lee, "Corrections of Gen. Anderson's Report of Jonesboro," *Southern Historical Society Papers* 5 (1878): 131.

10. *OR*, part 1, ch.57 698-99, 703; *Confederate Veteran* 12, no. 7, 350; and Sword, *Confederacy's Last Hurrah*, 387.

11. *Confederate Veteran* 18, no. 7, (July 1910): 327; *OR*, part 1, 692, 695, 698–99; and Warner, *Generals in Gray*, 52–53.

12. *OR*, part 1, 134, 181; and Warner, *Generals in Gray*, 28.

13. *OR*, part 1, 689–90, 724; and Buel and Johnson, *Battles and Leaders*, vol. 4, 437; Watkins, *"Co. Aytch,"* 240–41.

14. Buel and Johnson, *Battles and Leaders*, vol. 4, 437.

15. *OR*, part 1, 689, 695.

16. *OR*, part 1, 765–66; Horn, *Decisive Battle of Nashville*, 151; and *Confederate Veteran* 13, no. 1 (January 1905): 29–30.

17. *Confederate Veteran* 6, no. 7 (July 1898): 337; and Sword, *Confederacy's Last Hurrah*, 284–85.

18. *OR*, part 1, 564; Starr, *Union Cavalry in the Civil War*, 550–51; Sword, *Confederacy's Last Hurrah*, 386; Horn, *Decisive Battle of Nashville*, 151; and Wilson, *Under the Old Flag*, 118–21.

19. Stockdale, *Death of an Army*, 91; *Confederate Veteran* 13, no.1, 29–30; and *OR*, part 1, 591.

20. *Confederate Veteran* 13, no.1, 29–30; and *OR*, part 1, 591.

21. Buel and Johnson, *Battles and Leaders*, vol. 4, 469.

22. Horn, *Decisive Battle of Nashville*, 151–52; *OR*, part 1, 591–92; and Thomas Jordan and J. P. Pryor, *The Campaigns of Lt.-Gen. N. B. Forrest and of Forrest's Cavalry* (New Orleans, LA: Blelock & Company, 1868), 641–42.

23. Coon describes the banner as Rucker's "division" flag, which is erroneous since Rucker commanded a brigade. The standard could have been Chalmers's division flag. Rucker is also referred to as a general by Coon and in other Union accounts, which is inaccurate. *OR*, part 1, 591–92, 595.

24. Horn, *Decisive Battle of Nashville*, 151; Jordan and Pryor, *Campaigns of Lt.-Gen N. B. Forrest*, 642–43; Stockdale, *Death of an Army*, 92; and *OR*, part 1, 767. Some Rebels later claimed that Wilson ordered buildings at the university in Tuscaloosa burned in early April 1865 in retribution for the cadets' defense at Nashville.

25. *OR*, part 1, 766; and *Confederate Veteran* 13, no. 1 (January 1905): 29–30.

26. Wyeth, *Life of General Nathan Bedford Forrest*, 529; and Wilson, *Under the Old Flag*, 120.
27. *OR*, part 1, 750.
28. *Confederate Veteran* 16, no. 4 (April 1908): 192; Warner, *Generals in Gray*, 141–42; and *OR*, part 1, 706.
29. *Confederate Veteran* 2, no.2 (February 1894): 47; *Confederate Veteran* 18, no. 7 (July 1910): 327; and Sword, *Confederacy's Last Hurrah*, 387, 389.
30. Watkins, *"Co. Aytch"*, 240–41.
31. Cox, *Sherman's March to the Sea*, 127; and *OR*, part 1, 134.
32. Stockdale, *Death of an Army*, 108; and Buel and Johnson, *Battles and Leaders*, vol. 4, 470.
33. Buel and Johnson, *Battles and Leaders*, vol. 4, 437; *OR*, part 1, 756; Wyeth, *Life of General Nathan Bedford Forrest*, 531–32; Hood, *Advance and Retreat*, 332; and Scott Walker, *Hell's Broke Loose in Georgia: Survival in a Civil War Regiment* (Athens, GA: University of Georgia Press, 2005), 207.
34. Wyeth, *Life of General Nathan Bedford Forrest*, 530; and Wilson, *Under the Old Flag*, 127. Some accounts state that Rucker's arm was later amputated at a Nashville hospital. It is unclear whether Rucker's initial interrogation by Hatch occurred at the Tucker house or at a location near the Granny White cavalry fight.
35. *Confederate Veteran* 13, no. 1, 29–30.
36. *OR*, part 1, 50.
37. *OR*, part 2, 210–11.
38. Stockdale, *Death of an Army*, 109; *OR*, part 1, 40; and Cox, *Sherman's March to the Sea*, 127.
39. *OR*, part 1, 690; Welsh, *Medical Histories*, 117; and Warner, *Generals in Gray*, 158–59.
40. Sword, *Confederacy's Last Hurrah*, 390–91; and Stockdale, *Death of an Army*, 177–78.
41. *OR*, part 2, 214; and *OR*, part 1, 161.
42. Dodd, "Reminiscences of Hood's Tennessee Campaign," 523; James Porter, *Confederate Military History* 8: 167; and *Confederate Veteran* 17, no. 1 (January 1909): 19.
43. *New York Times*, 9 January 1865.

CHAPTER 6

1. Wilson, *Under the Old Flag*, 130; and Stockdale, *Death of an Army*, 120.
2. *OR*, part 2, 222.
3. *OR*, part 2, 239–40; Warner, *Generals in Blue*, 272–73; and Boatner, *Civil War Dictionary*, 466–67.
4. *Confederate Veteran* 13, no. 4 (April 1905): 161.
5. *Confederate Veteran* 18, no. 7 (July 1910): 327; *OR*, part 1, 698–99; and Sword, *Confederacy's Last Hurrah*, 394.
6. *Nashville Journal* quoted in the *Charleston Mercury*, 4 January 1865.
7. Chaplain Quintard claims that Gist initially was buried at St. John's Church in Ashwood, Tennessee, along with Gen. Hiram Granbury and Gen. Otho F. Strahl, also killed at Franklin, but this does not appear to be the case. Noll, ed., *Doctor Quintard*, 115.

8. Richard M. McMurry, ed., "A Mississippian at Nashville," *Civil War Times Illustrated* 12, no. 2 (May 1973): 14.

9. *Confederate Veteran* 13, no. 1, 29–30. No other accounts place Hood at the gap that morning, but it is not unreasonable, even if Johnston's recollection was some forty years after the event, to assume that he rode the four miles from Franklin to check on his rear guard. Hood makes no mention of this in his memoir. Colonel Kelley, Johnston's commander at the time, read this postwar narrative and made some corrections that were published with Johnston's article, but does not dispute the Hood sighting, although he may not have been in a position that morning to say otherwise.

10. Sword, *Confederacy's Last Hurrah*, 394; and Charles C. Coffin, *Freedom Triumphant: The Fourth Period of the War of the Rebellion from September, 1864, to Its Close* (New York: Harper & Brothers, 1890), 158.

11. *Confederate Veteran* 18, no. 7 (July 1910): 327; and *OR*, part 1, 699. Wilson says Knipe hit Stevenson's—not Clayton's—division here, which is inaccurate. Wilson, *Under the Old Flag*, 464.

12. *OR*, part 1, 689; and Sword, *Confederacy's Last Hurrah*, 447. Shacklett's men belonged to Col. Edward Crossland's brigade.

13. *OR*, part 1, 607, 703; *Nashville Journal*, 24 December 1864, reprinted in the *Charleston Mercury*, 4 January 1865.

14. *OR*, part 1, 607, 690; Sword, *Confederacy's Last Hurrah*, 395; Hattaway, *General Stephen D. Lee*, 145–46; and *OR*, part 1, 706.

15. *OR*, part 1, 703; and *Confederate Veteran* 18, no. 7, 327.

16. Clayton said Falconnet was a colonel commanding a brigade, which appears to be erroneous. Clayton also states Falconnet belonged to the 14th Battalion, Alabama Cavalry, which was incorporated into the 7th Alabama in 1863. *OR*, part 1, 699.

17. *OR*, part 1, 699, 703, 706.

18. Sword, *Confederacy's Last Hurrah*, 395–96; Wilson, *Under the Old Flag*, 464; and Richard W. Johnson, *A Soldier's Reminiscences in Peace and War* (Philadelphia: J. B. Lippincott Company, 1886), 289.

19. *OR*, part 1, 690; and Johnson, *Soldier's Reminiscences*, 290.

20. Sword, *Confederacy's Last Hurrah*, 396; and *OR*, part 1, 601–2.

21. *OR*, part 1, 701; and *Confederate Veteran* 18, no. 7 (July 1910): 327.

22. *OR*, part 2, 228; Johnson, *Soldier's Reminiscences*, 290; Sword, *Confederacy's Last Hurrah*, 396; and John W. Carroll, *Autobiography and Reminiscences of John W. Carroll* (Henderson, TN: N.p., 1898), 36.

23. *OR*, part 1, 134, 157, 291.

24. L. G. Bennett and W. M. Haigh, *History of the Thirty-sixth Regiment, Illinois Volunteers, during the War of the Rebellion* (Aurora, IL: Knickerbocker & Hodder, 1876), 695

25. L. W. Day, *Story of the One-Hundred-First Ohio Infantry: A Memorial Volume* (Cleveland, OH: W. M. Bayne Printing Co., 1894), 313–14; and *OR*, part 1, 135, 181.

26. Roman, *Military Operations*, 626; and *OR*, part 2, 699–700.

27. *OR*, part 1, 766; and Wilson, *Under the Old Flag*, vol. 2, 129.

28. *OR*, part 1, 237.

29. *OR*, part 1, 690, 706.

30. Horn, *Decisive Battle of Nashville*, 160; Buel and Johnson, *Battles and Leaders*, vol. 4, 437; Winston Groom, *Shrouds of Glory: From Atlanta to Nashville—The Last Great Campaign of the Civil War* (New York: Pocket Books, 1995), 259.

31. *OR*, part 1, 157, 238.

32. *OR*, part 2, 706–7.

33. *OR*, part 1, 690; and Buel and Johnson, *Battles and Leaders*, 470.

34. James Harvey Mathes, *General Forrest* (New York: D. Appleton and Co., 1902), 322; *OR*, part 1, 592, 696; John R. Lundberg, *The Finishing Stroke: Texans in the 1864 Tennessee Campaign* (Abilene, TX: McWhinney Foundation Press, 2002), 117–18; and Sword, *Confederacy's Last Hurrah*, 397–98. At least one account states this battery was Bledsoe's Missouri Battery from Cheatham's Corps, which is apparently wrong. On the morning of the seventeenth, Lee had ordered the five guns of Courtney's Battalion, which included Douglas's Battery, to assist Stevenson.

35. *Confederate Veteran* 18, no. 7 (July 1910): 328; and *OR*, part 1, 566-67. Whether by exaggeration—which seems more likely—or error, Wilson claimed in at least one postwar account that his men were battling Forrest here: "Forrest did his best to hold his ground, but it was impossible. Hedges rode headlong over the battery." Buel and Johnson, *Battles and Leaders*, 470.

36. *Confederate Veteran* 18, no. 7 (July 1910): 328.

37. Buel and Johnson, *Battles and Leaders*, 470; *OR*, part 1, 578, 592, 692, 696; Lundberg, *Finishing Stroke*, 117–18; and Sword, *Confederacy's Last Hurrah*, 399.

38. Buel and Johnson, *Battles and Leaders*, 470; and Lyman B. Pierce, *History of the Second Iowa Cavalry* (Burlington, IA: Hawk-Eye Steam Books, 1865), 151.

39. *OR*, part 1, 699, 707.

40. Buel and Johnson, *Battles and Leaders*, 470; *OR*, part 1, 607, 699–700; and Wilson, *Under the Old Flag*, vol. 2, 123–24.

41. James Dinkins, *1861–1865: Personal Recollections and Experiences in the Confederate Army, by an 'Old Johnnie'* (Cincinnati, OH: The Robert Clark Company, 1897), 251; Welsh, *Medical Histories*, 31; Jordan and Pryor, *Campaigns of Lt.-Gen. N. B. Forrest*, 644; and Sword, *Confederacy's Last Hurrah*, 398. For a slightly different version of this action, see H. A. Tyler's account in *Confederate Veteran* 12, no. 9 (September 1904). Tyler claims Buford was attacked by three Federals and killed one, hit another on the head with his pistol, breaking it in the process, and pulled the other out of the saddle by his hair, thus making his escape.

42. Pierce, *Second Iowa Cavalry*, 149, 151–52.

43. *OR*, part 1, 592–96; and Pierce, *Second Iowa Cavalry*, 150–51. At least one Union report states this captured Confederate flag belonged to Ross's cavalry brigade, which is erroneous, since Ross was then en route with Forrest's main body to join Hood.

44. *Confederate Veteran* 18, no. 7 (July 1910): 328; Pierce, *Second Iowa Cavalry*, 152; *OR*, part 1, 696; and Dinkins, *1861–1865*, 251.

45. Jordan and Pryor, *Campaigns of Lt.-Gen. N. B. Forrest*, 644; Horn, *Decisive Battle of Nashville*, 160; and Buel and Johnson, *Battles and Leaders*, vol. 4, 437.

46. Buel and Johnson, *Battles and Leaders*, vol. 4, 437; *OR*, part 1, 690, 706; and Warner, *Generals in Gray*, 137.

47. Buel and Johnson, *Battles and Leaders*, vol. 4, 470; Keenan, *Wilson's Cavalry Corps*, 115; and Wilson, *Under the Old Flag*, 133.

48. *OR*, part 2, 238–39.

49. *OR*, part 1, 566; and Wilson, *Under the Old Flag*, 130, 470. In his war memoir, Wilson states that he called off the pursuit around 10 P.M. and that his troopers took about an hour more to re-form. This appears to be erroneous according to battle reports that night, which indicate that the action apparently ended by 7 P.M.

50. *OR* part 1, 573–74; *OR*, part 2, 241; and Keenan, *Wilson's Cavalry Corps*, 115.

51. *OR*, part 2, 233, 239.

52. Stockdale, *Death of an Army*, 130; and Sword, *Confederacy's Last Hurrah*, 386.

53. *OR*, part 2, 228–29.

54. Ibid.; and *OR*, part 2, 239.

55. *OR*, part 2, 699–700.

56. *OR*, part 2, 229–30.

CHAPTER 7

1. *OR*, part 2, 256.

2. Wilson, *Under the Old Flag*, 133.

3. *Confederate Veteran* 17, no. 1 (January 1909): 20.

4. *OR*, part 1, 673, 724.

5. *OR*, part 2, 706.

6. Bennett and Haigh, *History of the Thirty-sixth Regiment*, 696–97.

7. *OR*, part 2, 706–7.

8. *OR*, part 2, 707.

9. *OR*, part 2, 256.

10. *OR*, part 2, 256–57.

11. *OR*, part 1, 158.

12. Bennett and Haigh, *History of the Thirty-sixth Regiment*, 699; and Day, *One-Hundred-First Ohio Infantry*, 316.

13. *OR*, part 1, 158.

14. Noll, *Doctor Quintard*, 121; McMurry, *John Bell Hood*, 180; and Sword, *Confederacy's Last Hurrah*, 404–5.

15. *OR*, part 1, 728; and *Confederate Veteran* 19, no. 11 (November 1911): 542.

16. Noll, *Doctor Quintard*, 121; and McMurry, *John Bell Hood*, 180.

17. *OR*, part 1, 741, 756; Walker, *Hell's Broke Loose in Georgia*, 207–8; and *Richmond Daily Dispatch*, 28 January 1865.

18. Catton, *This Hallowed Ground*, 99; and Dabney H. Maury, *Recollections of a Virginian in the Mexican, Indian, and Civil Wars* (New York: Charles Scribner's Sons, 1894), 205.

19. Warner, *Generals in Gray*, 92–93; Welsh, *Medical Histories*, 70–72; and Boatner, *Civil War Dictionary*, 288–89.
20. Boatner, *Civil War Dictionary*, 295–96; *OR*, part 2, 121; and Welsh, *Medical Histories*, 72.
21. Noll, *Doctor Quintard*, 122; McMurry, *John Bell Hood*, 180; Wyeth, *Life of General Nathan Bedford Forrest*, 537; Jordan and Pryor, *Campaigns of Lt.-Gen. N. B. Forrest*, 646; *OR*, part 1, 661; and Sword, *Confederacy's Last Hurrah*, 406.
22. Sword, *Confederacy's Last Hurrah*, 396–97, 401; Warner, *Generals in Gray*, 248–49; *OR*, part 1, 158–59; and Wilson, *Under the Old Flag*, 130.
23. *OR*, part 1, 566, 578; *OR*, part 2, 275; Buel and Johnson, *Battles and Leaders*, vol. 4, 470; and Wilson, *Under the Old Flag*, 134. Wilson states in a February 1, 1865, report that supplies arrived on the night of December 18. But in a dispatch to Thomas written at 6 A.M. on the nineteenth, he writes that other than Hatch's division, the cavalry was out of rations and almost out of ammunition. If both reports are accurate, it appears there were not enough rations for the entire corps, so Hatch's men were supplied in order to continue the pursuit on the nineteenth, although Wilson does not say so. In his postwar article in *Battles and Leaders*, he states the cavalry was "almost entirely out of rations" on the morning of the nineteenth. Hatch's campaign report does not address the issue. In his book, Wilson says that the supply trains caught up but that in the dark issuing rations to the men went slowly. Hatch appears to have been a priority so that he continued the chase by early dawn the next day.
24. Keenan, *Wilson's Cavalry Corps*, 118; and *OR*, part 2, 260.
25. *OR*, part 1, 158–59; and *OR*, part 2, 257.

CHAPTER 8
1. *New York Times*, 19 December 1864.
2. *OR*, part 1, 756; John W. Morton, *The Artillery of Nathan Bedford Forrest's Cavalry* (Nashville, TN: M. E. Church South, 1909), 286; and Jordan and Pryor, *Campaigns of Lt.-Gen. N. B. Forrest*, 646. It will be recalled that at least two of Morton's guns had been sent ahead with Buford on December 16–17.
3. James R. Chalmers, "Forrest and His Campaigns," *Southern Historical Society Papers* 7 (October 1879): 482–83.
4. *OR*, part 2, 275.
5. *OR*, part 2, 275; and *OR* part 1, 566. In a February 1, 1865, report about the campaign, Wilson stated that "supplies arrived during the night" of December 18–19. Whether this is inaccurate or whether these supplies were so few that they were issued only to Hatch's men to resume the pursuit on the nineteenth remains unclear.
6. *OR*, part 1, 135, 159.
7. *OR*, part 1, 42.
8. *OR*, part 2, 283–85.
9. *OR*, part 1, 135, 159.

10. William L. McDonald, *Civil War Tales of the Tennessee Valley* (Kileen, AL: Heart of Dixie Publishing Company, 2003), 132; and *OR*, part 2, 710.

11. Groom, *Shrouds of Glory*, 260; *OR*, part 2, 710; and Christopher Losson, *Tennessee's Forgotten Warriors: Frank Cheatham and His Confederate Division* (Knoxville, TN: University of Tennessee Press, 1989), 240.

12. *OR*, part 1, 135.

13. Warner, *Generals in Blue*, 141–42, 267–68.

14. *OR*, part 1, 578, 592–93; and Keenan, *Wilson's Cavalry Corps*, 119. The ford used by Coon's brigade was actually over Curtis Creek, which paralleled Rutherford Creek before eventually joining it.

15. *OR*, part 1, 159–60.

16. *OR*, part 2, 275–76.

17. *OR*, part 1, 42.

18. *OR*, part 2, 265.

19. Groom, *Shrouds of Glory*, 260–61; *OR*, part 1, 711; and Noll, *Doctor Quintard*, 122.

20. Hood, *Advance and Retreat*, 306.

21. Morton, *Artillery of Nathan Bedford Forrest's Cavalry*, 291.

22. Warner, *Generals in Gray*, 93–94, 325–26; Welsh, *Medical Histories*, 228–29; and Dinkins, *1861–1865*, 253.

23. *OR*, part 1, 724–26. Ector's brigade also included some dismounted Texas cavalrymen.

24. *Confederate Veteran* 15, no. 9 (September 1907): 405–6; Mathes, *General Forrest*, 324–25; Morton, *Artillery of Nathan Bedford Forrest's Cavalry*, 291–92; and Losson, *Tennessee's Forgotten Warriors*, 241. Some accounts claim this encounter involved Colonel Heiskell rather than Finlay, but this appears erroneous.

25. *OR*, part 1, 756–57; Starr, *Union Cavalry in the Civil War*, vol. 3, 553; Wyeth, *Life of General Nathan Bedford Forrest*, 539; Stockdale, *Death of an Army*, 138–39; and *Confederate Veteran* 15, no. 9, 402. Here is a breakdown of the strength of these brigades: Palmer—616; Featherston—498; Feild—278; Reynolds—528. Walthall's assistant adjutant Sanders contends that Palmer had only about 300 effectives, thus reducing the rear guard infantry to about 1,600.

26. *OR*, part 2, 710; and *Confederate Veteran* 12, no. 7 (July 1904): 349.

27. Bennett and Haigh, *History of the Thirty-sixth Regiment*, 699; and *OR*, part 2, 293.

28. Stockdale, *Death of an Army*, 133; and *OR*, part 1, 160, 566.

29. *OR*, part 1, 160.

30. Quintard gives a slightly different version of this encounter, claiming that Forrest notified the Federals by signal flag that if they did not cease fire, he would expose Union wounded to the cannonade. Whatever the case, the guns fell silent. Forrest's artilleryman, John Morton, states that Forrest still was north of the Duck when he made a "personal call" on Hatch to discuss the prisoners and the shelling. Since the pontoon bridges had already been taken up by this point, leaving Forrest basically stranded on the north bank, Morton's account appears erroneous. Morton, *Artillery of Nathan Bedford Forrest's Cavalry*, 293.

31. *OR*, part 1, 593, 757; *OR*, part 2, 291; Stockdale, *Death of an Army*, 138; Noll, *Doctor Quintard*, 123. One of Chalmers's troopers described Federal prisoners of war without sufficient clothing but placed the blame for their fate on Hatch and Thomas, who failed to negotiate. Adjutant Sanders of Walthall's staff claimed that in the prisoner exchange talks, Forrest asked specifically about retrieving the wounded Colonel Rucker, but that the negotiations went nowhere. *Confederate Veteran* 15, no. 9, 402; and Dinkins, *1861–1865*, 253.

32. *OR*, part 2, 287.

33. *OR*, part 1, 160; and Buel and Johnson, *Battles and Leaders*, vol. 4, 470.

34. *OR*, part 2, 714–15.

35. McMurry, *John Bell Hood*, 180–81; *OR*, part 2, 287, 291; and *OR*, part 1, 161.

36. *OR*, part 1, 673; McMurry, ed., "A Mississippian at Nashville," 14–15; Stockdale, *Death of an Army*, 144; and Suzanne Stoker Lehr, ed., *Fishing on Deep River: Civil War Memoir of Private Samuel Baldwin Dunlap, C.S.A.* (St. Joseph, MO: Platte Purchase Publishers, 2006), 377.

37. Hood, *Advance and Retreat*, 307; and Noll, *Doctor Quintard*, 122–23.

38. William R. Plum, *The Military during the Civil War with an Exposition of Ancient and Modern Means of Communication, and of the Federal and Confederate Cipher Systems; also a Running Account of the War between the States* (Chicago, IL: Jansen, McClurg & Company, 1882), 239. Plum says that all lines abandoned on Hood's approach to Nashville were restored in December, except the wire to Johnsonville, which was repaired in January 1865.

39. *OR*, part 2, 283–85.

CHAPTER 9

1. *OR*, part 1, 111; and Morton, *Artillery of Nathan Bedford Forrest's Cavalry*, 287.

2. *New York Times*, 9 January 1865; and *OR*, part 2, 299.

3. *OR*, part 2, 719; and Noll, *Doctor Quintard*, 123.

4. *OR*, part 1, 682, 692.

5. *OR*, part 2, 719; and *Confederate Veteran* 17, no.1 (January 1909): 20. Major Porter of Cheatham's staff disputes reports that oxen were used in the retreat: "I did not see an ox during the entire trip. We used horses and mules, and we had enough to do the work, doubling teams with heavy things like pontoons."

6. *OR*, part 1, 161; and *OR*, part 2, 300–301.

7. *Confederate Veteran* 15, no. 9 (September 1907): 406.

8. Walker, *Hell's Broke Loose in Georgia*, 212.

9. *OR*, part 1, 136; and *OR*, part 2, 299.

10. *OR*, part 1, 161.

11. *OR*, part 1, 42.

12. *OR*, part 2, 295–96.

13. Ibid.

14. *OR*, part 2, 296. This Union success was by General McCook in an engagement at Hopkinsville and Col. Oscar La Grange in a clash at

Ashbysburg. Wilson later claimed McCook accomplished little, riding more than 400 miles in seventeen days and being absent for the battle of Nashville and subsequent pursuit of Hood—"without the consolation of having done the Confederate cause the slightest injury." Wilson, *Under the Old Flag*, 145.

15. Stockdale, *Death of an Army*, 145; and John A. Simpson, ed., *Reminiscences of the 41st Tennessee: The Civil War in the West* (Shippensburg, PA: White Mane Publishing, 2001), 112.

16. *Confederate Veteran* 15, no. 9 (September 1907): 406.

17. *OR*, part 1, 578, 593; *OR*, part 2, 304; and Warner, *Generals in Blue*, 215–16. Hatch reported the Texans belonged to French's command, which was now being led by Walthall. There is no known relationship between the Iowan Samuel Foster and the Texan Samuel Foster, other than their link to the Nashville campaign.

18. *OR*, part 2, 299–300.

19. *OR*, part 2, 721.

20. *OR*, part 2, 721; *OR*, part 1, 673; and Stockdale, *Death of an Army*, 145.

21. Normand D. Brown, ed., *One of Cleburne's Command: The Civil War Reminiscences and Diary of Capt. Samuel T. Foster, Granbury's Texas Brigade, C.S.A.* (Austin, TX: University of Texas Press, 1980), 153–58.

22. *OR*, part 1, 136, 292, 296.

23. *OR*, part 2, 722; *OR*, part 1, 726; *Confederate Veteran* 15, no. 9 (September 1907): 406. These Texans were apparently the 14th and 32nd Texas Cavalry, led by Maj. William E. Estes.

24. *Confederate Veteran* 15, no. 9 (September 1907): 406; *OR*, part 1, 296, 766; and Jordan and Pryor, *Campaigns of Lt.-Gen. N. B. Forrest*, 647–48. Young survived the war to become a circuit judge in Memphis.

25. *OR* part 2, 721 Presstman believed he had reached the Lamb's Ferry and Powell Road intersection, which was not true. The route he referred to likely was the Bevels Springs Road, which forks from the Lamb's Ferry Road and runs parallel to it before rejoining it a few miles to the south.

26. Watkins, *"Co. Aytch,"* 241; *OR*, part 1, 673, 732; *OR*, part 2, 721; Stockdale, *Death of an Army*, 145; and Sword, *Confederacy's Last Hurrah*, 414–15.

27. *OR*, part 1, 136, 162. It is unclear if the lack of pontoniers contributed to the problems in bridging Rutherford Creek, but this appears to be the case.

28. Sword, *Confederacy's Last Hurrah*, 414–15; *OR*, part 1, 296, 766; and Jordan and Pryor, *Campaigns of Lt.-Gen. N. B. Forrest*, 647–48.

29. *Confederate Veteran* 15, no. 9, 402.

30. *OR*, part 1, 42, 136.

31. *OR*, part 2, 721; and Sword, *Confederacy's Last Hurrah*, 414.

CHAPTER 10

1. *OR*, part 2, 726.

2. *OR*, part 1, 162.

3. *OR*, part 1, 162. Wood stated in a 1:30 P.M. dispatch to Thomas that he was "just starting on the march." Kimball states it was 2 P.M. when he started.

4. Buel and Johnson, *Battles and Leaders*, vol. 4, 470; Horn, *Decisive Battle of Nashville*, 162; and Jordan and Pryor, *Campaigns of Lt.-Gen. N. B. Forrest*, 648.

5. *OR*, part 1, 136–37, 182, 757.

6. *OR*, part 2, 324–25.

7. Ridley, *Battles and Sketches*, 439.

8. *OR*, part 2, 324–25.

9. *OR*, part 1, 673.

10. *Confederate Veteran* 17, no.1 (January 1909): 20.

11. *OR*, part 1, 757; and Wyeth, *Life of General Nathan Bedford Forrest*, 538.

12. Roman, *Military Operations*, 626; and *OR*, part 2, 726.

13. *OR*, part 2, 319.

14. *New York Times*, 9 January 1865.

15. *Confederate Veteran* 2, no. 2 (February 1894): 46–47.

16. *OR*, part 1, 1,251; and *Confederate Veteran* 3, no. 8 (August 1895): 249. By December 16, Roddey had received orders to join Hood near Nashville and to destroy the railroad from Huntsville to Stevenson and from Stevenson to Murfreesboro on the way. He states that he was leaving a regiment to defend Decatur and that a company of engineers from Hood's army had arrived at Decatur "to replace the pontoon bridge" and assist in getting captured locomotives south of the Tennessee. *OR*, part 2, 698.

17. *OR*, part 2, 726, 729–30; Sword, *Confederacy's Last Hurrah*, 445; and Warner, *Generals in Gray*, 274–75.

18. *OR*, part 1, 727, 757, 767; and *Confederate Veteran* 15, no. 9 (September 1907): 403. In his January 24, 1865, report of the campaign, Forrest claims that Walthall and the infantry accompanied the cavalry back toward Columbia that morning, but this appears to be inaccurate, based on Walthall's reports. In a speech about the campaign given in 1881, D. W. Sanders, one of Walthall's staff officers, also says the infantry moved north with the cavalry. Sanders's version, however, relies heavily on Forrest's January 24 narrative. Other than Forrest's often erroneous report—which was repeated and magnified in many books about him and his exploits—and Sanders's remembrance, there is little evidence that Walthall's infantry fought north of Lynnville on the twenty-fourth.

19. Marshall P. Thatcher, *A Hundred Battles in the West, St. Louis to Atlanta, 1861–1865—The Second Michigan Cavalry* (Detroit, MI: L. F. Kilroy, 1884), 235–36; and *OR*, part 1, 757.

20. *OR*, part 1, 771; and Warner, *Generals in Gray*, 263–64.

21. Thatcher, *Hundred Battles*, 235–36.

22. *OR*, part 2, 334; Wilson, *Under the Old Flag*, 139; and *OR*, part 2, 730.

23. Wilson, *Under the Old Flag*, 139; Jordan and Pryor, *Campaigns of Lt.-Gen. N. B. Forrest*, 648; *OR*, part 1, 757; and Thatcher, *Hundred Battles*, 237–38. In his February 1, 1865, report and again in Buel and Johnson,

Battles and Leaders, vol. 4, 471, Wilson says Hatch attacked on the pike and Croxton on the flank, which is apparently inaccurate; Croxton and Hatch both stated otherwise.

24. Morton, *Artillery of Nathan Bedford Forrest's Cavalry*, 294.

25. *OR*, part 1, 573-74; Sword, *Confederacy's Last Hurrah*, 416; and Wilson, *Under the Old Flag*, 139. Various accounts describe the standard as Chalmers's headquarters flag or Buford's battle flag.

26. *OR*, part 1, 757, 771. Forrest states that Union troopers on his right flank forded the creek, which is inaccurate since Coon was halted by the high water.

27. *OR*, part 1, 757, 771; Sword, *Confederacy's Last Hurrah*, 416–17; Stockdale, *Death of an Army*, 143–44; and Morton, *Artillery of Nathan Bedford Forrest's Cavalry*, 294.

28. *OR*, part 1, 567, 573–74, 578; and Thatcher, *Hundred Battles*, 238.

29. Wilson, *Under the Old Flag*, 139; and *OR*, part 2, 334.

30. Walker, *Hell's Broke Loose in Georgia*, 213–14.

31. *OR*, part 2, 371; and Sword, *Confederacy's Last Hurrah*, 421.

32. *OR*, part 2, 331; and *OR*, part 1, 137, 163, 292.

33. *OR*, part 2, 331.

34. *OR*, part 2, 334–35.

35. *OR*, part 2, 335; and Wilson, *Under the Old Flag*, 143.

36. *OR*, part 2, 332.

37. *OR*, part 1, 673, 731; and Stockdale, *Death of an Army*, 144.

38. Sam Davis Elliott, *Soldier of Tennessee: General Alexander P. Stewart and the Civil War in the West* (Baton Rouge, LA: Louisiana State University Press, 1999), 255; and McMurry, "A Mississippian at Nashville," 15.

39. *Recollections and Reminiscences*, vol. 1, 257; Mcmorries, *History of the First Regiment*, 92 and McMurry, "A Mississippian at Nashville," 15.

40. *Confederate Veteran* 16, no. 4 (April 1908): 192; and Douglas John Cater, *As It Was: Reminiscences of a Soldier of the Third Texas Cavalry and the Nineteenth Louisiana Infantry* (Austin, TX: State House Press, 1990), 203.

41. Noll, *Doctor Quintard*, 124; and Brown, ed., *One of Cleburne's Command*, 153.

42. Van Horne, *Life of Major-General George H. Thomas*, 371.

43. *OR*, part 1, 758, 771; Jordan and Pryor, *Campaigns of Lt.-Gen. N. B. Forrest*, 648; and Walker, *Hell's Broke Loose in Georgia*, 214.

44. *OR*, part 2, 729–30.

45. Groom, *Shrouds of Glory*, 272.

CHAPTER 11

1. Walker, *Hell's Broke Loose in Georgia*, 214.

2. Stockdale, *Death of an Army*, 146.

3. *OR*, part 1, 603; and Stockdale, *Death of an Army*, 145, 149.

4. *Confederate Veteran* 12, no.7 (July 1904): 349; and *OR*, part 1, 579.

5. *OR*, part 2, 342.

6. *OR*, part 1, 43.

7. *OR*, part 1, 727; and Walker, *Hell's Broke Loose in Georgia*, 215.

8. *OR*, part 1, 727.

9. Chalmers, "Forrest and His Campaigns," 483; and Jordan and Pryor, *Campaigns of Lt.-Gen. N. B. Forrest,* 650. Chalmers is referring to Xenophon, the Greek historian, soldier, and philosopher, and the 10,000 primarily Greek mercenaries who made a legendary retreat in the Greco-Persian Wars.

10. *OR,* part 1, 567.

11. *OR,* part 1, 603, 727; and Walker, *Hell's Broke Loose in Georgia,* 215.

12. *OR,* part 1, 727; and Walker, *Hell's Broke Loose in Georgia,* 215.

13. *OR,* part 1, 578–79; and Sword, *Confederacy's Last Hurrah,* 418.

14. *OR,* part 1, 578–79, 772.

15. Morton, *Artillery of Nathan Bedford Forrest's Cavalry,* 297.

16. *OR,* part 1, 758; Stockdale, *Death of an Army,* 152; Chalmers, "Forrest and His Campaigns," 483; and *Confederate Veteran* 15, no. 9 (September 1907): 406.

17. Jordan and Pryor, *Campaigns of Lt.-Gen. N. B. Forrest,* 650–51; *OR,* part 1, 758; and Wilson, *Under the Old Flag,* 140.

18. *Confederate Veteran* 3, no. 8 (August 1895): 249; and Sword, *Confederacy's Last Hurrah,* 420.

19. Cox, *Sherman's March to the Sea,* 125.

20. McMurray, "A Mississippian at Nashville," 15.

21. Groom, *Shrouds of Glory,* 264; Lundberg, *Finishing Stroke,* 119; and *OR,* part 1, 732.

22. Lehr, ed., *Fishing on Deep River,* 379.

23. *Recollections and Reminiscences,* vol. 1, 257.

24. *Confederate Veteran* 15, no. 3 (March 1907): 126.

25. *OR,* part 2, 731–33; and *OR,* part 1, 674. Hood issued several orders from "Bainbridge" on the twenty-fifth, but since the bridge was still under construction, he would have had to cross the river by boat to reach the village. It is likely that he remained on the north bank until the span was completed.

26. *OR,* part 2, 731–33; and *OR,* part 1, 674.

27. *OR,* part 1, 163–64, 292; and *OR,* part 2, 348. Beatty reported that he received word from Wood around 1 P.M. that Wilson was "hotly engaged," but his time frame is inaccurate.

28. *OR,* part 1, 137.

29. *OR,* part 1, 164.

30. *OR,* part 2, 342. In this communication, Thomas forwarded to Halleck a copy of Wilson's 10 A.M. dispatch from Pulaski.

31. Walker, *Hell's Broke Loose in Georgia,* 215.

32. *OR,* part 1, 727; and Walker, *Hell's Broke Loose in Georgia,* 216.

33. *OR,* part 1, 43, 567.

34. Wilson, *Under the Old Flag,* 140. Wilson states that Croxton's command fought at Anthony's Hill on December 25, but this does not appear to be the case. Croxton says he was not engaged after the combat on the twenty-fourth. *OR,* part 1, 567; and *OR,* part 1, 574.

35. Roman, *Military Operations,* 328, 627.

36. *OR,* part 2, 733–34.

37. Hood, *Advance and Retreat,* 306.

38. *OR*, part 1, 845. Many of these Union wagons had been captured by Forrest during the Confederate victory at nearby Brices Cross Roads the previous June—or so Grierson and Karge believed.

CHAPTER 12

1. *OR*, part 2, 736.
2. Wilson, *Under the Old Flag*, 138–39, 141.
3. Wilson, *Under the Old Flag*, 141. The site today is open pasture and farm land.
4. *OR*, part 1, 727, 772; Jordan and Pryor, *Campaigns of Lt.-Gen. N. B. Forrest*, 651–52; and Stockdale, *Death of an Army*, 153–54.
5. *Confederate Veteran* 15, no. 9 (September 1907): 407.
6. *OR*, part 1, 758.
7. *OR*, part 1, 758; *Confederate Veteran* 15, no. 9, 402; and Chalmers, "Forrest and His Campaigns," 484. Forrest identifies the infantry brigades involved as Ector's and Granbury's, which is erroneous. Granbury's was not present at this action while Ector's had been consolidated with Reynolds's Brigade in Walthall's reorganization of the rear guard at Columbia on December 20.
8. *Confederate Veteran* 12, no. 7 (July 1904): 349; Lundberg, *Finishing Stroke*, 119; *OR*, part 1, 579, 758; Stockdale, *Death of an Army*, 156; Sword, *Confederacy's Last Hurrah*, 419; Jordan and Pryor, *Campaigns of Lt.-Gen. N. B. Forrest*, 653–54.
9. *OR*, part 1, 567, 607–8; Wilson, *Under the Old Flag*, 141; and Chalmers, "Forrest and His Campaigns," 484.
10. *OR*, part 1, 164.
11. McMurry, *John Bell Hood*, 181; and Sword, *Confederacy's Last Hurrah*, 421.
12. Groom, *Shrouds of Glory*, 264; Cox, *Sherman's March to the Sea*, 125–26; and McMurry, *John Bell Hood*, 181.
13. Lehr, ed., *Fishing on Deep River*, 379.
14. *OR*, part 1, 165.
15. Wilson, *Under the Old Flag*, vol. 2, 139; and Talcott E. Wing, *History of Monroe County, Michigan* (New York: Munsell & Company, 1890), 322–24.
16. *OR*, part 1, 846–47; and Robert C. Black III, *The Railroads of the Confederacy* (Chapel Hill, NC: University of North Carolina Press, 1998), 266–67.
17. *OR*, part 1, 165.
18. Ibid., 165–66.
19. Ibid., 724.
20. *OR*, part 2, 740; and Lehr, ed., *Fishing on Deep River*, 379.
21. *OR*, part 2, 370–71.
22. Ibid., 382.
23. *OR*, part 1, 165–66.
24. Ibid.
25. *OR*, part 2, 382; and Wales W. Wood, *A History of the Ninety-fifth Regiment, Illinois Infantry Volunteers* (Chicago, IL: Tribune Company's Book and Job Printing Office, 1865), 144.

26. *OR*, part 1, 724, 732; *Confederate Veteran* 2, no. 5 (May 1894): 151; and *Confederate Veteran* 20, no. 10 (October 1912): 477; and Douglas Hale, *The Third Texas Cavalry in the Civil War* (Norman, OK: The University of Oklahoma Press, 1993), 267–68.
27. *OR*, part 2, 744; and *Confederate Veteran* 15, no. 9 (September 1907): 406.
28. *OR*, part 2, 744; *OR*, part 1, 579; and *Confederate Veteran* 2, no. 2 (February 1894): 47.
29. *OR*, part 1, 758–59.
30. Ibid., 137, 167.
31. *OR*, part 1, 167.
32. Day, *One-Hundred-First Ohio Infantry*, 317; and Wood, *Ninety-fifth Regiment*, 145–46.
33. Lundberg, *Finishing Stroke*, 120; and *OR*, part 1, 767.
34. *OR*, part 2, 389.
35. *OR*, part 1, 167–68.
36. *OR*, part 2, 388–89.
37. Ibid., 400–401.
38. Wilson, *Under the Old Flag*, 142–45; and Buel and Johnson, *Battles and Leaders*, vol. 4, 471.
39. *OR*, part 2, 744; and Lehr, ed., *Fishing on Deep River*, 379–80.

CHAPTER 13
1. *OR*, part 1, 167–68.
2. *OR*, part 1, 50–51.
3. *OR*, part 2, 403–4; and *OR*, part 1, 43.
4. Black, *Railroads of the Confederacy*, 267.
5. *OR*, part 2, 439; and Pollard, *Lost Cause*, 588.
6. *OR*, part 2, 408–9.
7. Stone, "Hood's Invasion of Tennessee," 616.
8. *OR*, part 1, 137.
9. John William Draper, *History of the American Civil War* (New York: Harper & Brothers, 1870), 360.
10. *OR*, part 1, 170–71.
11. *OR*, part 1, 170
12. *OR*, part 2, 425, 428, 432.
13. *Richmond Daily Dispatch*, 30 December 1864.
14. Roman, *Military Operations*, vol. 2, 328.
15. *OR*, part 2, 419–21.
16. *OR* part 2, 420–21, 427–28, 441–42.
17. *OR*, part 2, 429–32; Buel and Johnson, *Battles and Leaders*, vol. 4, 471; and Wilson, *Under the Old Flag*, 143.
18. *OR*, part 2, 422.
19. *OR*, part 1, 674, 732; and Lehr, ed., *Fishing on Deep River*, 380.
20. *OR*, part 2, 439.
21. *OR*, part 2, 749–50.
22. *OR*, part 1, 45–46, 661; Hood, *Advance and Retreat*, 507; and *OR*, part 2, 521.

23. *OR*, part 1, 44; *OR*, part 2, 441–42; and Cleaves, *Rock of Chickamauga*, 276.
24. *OR*, part 1, 110–11.

CHAPTER 14

1. John B. Jones, *A Rebel War Clerk's Diary at the Confederate States Capital* (Philadelphia: J. B. Lippincott & Company, 1866), 371–73; and *Richmond Daily Dispatch*, 2 January 1865.
2. *OR*, part 2, 470, 481–83, 507.
3. Ibid.
4. *OR*, part 2, 756.
5. *OR*, part 2, 757–58; and Roman, *Military Operations*, 329–30, 627.
6. *OR*, part 1, 74; and Walker, *Hell's Broke Loose in Georgia*, 223.
7. Sword, *Confederacy's Last Hurrah*, 426; *Atlanta Appeal*, n.d.; and *Richmond Daily Dispatch*, 26 January 1865.
8. *OR*, part 2, 758–59; and Stockdale, *Death of an Army*, 171–72.
9. Stanley F. Horn, *The Army of Tennessee* (Norman, OK: University of Oklahama Press, 1993), 421.
10. Roman, *Military Operations*, 328–30, 627; and *OR*, part 2, 757–58.
11. *New York Times*, 9 January 1865; and Wilson, *Under the Old Flag*, 160–61.
12. *OR*, part 1, 51; and *OR*, part 2, 515; and Cleaves, *Rock of Chickamauga*, 276–77.
13. *Richmond Daily Dispatch*, 24 December 1864 and 28 December 1864; and *New York Times*, 21 December 1864.
14. *Richmond Senintel*, 29 December 1864; and *New York Times*, 2 January 1865.
15. *OR*, part 2, 770; and *Confederate Veteran* 16, no. 4 (April 1908): 192.
16. Richard Taylor, *Destruction and Reconstruction: Personal Experiences of the Late War* (D. Appleton and Co., 1879), 217.
17. *OR*, part 2, 722, 770.
18. *OR*, part 2, 774–75; and *OR*, part 1, 724.
19. *OR*, part 1, 661–62.
20. Ibid.
21. *OR*, part 1, 674, 732; Losson, *Tennessee's Forgotten Warriors*, 243. Hood's army journal states that Cheatham arrived in Tupelo on January 12, which appears inaccurate.
22. Wyeth, *Life of General Nathan Bedford Forrest*, 548.
23. *OR*, part 1, 772; and Frank A. Montgomery, *Reminiscences of a Mississippian in Peace and War* (Cincinnati, OH: The Robert Clarke Company Press, 1901), 221.
24. *OR*, part 2, 778–79.

CHAPTER 15

1. *Richmond Daily Dispatch*, 14 January 1865.
2. *OR*, part 1, 656; and Hood, *Advance and Retreat*, 307.
3. *OR*, part 1, 663–64; *OR*, part 2, 783; Thomas A. Head, *Campaigns and Battles of the Sixteenth Regiment, Tennessee Volunteers, in the War between the States, 1861–1865* (Nashville, TN: Cumberland Presbyterian Publishing

House, 1885), 155; and *Confederate Veteran* 17, no. 1 (January 1909): 20. It is unclear if Porter is writing about the entire army or just Cheatham's troops, although he could be describing either or both.

4. *OR*, part 2, 782.

5. *OR*, part 2, 783; and Morton, *Artillery of Nathan Bedford Forrest's Cavalry*, 301.

6. Hood, *Advance and Retreat*, 308–10; *OR*, part 1, 663–64; *OR*, part 2, 850–51; William J. McMurray, *History of the Twentieth Tennessee Regiment, Volunteer Infantry, C.S.A.* (Nashville, TN: The Publications Committee, 1904), 353–54; Porter, *Confederate Military History*, 8: 168; and Donn Piatt, *General George H. Thomas: A Critical Biography* (Cincinnati, OH: Robert Clarke & Co., 1893), 591.

7. Wyeth, *Life of General Nathan Bedford Forrest*, 543–44; and Hood, *Advance and Retreat*, 310.

8. Porter, *Confederate Military History* 8, 169; Hood, *Advance and Retreat*, 303–4; *OR*, part 1, 663–64, 676, 682, 692; and *OR*, part 2, 389.

9. *OR*, part 2, 780–82; and Hood, *Advance and Retreat*, 310–11.

10. Connelly, *Autumn of Glory*, 513; and Roman, *Military Operations*, 331–32.

11. *OR*, part 2, 786; and Sword, *Confederacy's Last Hurrah*, 429–30. Historian Wiley Sword claims Hood shrewdly called for his own removal even as he planted the familiar seeds of incompetent subordinates in an attempt to avoid public disgrace and retain command.

12. *OR*, part 2, 789.

13. Ibid., 785, 789.

14. McMurry, *John Bell Hood*, 182; *OR*, part 2, 786; and Sword, *Confederacy's Last Hurrah*, 425–26.

15. Roman, *Military Operations*, 332; and *OR*, part 2, 784–85, 791.

16. Cooper, *Jefferson Davis*, 540; Connelly, *Autumn of Glory*, 489–90.

17. *OR*, part 2, 593.

18. Cleaves, *Rock of Chickamauga*, 277–78; and Wilson, *Under the Old Flag*, 180.

19. *Richmond Daily Dispatch*, 26 January 1865; *OR*, part 2, 795; and McMurry, *John Bell Hood*, 183.

20. Horn, *Army of Tennessee*, 422–23; and *OR*, part 1, 664.

21. *Richmond Daily Dispatch*, 28 January 1865; and *OR*, part 2, 805.

22. Watkins, *"Co. Aytch,"* 242; and Head, *Campaigns and Battles*, 92.

23. Wilson, *Under the Old Flag*, 157; and James R. Rusling, *Men and Things I Saw in Civil War Days* (New York: Eaton & Mains Press, 1899), 103.

24. Taylor, *Destruction and Reconstruction*, 216–17.

25. *OR*, part 2, 804.

26. Isabella D. Martin and Myrta Lockett Avery, ed., *A Diary from Dixie, as Written by Mary Boykin Chesnut, Wife of James Chesnut Jr., United States Senator from South Carolian, 1859–1861, and Afterward an Aide to Jefferson Davis and a Brigadier General in the Confederate Army* (New York: D. Appleton and Company, 1905), 342–43; and C. Vann Woodward, ed., *Mary Chesnut's Civil War* (New Haven, CT: Yale University Press, 1981), 708.

27. Martin and Avery, ed., *Diary from Dixie*, 342–43; and Woodward, ed., *Mary Chesnut's Civil War*, 708–10.

28. Jones, *Rebel War Clerk's Diary*, 450.
29. Hood, *Advance and Retreat*, 336.
30. Ibid.
31. McMurry, *John Bell Hood*, 188; Sword, *Confederacy's Last Hurrah*, 437; and Woodward, ed., *Mary Chesnut's Civil War*, 783–85, 804–5.
32. Hood, *Advance and Retreat*, 311; Connelly, *Autumn of Glory*, 513; Warner, *Generals in Gray*, 280; Warner, *Generals in Blue*, 112; and McMurry, *John Bell Hood*, 192.
33. Wyeth, *Life of General Nathan Bedford Forrest*, 583.
34. Connelly, *Autumn of Glory*, 535.
35. Watkins, *"Co. Aytch"*, 245; *Confederate Veteran* 15, no. 9 (September 1907): 407.
36. *Confederate Veteran* 2, no. 2 (February 1894): 47; *Confedeterate Veteran* 18, no. 7 (July 1910): 329; and Simpson, ed., *Reminiscences of the 41st Tennessee*, 112.

APPENDIX A

1. Kennedy, *Civil War Battlefield Guide*, 85; and James V. Murfin, *The Gleam of Bayonets: The Battle of Antietam and the Maryland Campaign of 1862* (Baton Rouge, LA: Louisiana State University Press, 1965), 303–4, 319.
2. Kennedy, *Civil War Battlefield Guide*, 122 and Derek Smith, *The Gallant Dead: Union & Confederate Generals Killed in the Civil War* (Mechanicsburg, PA: Stackpole Books, 2005), 184–87.

Bibliography

Alfriend, Frank H. *The Life of Jefferson Davis.* Cincinnati: Caxton Publishing House, 1868.

Bennett, L. G., and W. M. Haigh. *History of the Thirty-sixth Regiment, Illinois Volunteers, during the War of the Rebellion.* Aurora, IL: Knickerbocker & Hodder, 1876.

Black, Robert C. *The Railroads of the Confederacy.* Chapel Hill, NC: University of North Carolina Press, 1998.

Boatner, Mark M. *The Civil War Dictionary.* Rev. ed. New York: David McKay Company, Inc., 1987.

Brown, Norman D., ed. *One of Cleburne's Command: The Civil War Reminiscences and Diary of Capt. Samuel T. Foster, Granbury's Texas Brigade, C.S.A.* Austin, TX: University of Texas Press, 1980.

Buel, Clarence C., and Robert V. Johnson. *Battles and Leaders of the Civil War: Being for the Most Part Contributions by Union and Confederate Authors.* 4 vols. New York: Century Company, 1887.

Burgess, Tim, ed. "Reminiscences of the Battle of Nashville." *Journal of Confederate History.* Paris, TN: Guild Bindery Press, No. 1 (Summer 1988).

Carroll, John W. *Autobiography and Reminiscences of John W. Carroll.* Henderson, TN: N.p., 1898.

Carter, W. R. *History of the First Regiment of Tennessee Volunteer Cavalry in the Great War of the Rebellion—1862–1865.* Knoxville, TN: Gaut-Ogden, 1904.

Cater, Douglas John. *As It Was: Reminiscences of a Soldier of the Third Texas Cavalry and the Nineteenth Louisiana Infantry.* Austin, TX: State House Press, 1990.

Catton, Bruce. *This Hallowed Ground: The Story of the Union Side of the Civil War.* Garden City, NY: Doubleday & Co., 1956.

Chalmers, James R. "Forrest and His Campaigns." *Southern Historical Society Papers* 7, no. 10, (October 1879).

Cleaves, Freeman. *Rock of Chickamauga: The Life of General George H. Thomas.* Norman, OK: University of Oklahoma Press, 1948.

Coffin, Charles C. *Freedom Triumphant: The Fourth Period of the War of the Rebellion from September, 1864, to Its Close.* New York: Harper & Brothers, 1890.

Connelly, Thomas L. *Army of the Heartland: The Army of Tennessee, 1861–1862.* Baton Rouge, LA: Louisiana State University Press, 1967.

———. *Autumn of Glory: The Army of Tennessee, 1862–1865.* Baton Rouge, LA: Louisiana State University Press, 1971.

Cooper, William J. *Jefferson Davis, American.* New York: Alfred A. Knopf, 2000.

Cox, Gen. Jacob D. *Sherman's March to the Sea—Hood's Tennessee Campaign & The Carolina Campaigns of 1865.* New York: Da Capo Press, 1994.

Cozzens, Peter. *No Better Place To Die: The Battle of Stones River.* Urbana, IL: University of Illinois Press, 1990.

Daniel, Larry J. *Cannoneers in Gray.* Tuscaloosa, AL: University of Alabama Press, 1984.

———. *Soldiering in the Army of Tennessee: A Portrait of Life in a Confederate Army.* Chapel Hill, NC: The University of North Carolina Press, 1991.

Davis, Burke. *The Long Surrender.* New York: Random House, 1985.

Davis, Jefferson. *The Rise and Fall of the Confederate Government.* 2 vols. New York: D. Appleton and Co., 1881.

Day, L. W. *Story of the One-Hundred-First Ohio Infantry: A Memorial Volume.* Cleveland, OH: W. M. Bayne Printing Co., 1894.

Dinkins, James. *1861–1865—Personal Recollections and Experiences in the Confederate Army, by an 'Old Johnnie.'* Cincinnati, OH: The Robert Clark Company, 1897.

Dodd, W.O. "Reminiscences of Hood's Tennessee Campaign." *Southern Historical Society Papers* 9 (1881).

Draper, John William. *History of the American Civil War.* 3 vols. New York: Harper & Brothers, 1870.

Elliott, Sam Davis. *Soldier of Tennessee: General Alexander P. Stewart and the Civil War in the West.* Baton Rouge, LA: Louisiana State University Press, 1999.

Evans, Clement A., ed. *Confederate Military History.* 12 vols. Atlanta, GA: Confederate Publishing Company, 1899.

Foote, Shelby. *The Civil War: A Narrative.* 3 vols. New York: Vintage Books, 1986.

Freeman, Douglas Southall. *Lee's Lieutenants: A Study in Command.* Abridged by Stephen W. Sears. New York: Simon & Schuster, 2001.

Grant, Ulysses S. *Personal Memoirs of U.S. Grant.* 2 vols. New York: J. J. Little & Company, 1885.

Groom, Winston. *Shrouds of Glory: From Atlanta to Nashville—The Last Great Campaign of the Civil War.* New York: Pocket Books, 1995.

Grote, George, and Phillippe-Paul Segur. *The Two Great Retreats of History: The Retreat of the Ten Thousand—Napoleon's Retreat From Moscow.* Boston: Ginn & Company, 1899.

Gue, Benjamin F. *History of Iowa—From the Earliest Times to the Beginning of the Twentieth Century.* 4 vols. New York: The Century History Company, 1903.

Hale, Douglas. *The Third Texas Cavalry in the Civil War.* Norman, OK: The University of Oklahoma Press, 1993.

Harwell, Richard, ed. *The Journal of Kate Cumming—A Confederate Nurse.* Savannah, GA: The Beehive Press, 1975.

Hattaway, Herman. *General Stephen D. Lee.* Starkville, MS: University Press of Mississippi, 1976.

Head, Thomas A. *Campaigns and Battles of the Sixteenth Regiment, Tennessee Volunteers, in the War between the States, 1861–1865.* Nashville, TN: Cumberland Presbyterian Publishing House, 1885.

Hood, John Bell. *Advance and Retreat: Personal Experiences in the United States and Confederate Armies.* Secaucus, NJ: Blue and Grey Press, 1985.

Horn, Stanley F. *The Army of Tennessee.* Norman, OK: University of Oklahoma Press, 1993.

———. *The Decisive Battle of Nashville.* Baton Rouge, LA: Louisiana State University Press, 1984.

Hughes, Nathaniel Cheairs, ed. *The Civil War Memoir of Philip Daingerfield Stephenson, D.D.* Conway, AR: University of Central Arkansas Press, 1995.

Johnson, Richard W. *A Soldier's Reminiscences in Peace and War.* Philadelphia: J. B. Lippincott Company, 1886.

Jones, John B. *A Rebel War Clerk's Diary at the Confederate States Capital.* 2 vols. Philadelphia: J. B. Lippincott & Company, 1866.

Jordan, Thomas, and J. P. Pryor. *The Campaigns of Lt.-Gen. N. B. Forrest and of Forrest's Cavalry.* New Orleans, LA: Blelock & Company, 1868.

Keenan, Jerry. "The Gallant Hood of Texas." *America's Civil War* 7, no. 1 (March 1994).

———. *Wilson's Cavalry Corps: Union Campaigns in the Western Theater, October 1864 through Spring 1865.* Jefferson, NC: McFarland & Company, 1998.

Kennedy, Frances H., ed. *The Civil War Battlefield Guide.* Boston: Houghton Mifflin, 1990.

Lee, Stephen D. "Correction of Gen. Anderson's Report of Jonesboro." *Southern Historical Society Papers* 5 (January–June, 1878).

Lehr, Suzanne Stoker, ed. *Fishing on Deep River: Civil War Memoir of Private Samuel Baldwin Dunlap, C.S.A.* St. Joseph, MO: Platte Purchase Publishers, 2006.

Losson, Christopher. *Tennessee's Forgotten Warriors: Frank Cheatham and His Confederate Division.* Knoxville, TN: University of Tennessee Press, 1989.

Lundberg, John R. *The Finishing Stroke: Texans in the 1864 Tennessee Campaign.* Abilene, TX: McWhinney Foundation Press, 2002.

Martin, Isabella D., and Myrta Lockett Avery. *A Diary From Dixie, as written by Mary Boykin Chesnut, wife of James Chesnut, Jr., United States Senator from South Carolina, 1859–1861, and afterward an Aide to Jefferson Davis and a Brigadier General in the Confederate Army.* New York: D. Appleton and Company, 1905.

Mathes, James Harvey. *General Forrest.* New York: D. Appleton and Company, 1902.

Maury, Dabney Herndon. *Recollections of A Virginian in the Mexican, Indian, and Civil Wars.* New York: Charles Scribner's Sons, 1894.

McDonald, William L. *Civil War Tales of the Tennessee Valley.* Kileen, AL: Heart of Dixie Publishing Company, 2003.

McMorries, Edward Young. *History of the First Regiment, Alabama Volunteer Infantry, C.S.A.* Montgomery, AL: The Brown Printing Co., 1904.

McMurray, William J. *History of the Twentieth Tennessee Regiment, Volunteer Infantry, C.S.A.* Nashville, TN: The Publications Committee, 1904.

McMurry, Richard M. *John Bell Hood and the War for Southern Independence.* Lincoln, NE: University of Nebraska Press, 1982.

———, ed. "A Mississippian at Nashville." *Civil War Times Illustrated* 12, no. 2 (May 1973).

Miles, Jim. *Paths To Victory: A History and Tour Guide of the Stone's River, Chicka-mauga, Chattanooga, Knoxville, and Nashville Campaigns.* Nashville, TN: Rutledge Hill Press, 1991.

Montgomery, Frank A. *Reminiscences of a Mississippian in Peace and War.* Cincinnati, OH: The Robert Clarke Company Press, 1901.

Morton, John W. *The Artillery of Nathan Bedford Forrest's Cavalry.* Nashville, TN: M. E. Church South, 1909.

Murfin, James V. *The Gleam of Bayonets: The Battle of Antietam and the Maryland Campaign of 1862.* Baton Rouge: Louisiana State University Press, 1965.

Newberry, J. S. *The U.S. Sanitary Commission in the Valley of the Mississippi during the War of the Rebellion.* Cleveland, OH: Fairbanks, Benedict & Co., 1871.

Noll, Rev. Arthur Howard Noll, ed. *Doctor Quintard—Chaplain, C.S.A., and Second Bishop of Tennessee—Being His Story of the War (1861–1865).* Sewanee, TN: The University Press of Sewanee, Tennessee, 1905.

Noyes, Edward. "Excerpts from the Civil War Diary of E. T. Eggleston," *Tennessee Historical Quarterly* 17 (December 1958).

Patterson, Gerard A. *Rebels from West Point.* New York: Doubleday, 1987.

Piatt, Donn. *General George H. Thomas: A Critical Biography.* Cincinnati, OH: Robert Clarke & Co., 1893.

Pierce, Lyman B. *History of the Second Iowa Cavalry.* Burlington, IA: Hawk-Eye Steam Books and Job Printing Establishment, 1865.

Plum, William R. *The Military Telegraph during the Civil War with An Exposition of Ancient and Modern Means of Communication, and of the Federal and Confederate Cipher Systems; Also a Running Account of the War between the States.* 2 vols. Chicago, IL: Jansen, McClurg & Company, 1882.

Pollard, Edward A. *The Lost Cause: A New Southern History of the War of the Confederates.* New York: E. B. Treat & Company, 1867.

Recollections and Reminiscences, 1861–1865, through World War I. 6 vols. South Carolina Division, United Daughters of the Confederacy, 1992.

Ridley, Bromfield L. *Battles and Sketches of the Army of Tennessee.* Mexico, MO: Missouri Publishing Company, 1906.

Ritter, W. L. "Sketches of the Third Maryland Artillery." *Southern Historical Society Papers* 11 (January–December 1883).

Roman, Alfred. *The Military Operations of General Beauregard in the War between the States.* 2 vols. New York: Harper & Brothers, 1884.

Rowland, Dunbar. *Encyclopedia of Mississippi History.* 2 vols. Madison, WI: Selwyn A. Brant, 1907.

———. *Jefferson Davis: Constitutionalist—His Letters, Papers and Speeches.* 10 vols. New York: J. J. Little & Ives Company, 1923.

Rusling, James F. *Men and Things I Saw in Civil War Days.* New York: Eaton & Mains Press, 1899.

Sandburg, Carl. *Abraham Lincoln.* 4 vols. New York: Harcourt, Brace & Company, 1939.

Schofield, John M. *Forty-Six Years in the Army.* New York: The Century Company, 1897.

Sherman, William T. *Sherman's Civil War.* New York: Crowell-Collier Publishing Co., 1962.

Simpson, John A., ed. *Reminiscences of the 41st Tennessee: The Civil War in the West.* Shippensburg, Pa.: White Mane Publishing, 2001.

Smith, Derek. *Civil War Savannah.* Savannah, GA: Frederic Beil, 1997.

———. *The Gallant Dead: Union and Confederate Generals Killed in the Civil War.* Mechanicsburg, PA: Stackpole Books, 2005.

Starr, Stephen Z. *The Union Cavalry in the Civil War.* 3 vols. Baton Rouge, LA: Louisiana State University Press, 1985.

Stockdale, Paul H. *The Death of an Army: The Battle of Nashville and Hood's Retreat.* Murfreesboro, TN: Southern Heritage Press, 1992.

Stone, Colonel Henry. "Hood's Invasion of Tennessee." *The Century* 34, issue 4 (August 1887).

Strode, Hudson. *Jefferson Davis: Tragic Hero—The Last Twenty-five Years, 1864–1889.* New York: Harcourt, Brace & World, 1964.

Swinton, William. *The Twelve Decisive Battles of the War: A History of the Eastern and Western Campaigns, in Relation to the Actions That Decided Their Issue.* New York: Dick & Fitzgerald, 1871.

Sword, Wiley. *The Confederacy's Last Hurrah: Spring Hill, Franklin, and Nashville.* Lawrence, KS: University Press of Kansas, 1992.

Sykes, E. T. "Walthall's Brigade: A Cursory Sketch with Personal Experiences of Walthall's Brigade, Army of Tennessee, C.S.A., 1862–1865." *Publications of the Mississippi Historical Society* 1 (1916).

Taylor, Richard. *Destruction and Reconstruction: Personal Experiences of the Late War.* New York: D. Appleton and Co., 1879.

Thatcher, Marshall P. *A Hundred Battles in the West, St. Louis to Atlanta, 1861–1865—The Second Michigan Cavalry.* Detroit, MI: L. F. Kilroy, 1884.

Thompson, Bradford F. *History of the One-Hundred Twelfth Regiment of Illinois Volunteer Infantry in the Great War of the Rebellion.* Toulon, IL: Stark County News Office, 1885.

U. S. War Department. *The War of the Rebellion: A Compilation of the Official Records of the Union and Confederate Armies.* 128 vols. Washington, D.C.: U. S. Government Printing Office, 1880–1901.

U. S. War Department. *Official Records of the Union and Confederate Navies in the War of the Rebellion.* 303 vols. Washington, D.C.: U.S. Government Printing Office, 1894–1922.

Van Horne, Thomas B. *History of the Army of the Cumberland—Its Organization, Campaigns, and Battles.* 2 vols. Cincinnati, OH: Robert Clarke & Co., 1875.

———. *The Life of Major-General George H. Thomas.* New York: Charles Scribner's Sons, 1882.

Walker, John. "Blood on the Snow." *Military Heritage* 8, no. 5 (April 2007).

Walker, Scott. *Hell's Broke Loose in Georgia: Survival in a Civil War Regiment.* Athens, GA: University of Georgia Press, 2005.

Warner, Ezra J. *Generals in Blue: Lives of the Union Commanders.* Baton Rouge, LA: Louisiana State University Press, 1964.

———. *Generals in Gray: Lives of the Confederate Commanders.* Baton Rouge, LA: Louisiana State University Press, 1959.

Watkins, Sam R. *"Co. Aytch": A Sideshow of the Big Show.* New York: Macmillan Publishing Co., 1962.

Welsh, Jack D. *Medical Histories of Confederate Generals.* Kent, OH: Kent State University Press, 1995.

Wilson, James H. *Under the Old Flag.* 2 vols. New York: B. Appleton and Company, 1912.

Wing, Talcott E. *History of Monroe County, Michigan.* New York: Munsell & Company, 1890.

Wood, Wales W. *A History of the Ninety-fifth Regiment, Illinois Infantry Volunteers.* Chicago, IL: Tribune Company's Book and Job Printing Office, 1865.

Woodward, C. Vann, ed. *Mary Chesnut's Civil War.* New Haven, CT: Yale University Press, 1981.

Wyeth, John Allan. *The Life of General Nathan Bedford Forrest.* New York: Barnes & Noble Publishing, 2006.

———. *That Devil Forrest.* New York: Harper, 1959.

NEWSPAPERS AND MAGAZINES

America's Civil War
Atlanta Appeal
The Century
Charleston (South Carolina) *Mercury*
Charlottesville (Virginia) *Chronicle*
Chicago Tribune
Cincinnati Commercial
Civil War Times Illustrated
Confederate Veteran
Daily Richmond Enquirer
Military Heritage
Nashville Journal
New York Times
New York Tribune
North & South
Richmond Daily Dispatch
Richmond Sentinel
Staunton (Virginia) *Vindicator*

Index

Page numbers in italics indicate illustrations

Stackpole Military History Series

Real battles. Real soldiers. Real stories.

Stackpole Military History Series

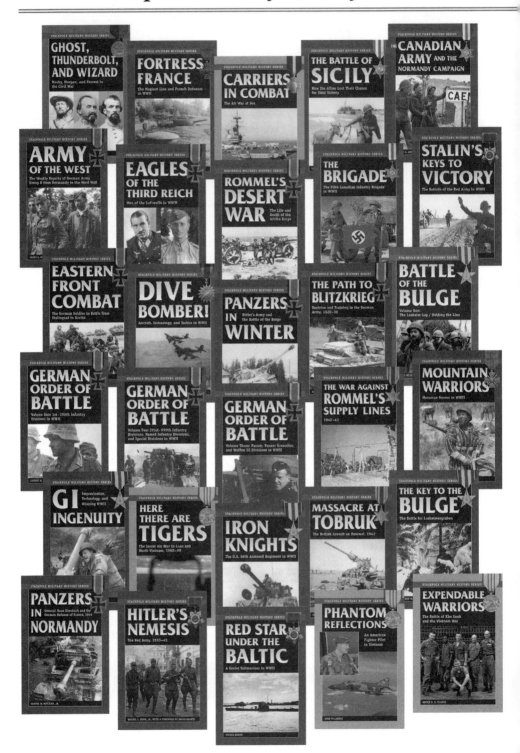

Real battles. Real soldiers. Real stories.

Stackpole Military History Series

Real battles. Real soldiers. Real stories.

NEW for Fall 2011

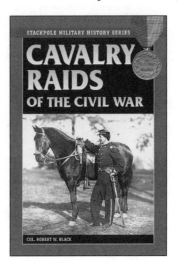

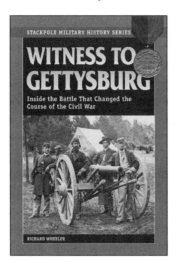

Stackpole Military History Series

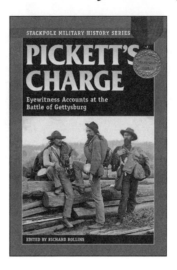

PICKETT'S CHARGE
EYEWITNESS ACCOUNTS AT THE
BATTLE OF GETTYSBURG
Edited by Richard Rollins

On the final day of the battle of Gettysburg, Robert E. Lee
ordered one of the most famous infantry assaults of all time:
Pickett's Charge. Following a thundering artillery barrage,
thousands of Confederates launched a daring frontal attack on
the Union line. From their entrenched positions, Federal
soldiers decimated the charging Rebels, leaving the field
littered with the fallen and several Southern divisions in tatters.
Written by generals, officers, and enlisted men on both sides,
these firsthand accounts offer an up-close look at Civil War
combat and a panoramic view of the carnage of July 3, 1863.

$21.95 • Paperback • 6 x 9 • 432 pages • 11 maps

WWW.STACKPOLEBOOKS.COM
1-800-732-3669

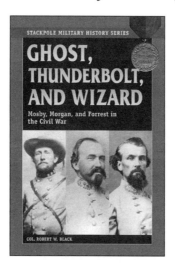

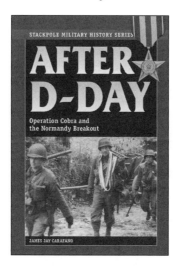

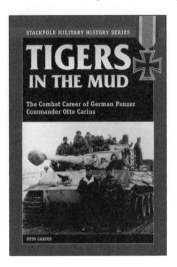

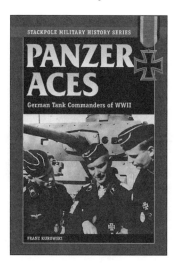

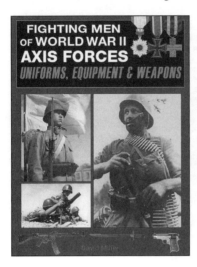
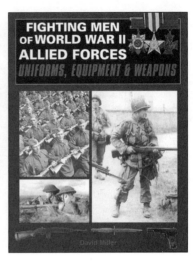